DIGITAL DETROIT

Digital Detroit

RHETORIC AND SPACE IN THE AGE OF THE NETWORK

JEFF RICE

Southern Illinois University Press
Carbondale and Edwardsville

Previous versions of portions of this book were published
in the following articles: "Building Interfaces: The Maccabees," *Pre/Text* 20 (July 2009); "Woodward Paths: Motorizing Space," *Technical Communication Quarterly* 18.3
(July 2009), 224–41; "Urban Mapping: A Rhetoric of the
Network," *Rhetoric Society Quarterly* 38.2 (March 2008),
copyright © 2008; "Networked Exchanges, Identity, Writing," *Journal of Business and Technical Communication* 23.3
(July 2009), 294–317 (final, definitive version; Sage Publications, Inc., http://online.sagepub.com; all rights reserved);
and "Folksono(me)," *JAC* 28 (August 2008), 181–208.

Library of Congress Cataloging-in-Publication Data
Rice, Jeff, 1969–
Digital Detroit : rhetoric and space in the age of the network
/ Jeff Rice.
    p. cm.
Includes bibliographical references and index.
    ISBN-13: 978-0-8093-3087-4 (pbk. : alk. paper)
    ISBN-10: 0-8093-3087-3 (pbk. : alk. paper)
    ISBN-13: 978-0-8093-3088-1 (ebook)
    ISBN-10: 0-8093-3088-1 (ebook)
1. Mass media—Philosophy. 2. Digital communications—
Philosophy. 3. Rhetoric—Philosophy. 4. Rhetoric—
Michigan—Detroit. I. Title.
P91.3.R523 2012
302.2309774'34—dc23   2011022745

To Jenny
To Vered
To Judah

You are my network.

CONTENTS

ILLUSTRATIONS

ACKNOWLEDGMENTS

This book was written while I was employed as an assistant professor of English at Wayne State University and then as an associate professor at the University of Missouri. I am grateful for my time in Detroit-Metro and for what the city has taught me about rhetoric and networked thinking. My understanding of space, of the places I live and work within, as well as the spaces I think within, has been greatly enhanced by my time in Detroit.

Just outside of Detroit, in Warren, I enjoyed two of the finest brewpubs Michigan has to offer: Dragonmead and Kuhnhenn. I'm appreciative of their outstanding beers and grateful for their helping introduce me to the craft beer culture I am currently in love with. I am also grateful to Bell's for that first six-pack of Kalamazoo Stout I bought at a corner grocery on Woodward Avenue during my first week of living in the Detroit-Metro area. Back then, HopSlam releases were no big deal. Now, Bell's annual release is a madhouse. Among many things, Michigan brought me into the world of craft beer, and I hope never to leave that world.

And just inside Detroit, music played while I wrote. My thanks goes out to the original WDET, before it traded its amazing and eclectic music programming in favor of drab and uninspiring talk radio. Since then, I've depended greatly on KDHX, broadcast over the Internet, from St. Louis.

I thank Victor Vitanza and the anonymous reader who reviewed the *Digital Detroit* manuscript and offered helpful comments and insights. I also thank Karl Kageff and Southern Illinois University Press for supporting my work again.

I thank Wayne State University for a 2006 research grant that helped fund early writing of the manuscript and the University of Missouri, which provided support for research as well.

Thanks also goes out to the University of Illinois's Digital Literacies group, North Carolina State's Materializing Communication and Rhetoric symposium, and the University of Kentucky, who invited me to give talks from this project. I am grateful for valuable feedback I received from conversations at these events.

Previous versions of parts of this book appeared in *Rhetoric Society Quarterly*, *Pre/Text*, *JAC*, the *Journal of Business and Technical Communication*, and *Technical Communication Quarterly*.

And of course, I thank my loving wife, Jenny. She is my inspiration and greatest love. She and I have the ultimate network: us, Vered and Judah, and our very hairy and always underfoot cat, Shiva.

DIGITAL DETROIT

INTRODUCTION

Long live the new, network-mediated
metropolis of the digital electronic era.
                            —William Mitchell, *e-topia*

*I*t has become common to begin a work about space with a quotation from Michel de Certeau. Indeed, de Certeau's "Walking in the City" serves as a canonical marker of the possibilities space offers rhetorical studies. Its opening fragment, "Seeing Manhattan from the 118th floor of the World Trade Center," begins a breathtaking exploration of the kinds of meanings and ideas spaces can produce (91). "A city composed of paroxysmal places in monumental reliefs," de Certeau describes it. "The spectator can read in it a universe that is constantly exploding" (91). De Certeau's essay, a rejection of the "totalizing" experience many of us make when we imagine space, is a call for the details, the banal, the mundane interactions that can reinvigorate a spatialized experience—whether of the page, the city, the street, the concept, or some other moment. And in details, de Certeau writes, "walkers" remake spaces via a variety of metaphoric turns and detours, actions that rewrite spaces and one's connections to such spaces. It's an attractive, if not romantic, notion. It is a notion that long served as a commonplace for my understanding of space.

While still in graduate school, I, like many others who imagine themselves as spectators of a given place or space, was mesmerized by my first reading of "Walking in the City." "A universe that is constantly exploding" speaks to the potential critical theory and rhetorical studies promise regarding the study of space, and that I, at that moment early in my studies, was being introduced to. Who, when reading de Certeau's essay, does not imagine him- or herself as the imaginary walker who generates a rheto-

1

ric out of an engagement with the city? As someone new to the study of rhetoric, I imagined myself as this fictitious walker as well, a writer gleaning inspiration from street corners, stoplights, shop awnings, graffiti, architecture, random conversations, and other items that comprise the materiality of a given generic city. "The walking of passers-by offers a series of turns (tours) and detours that can be compared to 'turns of phrase' or 'stylistic figures.' There is a rhetoric of walking" (100). This rhetoric of walking, I—like so many others before me—found alluring, seductive, and worth further thought. I, too, wanted to walk the city. I, too, wanted to participate in a rhetoric of tours and detours. Getting to that thought process, however, was delayed until I left the college town atmosphere of Gainesville, Florida, and received my first tenure-track job in the big city of Detroit.

During the five years I lived in Detroit, and in two different tenure-track positions at two different Detroit universities, I extended such romantic visions, while also fine-tuning them to new observations and thoughts regarding cities and space. Walking Detroit is not the same as walking de Certeau's imaginary New York. Detroit, among other things, is not condensed; the city is not set up for casual walking nor for strolling. The most horizontal major city in America, Detroit sports few sky scrapers and has more residential homes than almost any other major city in the country. Detroit's origins are in residential homes, not city spaces complete with cafes, wide sidewalks, pedestrian thoroughfares, and secluded alleyways that encourage walking, passing time, or experiencing Walter Benjamin's flaneur behavior. As the city grew in the post–World War II era, Thomas Sugrue writes, much of Detroit's city space consisted of blue-collar neighborhoods. "Small bungalows, most of frame construction, some of brick, crowded together on twenty-five-by-one-hundred-foot lots that allowed just enough room for small vegetable gardens or flower patches" (22). That legacy of the small home—as opposed to the cityscape—is felt today, from Detroit's most expensive to its poorest residential areas. The implications of such a legacy are found in the city's distances, its long stretches of empty space from one point to another. Such a legacy other major midwestern cities, like Chicago and St. Louis, lack. Today, most of Detroit's major areas, those spaces one would want to walk to and among—the New Center, downtown, Belle Isle, the Renaissance Center, the Heidelberg House, Eastern Market, Michigan Avenue—are hardly within walking distance of each other. In the Motor City, the automobile is still the choice for getting from point A to point B. Regardless, even if able to walk these spaces, most people would be afraid—whether correctly or not—to walk many of Detroit's neighborhoods on the east side or to stroll among the several blocks that separate Detroit from Dearborn along Warren Avenue or to venture alone along parts of the Cass Corridor, particularly from early evening to early morning. And yet, despite this lack of walking potential, despite this lack of actual walking, we can claim that Detroit, as de Certeau claimed of New York, does generate a rhetoric. Its rhetoric, however, is not about the commonality of sightseeing and spectatorship, what we might identify as fixed place or commonplace (topos), but is about, as this book demonstrates, the network.

Before I can expand that point and elaborate on the focus of this book, however, I am reminded of several efforts to make cities rhetorical, many of which are as alluring is de Certeau's metaphoric walk. De Certeau is not the only writer to consider a city's walking spaces, routes, streets, buildings, or other features as rhetorical. Georges Perec, too, writes poetically about place; his *Species of Space* is as canonical as de Certeau's "Walking in the City." In the chapter "The Street," Perec outlines his own plan for writing the city:

> Sitting in a café or walking in the street, notebook and pen in hand, I do my best to describe the houses, the shops and the people that I come across, the posters, and in a general way, all the details that attract my eye. The other description is written somewhere other than the place itself. I then do my best to describe it from memory, to evoke all the memories that come to me concerning it, whether events that have taken place there or people I have met there. (55)

To walk the city, Perec notes, is to write with the city. And when one writes the city, as Perec's text demonstrates, all kinds of stories emerge, from the predictable to the unpredictable. Such is the nature of memory, but such, as well, is the nature of the ways we describe or tell stories about spaces. Descriptions come from the place itself, as Perec notes, as well as from elsewhere: allusions, recollections, references, and imagination. One can hear Perec's sense of storytelling in yet another canonical essay on the city, Roland Barthes's "The Eiffel Tower." The Eiffel Tower, Barthes writes, "attracts meaning"; it is an empty space that means everything but emptiness (5). In a continuation of the project Barthes labeled in 1957 "mythologies" (assumptions taken to be natural truths but which are, in effect, constructions), Barthes calls the subject of the collection's first essay an empty sign "because it means everything" (4). Like de Certeau's equation of walking with literate practices (reading/writing), or Perec's evocation of all memories, Barthes imagines the Eiffel Tower's generic meaning as one that emerges out of a reading of city space.

> By rising above Paris, the visitor to the Tower has the illusion of raising the enormous lid which covers the private life of millions of human beings; the city then becomes an intimacy whose functions, i.e., whose connections he decipher; on the great polar axis, perpendicular to the horizontal curve of the river, three zones stacked one after the other, as though along a prone body, three functions of human life: at the top, at the foot of Montmartre, pleasure; at the center, around the Opéra, materiality, business commerce; toward the bottom, at the foot of the Pantheon, knowledge, study; then, to the right and left, enveloping this vital axis like two protective muffs, two large zones of habitation, one residential the other blue collar. (12–13)

When Barthes looks out from the tower, he finds himself telling a story, a story about neighborhoods, emotions, commerce, and other related associations. Barthes is telling a story about the Eiffel Tower and Paris, but he is also telling a story about space's connection to himself, the one who encounters this space. Barthes creates what de Certeau calls "a spatial story."

Detroit, too, has a spatial story. Spatial stories, de Certeau writes, are "proliferating metaphors—sayings and stories that organize places through the displacements they 'describe'" (116). Canonical tales, like the ones I introduce here via these three well-known writers, are metaphorical markers for a given theoretical exploration of space. These writings stand for introductions to the study of space. Their legacy is felt in the extensive literature of space and the imagination. Italo Calvino's *Invisible Cities*, W. G Sebald's *The Rings of Saturn*, and Nigel Coates's *Guide to Ecstacity* belong in that tradition, a tradition that blends physical space with the imagination so that a writer may explore their intersection and interaction. These texts, like de Certeau, Perec, and Barthes, place the writer in a precarious position: How does space affect me, and how do I affect the spaces I encounter? More recently, Bryan Talbot's stunning graphic novel *Alice in Sunderland* furthers this thinking. Its dense history of factual and imaginative tracings of Lewis Carroll's relationship to the English town of Sunderland map out a space that is both real and unreal simultaneously. "Here myth meshes with reality," Talbot's narrator professes (250). Indeed, Talbot's extended references, moments of narrative self-reflection, historical conjecture, and coincidental overlaps propose that a given space, like Sunderland, England, holds endless variations of spatial relationships and meanings. A given encounter with space, as the novel's other main character experiences when he "goes to this theater" (3) can transform into a variety of sensations, moments, references, histories, texts, and narratives. These links move outward and within two hubs: Sunderland (a physical space) and *Alice in Wonderland* (a textual space); neither is anchored to any one reference point. Space, Talbot's book suggests, can function like a network.

Talbot's contribution to the tradition of writing about space is based on viewing space as a metaphorical site of interactions. The possibility of such interactions, as Talbot's book demonstrates with Sunderland, is endless. In this book, I want to extend such gestures to Detroit. Bruno Latour calls interactions within space the basis of a new rhetoric. Latour, the student of technology and science's complexity within disciplines that often portray either as simplistic or unified, differentiates between rhetoric and science in order to understand how writers might come to understand the ways interactions shape various spatial stories.

> So what is the difference between rhetoric, so much despised, and science, so much admired? . . . The difference between the old rhetoric and the new is not that the first makes use of external allies which the second refrains from using; the difference is that the first uses only a *few* of them and the second *very many*. (*Science in Action* 61)

Latour's point is that rhetoric, too, should be a practice in the *very many*. Talbot's Sunderland, like other texts before it, is an exercise in the very many. At its most simplistic definition, the very many demonstrates the very many things, people, ideas, concerns, and spaces that make up a given position, concept, and place. The very many is the basis of network rhetoric. This book, too, claims to be such an exercise in the very many; only its focus is Detroit. Because of the role the very many plays in spatial storytelling and construction, the metaphor I have come to see Detroit as embodying is the network.

We live in the age of the network. Interest in economics, labor, the World Wide Web, marketing, media, war, and other areas foregrounds the network and the changing apparatus we experience in a world shaped by technological innovation. To say that is not to romanticize the network nor to ignore the canonical but rather to recognize the complexity of relations, interactions, and movements that digital culture generates. Space is one locale where such connections occur. The complex space many of the texts I note here describe can be understood as a network. In *Reassembling the Social*, Latour writes that networks are no more than accounts, writings that trace relationships. Networks, Latour notes, are "a string of actions where each participant is treated as a full blown mediator" (128). Among mediators, and among their mediations, meanings are produced in various complex ways. Latour defines as actors those "agents" who participate in this process. "As soon as actors are treated not as intermediaries but as mediators," Latour continues, "they render the movement of the social visible to the reader. Thus, through many textual inventions, the social may become again a circulating entity that is no longer composed of the stale assemblage of what passed earlier as being part of society."

Since 2002, when I first arrived in the city of Detroit to begin life in academia, I have come to see both the generic term "city" as well as the specific locale of Detroit as such a circulating entity. Detroit has come to be, for me, an actor mediating a variety of meanings and interactions; it is not a fixed locale whose meaning is caught up in some type of grand narrative. Instead, it is an account, albeit a complex one, that embodies the rhetorical characteristics of "the very many." Detroit has come to signify what Katherine Hayles calls a digital subjectivity, a place of mediations and interactions. "Meaning emerges not through correspondences between the flat marks but through the interactions of human and nonhuman cognizers distributed throughout the environment" (212). In her work on fiction and computers, Hayles describes an identity that is as much an event or situation (that is, a reoccurring and continuing phenomenon) as it is a text. Hayles describes the basis of the network as the place where meanings come together, break apart, form hubs, connect and disconnect. Identity is not fixed; it is moving.

This is a book about Detroit as a moving network, a moving identity. "Network is a concept, not a thing out there" (Latour, *Reassembling* 131). The concept of the network is the focus of this text, the ways ideas and information function in the age of new media. To call Detroit a network is to call it an account, not a fixed representation of space. It is to simultaneously call it the physical locale we have always known to be Detroit, but it is also to call this space something else. "No longer just made of objects, computing now consists of situations," Malcolm McCullough writes in his examination of technology and space (21). Situations are not permanent fixtures. To think of Detroit as a situation and not only as a physical space is to engage in a project about invention, rhetoric, and how we engage with spaces of meaning. It is to think about relationships. To pose the city as a series of relationships is not, as a cultural critique might require, to identify its economic, gendered, or racial histories and the consequences of such histories. To pose the city as a series of relationships is not to perform a genealogy either. Rather, it is to extend such familiar, critical gestures to other kinds of relationships as well so that "the stale assemblage" yields to the "circulating entity." This gesture, in effect, is a response to calls like the one Richard Lanham makes in the *Economics of Attention*: "What happens when the economy is not based on stuff but on information and the attention that makes sense of it? And what happens when we move from the fixity of print to the volatility of digital expression?" (138). If print (as a generic category of information production, organization, and distribution) has created a Detroit based on "stuff" (race, economics, industry), what might it mean to base Detroit on information? In this book, I want to extend the gestures writers like Latour, Lanham, and McCullough make by considering a specific situation, Detroit, as a more complex situation and system of information; that is, as a network. In this sense, I extend Henri Lefebvre's concerns that cities not be understood as closed systems of meaning but rather as an oeuvre, an open text formed by those who engage with it (that is, a network) and not a body that imposes "itself upon [these people] as a system, as an already closed book" (*Writings on Cities* 117).

It may not be a coincidence, then, that I begin a discussion on Detroit and the network with four French theorists whose concepts shape my initial interest in place. Detroit, after all, was designed as a network (or grid) patterned after Paris's streets and boulevards; its name means in French "of the straight." But the trajectory that initially takes me from de Certeau to Perec to Barthes to Latour is not straight at all; it is multifaceted, suggestive, and not entirely representational. It is, I contend, the concept of being digital. As William Mitchell writes in *Placing Words: Symbols, Space, and the City*, "The vast web of intertextual relationships that we continually navigate in our intellectual and cultural lives is inextricably interwoven with the physical objects and spatial relationships that constitute the city" (11). In this book, I want to navigate a spatial story of Detroit as one such web of relationships.

Detroit

In the beginning pages of *Placing Words*, Mitchell foregrounds how the expectations one has before encountering a given place are based on the metaphoric walks one has already taken: what you've read, what you've heard, what you've thought, and what you've seen previously in a variety of media-shaped encounters with spaces. Mitchell poses a type of engagement with the city inspired by de Certeau. "The more you immerse yourself in texts, films and records somehow associated with a place, the more extended and asynchronous is the process of making sense of that place and of the communication that it provides context for" (14). In one passage, Mitchell connects his encounters with the Pythian Temple on West Seventieth Street in New York to reading about the temple previously in Bob Dylan's semiautobiographical *Chronicles*. Despite his familiarity with the temple, the site has no meaning for Mitchell until he reads Dylan's description of it. Once he forges a connection between Dylan's description and his own encounter with the place, Mitchell finds the development of a new meaning. Prior to this connection, Mitchell is unable to experience this specific space; it functions as a non-space, a space void of relationships. Such is the concern Marc Augé raises regarding space in his discussion of non-places as a generic problem resulting from twentieth-century technological progress and excess. "And while we use the word 'space' to describe the frequentation of *places* that specifically defines the journey, we should still remember that here are spaces in which the individual feels himself to be a spectator without paying much attention to the spectacle" (86). Non-places (or, we might add, non-spaces)[1] lack relationships. They, as Augé describes them, include shopping malls or airports. People pass through these spaces, but the spaces' meanings remain as individualized, solitary encounters. "If a place can be defined as relational, historical, and concerned with identity," Augé writes, "then a space which cannot be defined as relational, historical, or concerned with identity will be a non-place" (78–79). It is not difficult for me to recognize the ways Detroit has been identified as a non-place, a locale void of relationships. This book works to overcome that identification and begins with Mitchell's brief anecdote of connection, for Mitchell's connection between a space he encountered physically and that he encountered in another experience (Bob Dylan's text) is a challenge to the notion of non-space in general. Do all spaces, however banal or uninformative they may appear to be, no matter how destitute or wealthy they may be, maintain such relationships? Can a supposed non-space (the temple) become a space merely through specific types of connections? Are all spaces networked (like the temple that connects Mitchell to Dylan)? Are all spaces, then, digital?

I am tempted to answer in the affirmative. Have we yet explored the digital city as a space antithetical to the non-place? While Mitchell's anecdote about the temple suggests "yes," for how it forms connections among experiences—literary, digital, personal, and the physical—it also contrasts with the kinds of dichotomies of experience previously detailed in Mitchell's other space and technology writings like *e-topia*. By *e-topia*'s conclusion, for instance, Mitchell reemphasizes the importance of the non-place merely for the way it lets the individual be alone in her or his spatial, solitary enjoyment. Digitality, Mitchell concludes after a lengthy romanticization of the future of electronic space, no matter how influential it may be, still "will not diminish the thrill of having your eardrums assaulted by the mega-amplified Rolling Stones as you gulp Rolling Rock in a wildly reverberating football stadium somewhere" (*e-topia* 143). Of course digitality will not prevent such an activity. But to return digitality and space to an emphasis on *being alone* is to miss the point raised in the introduction to *Placing Words*. The *e-topia* move Mitchell makes resists the networked relationships that may exist in that given concert. To reduce digital space to an either/or situation is to make the inhabitant of a given digital space occupy only the role of a spectator. Such a gesture reinforces the non-place.

Engaging with spaces means being more than a spectator. Being a spectator is a position many of us feel comfortable with when we circulate within a city. Being a spectator means observing from a distance. Being a spectator means enforcing the "totalizing of the most immoderate of human texts" as de Certeau describes the act of "looking down" from the World Trade Center ("Walking" 92). The "spectators" of Detroit—the popular press, the nightly news, the daily conversations we hear and speak, and ourselves as we pity the city or look upon it in disgust—tend to totalize Detroit and make it a non-place. Before arriving in Detroit, I found little meaning in this city I later worked in, and if anything, I was a spectator of Detroit. I saw Detroit from the distance of the automobile I traveled in, the headline I glanced at, or the financial report of the auto industry broadcast on a CNN report. What meaning Detroit did have, no doubt, was connected to the popular imaginary of ruins and riots, representational imagery I had formed out of newspaper headlines, TV news, jokes, and other references. This impression was reinforced when I got my first look at the city as the car I was a passenger in exited the Lodge Freeway at Livernois: Burned-out shops. Run-down buildings. Check Cashing. Fast food. Few people walking around. While I don't deny that some elements of the popular, negative perception are, in fact, true, my expectations and initial perceptions based on those expectations were also not entirely legitimate either. My expectations were based too strongly in a topos of Detroit. They were based on observing, but not experiencing, the meaning of the city. They were based on being a spectator, a proverbial solitary "concertgoer" who tunes out the world for an immediate moment's experience. They were based largely on the non-space meaning of Detroit.

And for this reason, I find Mitchell's brief anecdote informative and his earlier comment problematic. The unanticipated encounter he retells in *Placing Words*, the one tied to a previous encounter (reading a book), resists a given topos-based meaning in a way that going to a concert and drinking the widely advertised beer often cannot. The topoi are based on expectation. The encounter experienced via topoi often (though it could be) isn't predicated on expectation. Going to a concert so that one can hear the music is not a negation of the idea of the encounter, but by itself it can reinforce the role of the spectator because of its dependence on fixed and expected meaning (the songs that will be played, the repeatable experience of purchasing the merchandise, the recognizable moment where participants hold up lighters and request the biggest hit as encore, the feeling of excitement when the band hits the stage, and so on). The lack of expectation, which I think is foregrounded more in the Dylan example of linkage Mitchell provides, captures much of what I have come to understand as the network, a general term for a variety of interconnected information systems encountered on the web, in industry, in telecommunications, in city spaces, in personal relationships, and in rhetorical expression. The network, as I've come to understand it, operates by movement, not fixity. That movement involves how we move within information and spaces simultaneously. That involvement can dramatically change a space's meaning by the juxtaposition of something as innocuous as a Bob Dylan reference and a personal anecdote.

Thus, this book is, in many ways, a mapping of Detroit as a network. "All maps," Denis Wood notes, "from the most apparently 'objective' to the most blatantly 'subjective'—embody the interests of their authors in map form" (71). Wood's own anecdote involves his frustration over maps that leave out encounters and observations because these are items impossible to fix on a piece of paper. "'Birds and Bees? The mapmakers weren't interested in those things,'" he mocks. "Exactly. So what did they map? What they were interested in. And this is the interest the map embodies . . . inevitably" (72). In this book, I adopt Wood's focus on one's interest, on making that interest a principle feature of writing about space. Those areas I opt to concentrate on are areas that *interest me*. My interests are not egocentric nor even eccentric but are examples of alternative ways to organize informational spaces (thus, another's interests would organize the space differently). This organization, like all acts of organization and arrangement, is rhetorical. While the tradition of organization and arrangement (which I will expand upon in chapter 1) has followed the Ramist practice of objectivity and personal distance, in the age of new media, where the network's presence is foregrounded, personal interest is always a part of a given arrangement. Personal interest is a principle of information organization.

Affirmation of personal interest as a major feature of rhetorical expression is also what Roland Barthes stressed in a number of later texts, from his discussion on the Eiffel Tower, to his exploration of Japan as a series of signs, to a pseudoautobiography, to a discussion of photography and allusive meanings. In the opening of *Roland Barthes*, much of this approach is spelled out.

> In what he writes, there are two texts. Text I is reactive, moved by indignations, fears, unspoken rejoinders, minor paranoias, defenses, scenes. Text II is active, moved by pleasure. But as it is written, corrected, accommodated to the fiction of Style, Text I becomes active too, whereupon it loses its reactive skin, which subsist only in patches (mere parentheses). (43)

By acknowledging that "pleasure" is a part of my writing, I also note that my understanding of Detroit is not entirely topos-based. The topoi, Aristotle states, are the places of argument "applicable in common to questions of justice and physics and politics and many different species [of knowledge]; for example, the topos of the more and the less" (*On Rhetoric* 1.2.21). The topoi maintain commonality, predictability, expectation. Any inquiry that mixes in the personal pleasure of the writer challenges how common a given topos, like Detroit, will be for its readership. The objective of this text, therefore, is not to present an expected reading of the city, but instead to offer something else, something that isn't entirely expected, nor completely absurd; something that is networked.

"A building," Nigel Coates writes, "like a film or a piece of music, can help to amplify your own responses and emotions" (42). But what about when those initial emotions—like the feeling of shock upon seeing burned out buildings for the first time—change into another perspective or emotional stance? We experience what Coates calls the "total dynamic fields that hold together events, cultures, time and space, as if it were a continual performance" (43). We experience a non-topos driven topography. The connection between rhetoric and topography is well played out in rhetorical and classical studies, whether in discussion of the Agora or commentary on Socrates's leaving the comfort of the city in the *Phaedrus*. Francis Yates simplifies this connection in a brief definition: "Topics are the 'things' or subject matter of dialectic which came to be known as topoi through the places in which they were stored" (31). This definition, however, treats topics as areas already in place. What Mitchell and Coates suggest is that when noncommon elements are introduced (memories, anecdotes, encounters, emotions, responses), such areas are not stored as much as they are circulated. For some contemporary writers on new media, this circulation is also known as *chora*. In *Heuretics: The Logic of Invention*, Gregory Ulmer updates the topos with chora, an electronic method of meaning making in which places of discussion are fluid and moving, rather than fixed or stored in one place. Chora, Ulmer writes, is Plato's forgotten explanation of space. Ulmer continues his extensive project regarding chora in *Electronic Monuments*, a more complete investigation into electronic spaces. "Chora is a holistic ordering of topics into an electrate image system of categories" (*Electronic Monuments* xx). The electrate system Ulmer names I situate here as networked-based invention and rhetorical practice. "'Chora' names the memory or memorial operation of sorting or ordering of that which remains undifferentiated" (*Electronic Monuments* 125). Chora is a rhetoric of organization updated for new media work.

> A topos collects entities into universal homogenous sets based on shared essences, necessary attributes; chora gathers singular ephemeral sets of heterogeneous items based on accidental details. Yet chora paradoxically becomes categorical (general) through the aesthetic evocation of an atmosphere by means of these details. (*Electronic Monuments* 120)

Another way to phrase this activity (the move from topos to chora within digital culture), I contend, is networked writing. Networked writing, like chora's ability to move meaning from place to place, serves as a model for contemporary rhetorical production. It shifts rhetorical production from the singularity of place to the gathering of items and details.

This model is not easy to construct. Denis Wood makes that clear when he locates a topos-bound mapping of Detroit. Wood reads a Detroit Geographical Expedition and Institute map against a United States Geological Survey map. Of the Detroit map, he writes, "At the moment I am looking at two other maps, one of a block in Bloomfield Hills, the other of a block in the Mack Avenue area of Detroit." Wood identifies a wealthy suburb and a road that runs east and west through the city, and he notes that the map's legend, which consists of symbols for grass, green shrubs and trees, and bicycles as well as broken bottles, litter, and cans, places predictable symbols in the expected places: greenery in Bloomfield Hills, trash in

Detroit. But, Wood notes, treating space as permanent is an ideological gesture often meant to keep *things in their place.* "The grass and toys of Bloomfield Hills are as permanent features in Detroit as the trash and broken bottles of Mack Avenue, more permanent, in fact, than the buildings that went up in the flames of 1967 or in the slower conflagration that followed. But permanence never had anything to do with it: The Survey has no interest in the durative" (84). The durative, the ongoing process of meaning making, mixes our expectations of space and the meanings that follow. Possibly, only networks can foreground that kind of mapping since they, too, are based on similar principles.

In the next five chapters, I take the "ongoing process" seriously as a writing and inventive methodology for new media. Because networks are messy, confusing spaces where information, people, things, places, and ideas are coming together and drifting apart, I attempt to write this book as a network as well. That means, of course, that the following chapters will foreground a great deal of information coming together, so much information that one may find discomfort in the references, allusions, quotations, and connections that are used because I am not explicating every piece of information I encounter; I am using it and then not using it. I am, in other words, networking Detroit by *tracing* its accounts. Despite the possible readerly discomfort, I find this method advantageous for how it allows me new kinds of opportunities to explore a space; by using a network to examine Detroit as a digital concept, I am made aware of connections I would not have discovered otherwise. The disadvantage to this method, however, is that it can, at times, feel confusing. The amount of references, allusions, quotations, and connections may throw some readers off. The topos of the scholarly book often requires "a single theory" that drives its composition. My methodological choice, however, follows Edward Casey's notion of space in *The Fate of Place.* Contrasting chora with the Aristotelian topoi, Casey writes, "space characteristically moves out, so far out as to explode the closely confining perimeters within which Aristotle attempted to ensconce material things. In this unequal battle, spacing-out triumphs over placing-in" (77). The information I bring together in this book reflects my effort to move out of a fixed space called Detroit; I am searching out connections, some of which are explicit, some of which are implicit. Each chapter of this book, therefore, explores networked writing through an undifferentiated section of Detroit that continuously moves out of its space and engages with other spaces: Woodward Avenue, the Maccabees Building, the Michigan Central Train Station, and 8 Mile. These explorations do not explain the topos of each space; instead they sort out and reorder each space as part of a larger network of meaning, a network I initiate here but that also can represent how such ordering might work elsewhere, in different spaces and in different cities, or by different people. And as I explore each space within the network, I simultaneously learn about networked rhetorics. I learn about digital mapping, affective interfaces, folksonom(me), digital response, and "good enough" decision making. Thus, this is not a doctrine of rhetorical practice I propose, but a rhetorical model conducive for electronic culture. This book, I contend, is a step towards a theory and pedagogy of the network. "What could be the vision of Detroit—a city built in the twentieth century—in this new century?" asks Kyong Park (92). The network, I respond.

1

NETWORKS, PLACE, AND RHETORIC

> This is how space begins, with words only,
> signs traced on the blank page.
> —Georges Perec, *Species of Spaces and Other Places*

Navigation

December 15, 2005, *Saturday Night Live* prerecorded skit entitled "Lazy Sunday" featured comics Chris Parnell and Andy Samberg as urban New Yorkers who rap about their day in the city and subsequent decision to see the film *The Chronicles of Narnia*.[1] At one point in the sketch, the comics must figure out the best route to the movie theater. They debate which online service is best.

"I prefer MapQuest!"

"That's a good one, too."

"Google Maps is the best."

"True dat."

"Double true!"

In this brief exchange, the characters emphasize the role mapping services such as MapQuest and Google Maps play in the navigation of online and physical spaces. While the characters explore how to navigate New York City, they could be discussing any major metropolitan area in the world. Cities often consist of complicated routes, well-worn paths of travel, and sudden surprises when traveling through them. "It must be granted that there is some value in mystification, labyrinth, or surprise in the environment," Kevin Lynch writes about urban navigation (5). Urban residents, Lynch argues, make sense of such routes via the "'public image,' the common mental pictures carried by large numbers of a city's inhabitants: areas of agreement which might be expected to appear in the interaction of a single physical reality, a common culture, and a basic physiological nature" (7). The public image today, as the *SNL* characters demonstrate, is the online map, for it establishes the commonality of space for city residents. "There seems to be a public image of any given city which is the overlap of many individual images. Or perhaps there is a series of public images, each held by some significant number of citizens" (Lynch 46). Online maps, via their complex database setups, bring together various public images and present them as a form of navigation. One public image—the city I live in—contests with the mapping services' public image—the collection of information gathered and assembled in one space. "To choose which theater to go to," Denis Wood writes about maps and city navigation, "*much less how to get there*, we have to organize all the relevant bits of information into some kind of structure" (15). The online map alters our sense of spatial structure by transforming space into digital information, and, in turn, by making digital information public imagery.

Even with the rise of the digital sphere's influence on navigation, the shaping of the public image, as Lynch also notes, is a physical activity. It results from the intricate ways navigators and the geographies they navigate interact in specific, physical locations. The *SNL* characters, for instance, must forge some sort of bodily relationship with New York itself in order to fashion a route to the movie theater via the online service (they walk its streets, visit its stores, work in its buildings). The relationship between physical interaction and space has been predominant from early seafaring peoples to modern urban dwellers. "The very fact that skilled navigation arose in what would seem to be perceptually difficult environments indicates the influence of [the shape of the physical world]" (Lynch 133). In the highly congested and very physical modern city, discovering how to avoid popular (and thus, over-trafficked) routes in favor of speedier routes has, as well, become a skill. The question is no longer "Where do we want to go today?" but rather, "How quickly can we get to where we want to go with minimum obstacles and interruptions, with minimum hassle and obstruction?" Indeed, a request to the computer servers that house MapQuest or Google Maps will produce a result in less than a second. The distance between the user and the map interface is barely recognizable. Even with that point, speed is not the only dominant aspect of communicative practices in the digital age, as Paul Virilio has famously stated. "We had to wait for the fusion/confusion of information and data processing to obtain the fusion/confusion of the secret of speed," Virilio writes (*Art of the Motor* 33). Massive computer servers may produce speed, but the speed of navigation is no longer a secret of fusing and confusing routes or even a mystification of routes, as Lynch argues. If anything, the emergence of information culture requires the emergence of a culture of navigation that does not necessarily avoid the secrecy of how to get from one location to the next, but that also does not build its foundations upon mystifying the navigator or the process of navigation. How quickly we navigate information depends on how the system we navigate within allows us access to the appropriate tools of navigation. Google Maps makes navigation simple: Get directions. Search nearby. Calculate your distance by car, public transit, or walking. These tools, I note, are database driven. These databases, I add, are the basis of a rhetoric of the network that can be read and understood via the city. The city I focus on in this book is the one I once lived in and engaged with in physical and nonphysical ways, Detroit, Michigan. It is the city I have begun to map in complex ways because of the networked rhetoric it shows me.

Since initially viewing the *SNL* skit, both the first time it was aired and later through repeated viewings on YouTube, I've wondered what it might mean to navigate a city like Detroit. My intent would not be to navigate Detroit quickly, but to navigate the city as if it were a digital space. Where do I want to go in Detroit, then, is not a question of getting from Jefferson Avenue to the New Center or of arriving at Corktown via Michigan Avenue. Instead, it is a question of imagining and actualizing the city as a data space to navigate, as a type of public image among public images. What is it about digital navigation that allows me the opportunity to "walk" Detroit in a less than totalizing way, as de Certeau calls for? In the *SNL* skit, I see the less than totalizing move de Certeau emphasizes in "Walking in the City." Beyond the characters' usage of Google Maps, their engagement with cell phones, cultural references, and parody to navigate an area stretching from Greenwich Village to Broadway breaks down the city as data consisting of space, culture, and expression. New York, therefore, is digital in a conceptual and actual way (from the juxtapositions of things and nonthings to the usage of online technology). To frame New York City as an online map, the way the *SNL* characters do, seems profound to me. Such a gesture feels like an innovation in space, one that suggests online mapping as speed, but also as an entirely new experience, a network of moments, movement, things, people, and places. A Digital Detroit, then, a public image of Detroit as digital, might begin as such an online map.

Thousands of people each day, no doubt, do navigate Detroit and its metro area via online mapping services: Posts on the Metroblogging

Detroit blog indicate the services' importance to Detroit.[2] The Detroit Yes! message board (the city's popular online forum) contains over 135 posts related to using Google Maps in the city.[3] And a former colleague of mine, as a newly arrived transplant to Detroit, regularly used a mapping GPS service to navigate his way through the various streets unfamiliar to him of the metro area when he first arrived. Online mapping, like Google Maps, is both a comfortable means of navigation as well as a novel approach to space. Conceptually, it offers a way to rethink what makes up a given environment, how we respond to such an environment, and how we use such environments to further make connections among spaces. Online mapping, as I will shortly argue, is a type of information system relevant to contemporary rhetorical work. It is also the first feature of Digital Detroit I will discuss in this book.

Online mapping services attempt to provide ways to navigate the vast network of information that the web has emerged into, and that is, as well, reflected in the material world of shops, streets, homes, and other physical locales. In this emerging space, "locations self-identify, notices of congestion immediately generate alternative paths to the destination, and services announce themselves" (Greenfield 65). These services arrange space so that users may navigate such spaces in meaningful and productive ways. Their role in the arrangement of online information cannot be minimized. One 2006 estimate proposes that "the number of navigation systems, whether in cars, portable devices or in cell phones, sold in North America will increase nearly 50% from 4.5 million in 2006 to 6.7 million next year [2007] and to 25 million by 2011" (Gopwani). The invention and sales of new types of phones, PDAs, computers, GPS systems, and other devices make the *SNL* skit more than a joke: These devices reflect the way space and technology are merging. The Internet— as a giant hypertextual space—foregrounds this process. "Our symbolic environment is, by and large," Manuel Castells contends, "structured by this flexible, inclusive hypertext, in which many people surf each day. The virtuality of this text is in fact a fundamental dimension of reality, providing the symbols and icons from which we think and thus exist" (13). Symbolic and iconic moments make up new spaces for habitation by creating large databases that users draw from. "The Web has gone map mad," a recent *Forbes* article on online mapping begins. "Ever since Google released easy-to-use software tools for its nifty on-screen maps of streets and satellite images a year ago, fans have set off an explosion of creative overlaps, adding their own useful and sometimes quirky data" (Bahree). All of this "data"—symbolic, iconic, personal—generates an evolving definition of spatial mapping, one that negotiates fixed spaces (streets) as well as ephemeral spaces (quirky data). "Centuries ago," Paul Virilio writes, "matter was defined by two dimensions: mass and energy. Today there comes a third one to it: information" ("Architecture" 180).

Detroit, the Motor City, has a specific relationship with information that includes innovations in mapping but that precedes these new technologies. Detroit, like many other storied cities, is a site of information distribution. According to one narrative, the first printing press in the Northwest was set up in Detroit.[4] As a general site of information distribution, Detroit teaches us much about American culture (it was once the country's automotive capital, it is the birthplace of Motown, it suffered greatly during the 1967 riots). Detroit, as well, is a site of technological development; it is the place where innovations occur (the automotive industry, techno music). And Detroit, like other major cities, informs. Its iconic imagery, economic status, and technological innovations in transportation are often generalized from in the popular media as indicators of larger national achievements or failures.

My own relationship with this city is based on perceiving the city as a site of information creation and as a site of informing. What I knew about Detroit before my arrival in 2002 was based primarily on the places of meaning I had previously encountered and gathered into my own public image. That information system, however, did not reveal to me the pessimistic technological situation Paul Virilio details in *The Art of the Motor*. In the "information universe," Virilio tells us, "Everything rushes at man, man-the-target is assailed on all sides, and our only salvation is now to be found in illusion, in flight from the reality of the moment" (132). In the age of information, Virilio warns, "control becomes the environment itself" (131). Indeed, the controlled economies of Michigan dependent on automotive success might lead one to perceive Detroit as an assembly-line-driven city unable to control its own destiny outside of one specific type of manufacturing. In his chronicle of Detroit, Thomas Sugrue makes such an argument, writing that "the most important force that restructured Detroit's economy after World War II was the advent of new automated processes in the automobile, auto parts, and machine tool industries" (130). Speed—of production—and control—automation— drove the Detroit economy to both success and failure, this narrative claims. Such declarations echo warnings of the dangers of the technologically driven control society delivered by theorists like William S. Burroughs and Gilles Deleuze. These writers advocate resisting or reshaping information control, proposing strategies like the nova technique or nomadism as tools for fighting the automation and speed of information as well as the tendency of each to dominate thought, action, politics, and other areas of experience. Of course, resisting control is not getting away from control, for even the nova technique is a control mechanism that strives to place power with a given rhetor: "The basic nova technique is very simple: Always as many insoluble conflicts as possible and always aggravate existing conflicts" (Burroughs, *Ticket That Exploded* 54–55). Even as the automotive industry lost control, it still maintains a type of control over the city's future as the effects of financial collapse continue. A conflict remains.

Very few cities have seen or produced conflict the way Detroit has. From city politics to urban design to race relations, conflict and Detroit have been in a difficult relationship for some time. The kinds of navigation that interest me regarding Detroit are not about resisting control or conflict but are about reshaping control, particularly how meanings are controlled and how information conflict may function in productive ways in rhetorical production. Detroit as a control society, as I will counter in this book, does not experience conflict in the way traditional resistance strategies do. Instead, and more in line with Burroughs's work, the city's rhetorical positioning evokes innovative methods that shift control from the circulated meanings disseminated in a variety of formats to media-based strategies the network provides. The meanings spaces generate always work to control representations or responses to representations. Within the network, as I want to show, this practice of control does not resemble the control society writers like Burroughs resisted. Instead, control continues to shift and change as new meanings are added and subtracted. While I recognize that such a statement may, at first, feel convoluted, in this book I work to flesh out what I mean by this shift in control as I form Detroit into a network. In the network, control may, indeed, become the environment as Virilio warns. That move towards environment, however, may not be entirely negative or negative at all.

When I first encountered the Motor City at the Lodge Freeway exit at Livernois Avenue, I, like many others before me, may have thought about the roles conflict and control play in Detroit, Michigan. Indeed, I carried with me a database of narratives regarding the city and control. As various narratives of Detroit make clear, economic and racial conflict have played major roles in the city's continued despair. A recent opinion piece in the *Detroit Free Press* by *Michigan Chronicle* publisher Sam Logan goes to great lengths to point out the city's failure as one of control: Competing entities attempt to control the city but fail in the process.

Logan notes the complicity of then-mayor Kwame Kilpatrick in these types of struggles but also indicts the school board, the state legislature, and the city council. Logan's response is to demolish the political infrastructure, and to replace it with new figures and ideas. "Yet the only way this city will survive is if there is a re-population with a new class of virtuous, ethical people. Only when we transition to a more politically appropriate realignment and expand our demographic bases of power can we dream of a new status quo. Without a major dose of gentrification, we simply do not have much of a future." In a February 7, 2011, op-ed, David Brooks repeats Logan's sentiments; he dismisses the promises of development project managers whose control over local finance often collapses. Instead, Brook favors fostering energetic people. Brooks challenges the narrative of capital improvement. "For years, cities like Detroit built fancy towers and development projects in the hopes that this would revive the downtown core. But cities thrive because they host quality conversations, not because they have new buildings and convention centers." Similar to Brooks's and Logan's commentary, the city-run website BelieveinDetroit. org runs public service announcements on Detroit television called *I'm a Believer*. In the commercial, local celebrities and politicians pronounce "I'm a Believer." Rejuvenation, we are told, will come from belief, not from investment or city planning. "If we all do something," the commercial proclaims in multiple voices, "we can do anything" ("Believe in Detroit"). This well-worn cliché places control back with the citizenry. If you believe it, success will come.

As if they are attempts to navigate a conflicted present and past, Detroit narratives often fluctuate between demolishments of some sort and rejuvenations as response. These narratives act as controlling mechanisms for how we interpret the city's positioning in American culture; they function as circulated, yet fixed, topoi; they map the city's spaces. Neither Logan nor the city are the first to express the sentiment of renewal; they are not the only ones who attempt to control a particular city image with this tale of a body that rises from the ashes of its failures, whether through new people or new beliefs. In his highly romanticized 1946 history of the city, Malcolm Bingay depicts Detroit as a city born in conflict and presumed despair. Like a phoenix, however, it always rises out of its problems. "Blow after blow has been rained upon this city throughout its history and always it has arisen from its ashes—cleaner and finer and better because it has conquered adversity" (15). More recently, in Sammy Davis Jr.'s sappy and over-produced Vegas-sounding song "Hello Detroit," this narrative of "down and out" is introduced so that it may eventually be overcome. Davis begins the song with an ode to Detroit's rough heritage. He calls the city a fighter and lover, noting how it is "strong" and has always "recovered" from whatever gets it down. Davis follows up this introduction with a quick beat and jump to the glorious areas of the city that have overcome "whatever" might have once left them broken or neglected. Davis sings "hello" to the city and maps his favorite sites that have resisted these un-provoked and unwarranted attacks. He lists strolling through Belle Isle Park and visiting Greektown after dark as encounters that will make the young spirited once again after experiencing troubled times.

Davis's rise–and-fall narrative is echoed in the one that White Stripes front man and one-time Detroit resident Jack White utilizes in his poem for Detroit, published July 6, 2008, in the *Detroit Free Press*. White's narrative of the city's idyllic spots such as Belle Isle and its showcase of automobiles concludes with the stanza of rebirth.

> Detroit, you hold what one's been seeking,
> Holding off the coward-armies weakling,
> Always rising from the ashes
> not returning to the earth.

White's automotive phoenix, like these other examples, follows the tradi-tion of connecting Detroit and destitution as parallel topoi. These topoi are strong in the popular vocabulary and public image of Detroit, and it is important to note their continued use by various kinds of writers, speakers, and performers as a type of database that informs rhetorical expression. Even those far removed from Detroit, like the novelist Henry Miller, who returned to the United States during World War II after ex-tended living in Europe, drew on this type of database. Visiting Detroit, Miller immediately grasped the city as one of despair, albeit without the same type of renewal finale other writers often fall back on. In his own mapping of America, Miller identifies Detroit as the focal point of the country's problems, as the space from which we can navigate all of America's issues. "The capital of the new planet—the one, I mean, which will kill itself off—is of course Detroit. I realized that the moment I arrived. At first I thought I'd go and see Henry Ford, give him my con-gratulations. But then I thought—what's the use? He wouldn't know what I was talking about" (41). Unlike Bingay's romanticism or Sammy Davis's whimsicalness, Miller offers his own version of redemption, war. If De-troit represents the country killing itself, it is because the city's economics are tied to conflict. In this rhetorical gesture, Miller sounds very much like Logan. The city's problems are systemic and politically structural.

Things are picking up in Detroit. Defense orders, you know. The taxi driver told me he expected to get his job back soon. In the factory, I mean. What would happen if the war suddenly stopped I can't imagine. There would be a lot of broken hearts. Maybe another crisis. People wouldn't know what to do for themselves if peace were suddenly declared. Everybody would be laid off. The bread lines would start up. Strange how we can manage to feed the world and not learn how to feed ourselves. (Miller 43)

Finally, during the 2011 Super Bowl, Chrysler ran a commercial that continued this narrative of destruction and renewal. Chrysler, as one of the "Big Three" automobile manufacturers, must demonstrate its own phoenix rise from a collapse easily identified in the 2008 bailout, but also viewable all over Detroit's faded landscape. Over a backdrop of canonical images of Detroit (steam rising off the street, abandoned factories, industry along the river, the Joe Louis fist), a voiceover in the commercial states: "I've got a question for you. What does this city know about luxury? What does a town that's been to hell and back know about the finer things in life?" The answer, we are told, is "more than most." Hard work. Conviction. The know-how that runs generations. "That's our story," the narrator says. And "it's probably not the one you've been reading about in the papers." This alternative story projects renewal of the automobile framed as belief in the car's future. As Eminem declares at the end of the commercial before the image of a new Chrysler he's been driving in appears, this alternative story symbolizes the mantra "This is what we do." What "we" do, it seems, is become reborn via the very item that led to the city's destruction: the automobile.

One might argue against or resist such simplified histories, narratives, or descriptions of space that these very different moments exemplify. Each narrative, in fact, offers its own moment of resistance to some version of control (Detroit is corrupt at its core; Detroit is not the bad place we think it is; Detroit's need for mass production will not save the nation but rather make it dependent on global suffering, Detroit can still be saved by its dependence on the car). Still, despite the conflict that gives Detroit its basic informational characteristics (as either down and out or on the verge of recovery) and that typically allows the average person to navigate this city, I have never found "resistance" to be a strong model for the city or for space in general. Nor have I worried too much over issues of control since I know such controls are often for more control (mine), not less control (someone else's). As hard as it is to do, I don't spend much time recovering these topoi when I need to navigate Detroit.

Instead, I have opted to work within information systems rather on them, as these other writers do. To work within is to understand the topoi, yet it is also to produce new kinds of information from within them, to produce a story we have not read about in the papers, as the Chrysler commercial proclaims. This process occurs particularly in terms of networks; it is based on how I map information in a variety of ways. As Virilio also writes—when not speaking in dire terms—"From now on, the beings and things that surround us are merely FIELDS and the real a single NETWORK—only a CYBERNETIC network since everything is exclusively internal to the 'field'" (*The Art of the Motor* 130). All of my information is a network. All of my information I gather and assemble is internal to that network. These previous references—a contemporary op-ed article, a 1940s historical book, a kitschy song, a novelist's travel memoirs, a car commercial—are database items within that network. Everything I produce, therefore, is a network as well. In this production, I "find wider possibilities, create networks and links, and make places and selves in ways beyond standardized purposes" (Kolb 192). The network I call Detroit includes Sammy Davis Jr. as much as it includes the Lodge Freeway. It includes a *Saturday Night Live* skit as much as it includes the university I first worked at in Detroit. This book is an exploration and creation of that network. It attempts to be an information system.

Detroit as a network is a deviation from Detroit as the supposed problematic city that most narratives reenforce. In what I have come to see as the information network called Detroit, I never felt assailed, nor did I feel the need to flee what surrounded me while I lived in the Detroit–Metro area. Eventually, as an educator for five years in the city—first at a private liberal arts university and then at a research university—I played a role as creator of information, both in research and in teaching. And I played that role willingly and with curiosity. I began to call Detroit a network because of how I saw its history, cultural moments, public buildings, neighborhoods, streets, stories, cultural references, and so on function as a system of information in which each node in that system fed off of and contributed to the next. In 2002, as a newly hired faculty member at the University of Detroit–Mercy, I felt much different than the University of Detroit professor William Bunge critiques as a figure divorced from his surroundings. Bunge, who mapped the nearby neighborhood of Fitzgerald as a socio-economic, cultural, and ethnic space, reserves harsh words for the university's intellectuals who refuse to recognize the neighborhood where they work as networked to the university workplace. "The blight along Livernois is associated with the University of Detroit. Students tend to form code-violating rooming houses and have the transients' disrespect for property up-keep. Fitzgerald Community Council membership is non-existent among University of Detroit professors" (145). Bunge, writing in the late 1960s and early 1970s, critiques a lack of networked thinking among those who work in the city, but who feel no connection to the city itself. While I was not above such problematic thinking, the longer I lived and worked in the city, the more I felt the desire to map out a part of that network and present it as a way to think about the rhetoric of networked spaces. I wanted to map a part of Detroit in order to demonstrate how networks function rhetorically (as opposed to the infrastructural networks that run the city's water, sewage, transportation, and electricity). I wanted to map a rhetoric of the network. This book is that eventual mapping. "All maps," Denis Wood argues, "inevitably, unavoidably, necessarily embody their authors' prejudices, biases and partialities (not to mention the less frequently observed art, curiosity, elegance, focus, care, imagination, attention, intelligence, scholarship their makers' bring to their labor)" (24). My interests in and emotional bonds to this adopted city inspired me to map Detroit as such a digital project.

Beginning mapping with a moment of pleasure. Enjoying Detroit. Photograph by the author.

My mapping, therefore, is a rhetorical project, for its concerns are with how information affects and produces information. My mappings and navigations of Detroit initially, though, were a combination of the conceptual (impressions left with me) and technological (use of actual online mapping services like Google Maps). A great deal of this navigation resembled a database. The recognition of that database stems from my professional position within Detroit. As a professor whose teaching and research involves web-based platforms, many of which—like wikis, weblogs, and other social software—depend on databases, I, like Castells's imaginary producer of virtual environments, work with students to manipulate, shape, and generate symbolic movements through these databases (that is, how to arrange writing within a wiki; how to formulate, construct, and extend writings and responses across weblogs; how to visualize and participate in the vast network of pages and sites that collectively form the web; how to invent within a networked space). To navigate these types of databases, one needs a metaphoric map, a set of tools to assist in making sense and utilizing all of this information. As if such work were not difficult enough, with the launch of the Google Maps embeddable web map in 2007, the mapping of space, it appears, has made navigation even more complex. In this new application, the database-driven product and the new media object juxtapose to generate a new type of web expression.[5] In what may already be a database (a specific kind of website whose data is not page driven but database driven) another database is embedded. The layout of a given site (personal site, business site, commerce site) engages with a completely different set of information (that formulated by Google and its partners elsewhere). Two complex spaces of information are put, not in proximity to one another, but within one another.

Symbolically, at least, two problems are foregrounded in this gesture. The layering of rhetorical space where one finds and uses meaning is complicated so that one has to figure out how to navigate between the two mappings of ideas. First there is the space one has arrived at (the website); second there is a space embedded in the first space (the Google map). In that second embedded space, visual depictions of the space can be found (panoramic images of the street, exit, store); links connect the user from the street viewed to a website representing what is on the street (shop, restaurant, bar); and nearby locations are mapped, visualized, and linked to as well. Terrain, satellite imagery, and, of course, distance are additional features of the database. The database quality of such maps create layers upon layers of mappable space. The layer, as I will note in chapter 4, is a major feature of network rhetoric. The drop and drag interface of Google Maps as well as its reliance on the hypertext link (an everyday feature of web writing and reading) makes database navigation as simple as any other computer application. Underneath that interface, a variety of complex decisions are made regarding information. I will expand the role of the interface in networks in chapter 3, but for now, I see its complexity in the overview of destruction and renewal I have touched upon in this chapter. Over long periods of time, and amid very different personalities, these topoi are mapped like database entries within a type of interface. That mapping is embedded in a larger narrative about Detroit and its failures.

Interfaces and layers are rhetorical features of new media writing. Rhetorically, then, one must figure out how to employ embedded maps for invention, arrangement, and delivery purposes. None of the options is obvious. Nor am I yet positive that there is one option to follow when working with such embedded maps, whether they are conceptual (a point I have been alluding to but that will become clearer shortly) or technological (as Google promises). Nevertheless, I identify a rhetorical problem that reflects my own interests in space and meaning. I want to flesh out the map (Detroit) within the map (Detroit as well) in similar ways as an embeddable web map might allow. This chapter begins with the promise of such work, tracing out the role databases play in networked spaces. In that sense, there exists a network (Detroit) within a larger network (new media). The following chapters continue this thinking in such a manner so that, I hope, this book as a whole can be read as a kind of database shaping a network. Like a database, the spaces are not permanent. And like a database, the spaces are always in relationship to one another. What is introduced in one chapter relates to what has been already introduced and what will be later shown. Each chapter is an element in the larger database called Digital Detroit. And each chapter, in turn, is itself a database with various relating elements within it. Before I get ahead of myself, however, I need to say a little more about databases and navigation.

The Database

Google Maps and MapQuest are databases; they store and assemble vast amounts of information hosted by their own and related services. Neither functions on its own; both are dependent on a variety of other databases in order for their own database to generate information. In a sense, then, databases engage in a type of communication system, one in which an agent (one database and its user) attempts to understand/address/respond to another agent (another or a series of databases and their users as well as what is contained in each database). In response to this activity, one might speculate that databases—as part of a larger body often called new media—are providing an emerging rhetoric regarding how to map space as well as how to move through places. That rhetoric is enacted by both a given system (one like Google Maps) and the rhetor who engages with the system (the user). Where oration, memory palaces, basic argumentation, the general category of print, and other types of new media have provided such rhetorical guidance for spatial arrangements previously, online mapping adds new dimensions to how we navigate and arrange space. One brief example of this database communication might be a related Google Maps service like Wayfaring, whose title page informs users how it creates maps: "Maps, Your Way." Wayfaring users can annotate spaces, add images, write notes about spaces encountered, compose reviews and thoughts on spaces visited, and hyperlink this work to others. Like Google Maps, its users layer information upon other information; each image, space, text that is layered is done in relationship to another. Wayfaring's basic "Create" page lists its purpose accordingly: "Create a map of your life; Build a map of your event; Make a Travelogue; Create a map with photos and video." From the instrumental (photos and video) to the conceptual (a map of your life), Wayfaring frames database information delivery as exchanges among agents. By connecting with other users' maps, Wayfaring users take the Google Maps service beyond mere street instruction; space, personal investment, and commentary become new elements of mapping databases. These elements are engaged with internally (one user) and externally (multiple users). Other sites like Rrove[6] and Google Maps EZ,[7] too, juxtapose commentaries with spaces and thus help create a fabric of moments, and not just a moment one attempts to reach (as a more traditional, print map might dictate). Sites like Amazon's now defunct Yellow Pages[8] previously allowed users to engage with panoramic imagery as they made their way through city districts, stopping to see and find stores, restaurants, hotels, and other places of commerce. "Find it on the block. Walk up and down the street," Amazon's site once invited, and Amazon customers could make their way through MapQuest maps and images simultaneously. Walks, like those that these sites promote, are digital de Certeau "walks" through connections, interactions with images, ideas, places, and maps; they are virtual quests. More important than the virtual dimensions of space any of these sites propose, however, is that these sites can be interlinked with nonmapping programs like the image sharing site Flickr, a given weblog, a bookmarking site like del.icio.us, a wiki, or other applications. Various forms of information, therefore, are being placed in relationship with one another as the tools used to create and disseminate this information are also generating relationships. Information is conceptually and digitally mapped across a number of spaces—some map based, some simply informational. There are implications here for the urban as well. For technology theorist Steven Johnson, spaces like these—which merge web applications via data associations—represent a new type of city.

> Imagine the universe of HTML documents as a kind of city spread out across a vast landscape, with each document representing a building in that space. The Web's city would be more anarchic than any real-world city on the planet—no patches of related shops and businesses; no meatpacking or theater districts; no bohemian communities or upscale brownstones; not even the much lamented "edge city" clusters of Los Angeles or Tyson's Corner. The Web's city would simply be an undifferentiated mass of data growing more confusing with each new "building" that's erected—so confusing, in fact, that the mapmakers (the Yahoos and Googles of the world) would generate almost as much interest as the city itself. (*Emergence* 117)

Johnson's analogy with the city is important. Within this data Johnson describes, a network is generated. That network is as personal as it is "data" oriented. Since originally making this analogy, Johnson has founded the online mapping system Outside.in,[9] an online space of maps categorized by cities that claims to represent 57,830 neighborhoods. As its logo describes, Outside.in is a place where "neighbors define places, stories, and people that shape a community." Its user-gathered data on each city, however, does not—as Johnson initially wrote—become more confusing as users navigate through the data. Quite the contrary, Outside.in utilizes HTML and database software to create a highly organized series of city spaces, each meant to put its citizens in connection with each other so that events, places to visit, and news become interlinked. The elements that make up a data-driven map like that featured in Outside.in, Wayfaring, or Rrove are fabricated out of physical spaces and personal interactions with physical spaces. Those personal interactions break down further into feelings, thoughts, concerns, and other related issues. Users of each map include such personal interactions as they describe or identify physical space. Users, as well, share such information with other users who are mapping other spaces. Thus, the database grows. Detroit, one city featured on Outside.in, is a database of newspaper headlines, aggregated blog posts, and Google maps that continuously grows as new producers of information go online and have their content integrated into Outside.in. In this sense, it is indeed an HTML city organized around a number of sensations; these sensations are professional (newspapers and Google) and personal (blogs). These sensations allow a city, like Detroit, to be mapped in unique ways.

"Any theory of the city that omits feelings, symbols, memories, dreams, myths, and all the subtle energies that go into the expressive dimension ignores the most human region of urban life," Eugene Walter claims (16). Moving through these networks that combine a variety of experiences—which include the personal—is not necessarily an easy experience; it can reflect the difficulty and uneasiness of urbanity in general (the various economic, racial, and political issues an urban environment faces daily). Or it can reflect the difficulty of navigating a MapQuest or Google Maps sense of direction which, at times, gives roundabout directions, shows shops that no longer exist, and fails to identify new traffic throughways. This movement can also reflect distaste with a city, infatuation with a city, or apathy toward a city. The network is a complex site of interactions. Directions to a theater may not always turn up the best route. It may turn up a series of other informational points as well. Enjoying, disliking, remembering, or visiting an urban space may turn up any number of informational points as well. Reading a blog post in an Outside.in aggregation can be pleasant ("I want to know more") or frustrating ("That's not how I feel"). These difficulties, too, are part of what is often called the affective. I will return to this point later in this chapter and in more detail in the next chapter.

I am starting, then, to bring affective, informational, urban, and other difficulties into relationship with one another in order to tell a spatial story of a space called Digital Detroit. Digital Detroit is the technological intervention I make as part of a larger exploration of the city, space, rhetoric, and networks. "The problems of technology attract little theoretical or practical attention from traditional rhetoricians, who regard words as the subject matter of their art," Richard Buchanan points out (185). Buchanan asks a fundamental question regarding the role of design in rhetorical studies, a question applicable to my own study of Detroit and networks. "How may we profitably consider the many innovations that have occurred in fields far removed from those traditionally associated with rhetoric, but with a degree of independence from the field in which they are usually celebrated? " (184). Databases might provide a place to attract more attention for rhetorical arrangement and invention; they might provide a place to explore how digital spaces expand the role of words in arrangement and invention. Removed from—or, we might say, extended from—computer science and physics—databases (and the networks they construct) might provide insight into how we arrange and invent within a variety of spaces, from the physical to the conceptual. "A new technology," Buchanan writes, "does not lead automatically to the creation of successful products. This step depends on the expertise of design and 'making,' where knowledge from many fields must be integrated in the product development process" (194). The database as rhetorical *inventio*, then, might allow for the design and making of a space. That space, as I will call it in this book, is Digital Detroit.

Arrangement, Invention, Ramism, Technology

In this first chapter, my claim that databases are generating an emerging rhetoric speaks to both new media expectations as well as traditional rhetorical concerns regarding arrangement, delivery, and place. The production of Digital Detroit, and the network spaces that give it its name, first begins with a discussion of such concerns, particularly that of arrangement and arrangement's relationship to invention. How a rhetor puts ideas, people, places, and things into relationship with another is how one, in general, invents. Digital Detroit is an invention. The spaces I bring together (arrangement) and develop conceptually via the network (invention) create this other space I have named Digital Detroit. For these reasons, this project, as I understand it, is a rhetorical one. This chapter has begun my invention process by way of the Google Maps exigence. While we may be used to thinking of invention as a nontechnological process, or at least one in which technology and user are distinct agents, this exigence shows that invention may occur in an application like Google Maps as much as it may occur with the rhetor who uses Google Maps. Both the application and the user are structured by invention. In the network shaped by database information, structure and arrangement become technological processes. As Kai Eriksson writes, "Structure is obviously one of the most central general metaphors against which network is organized" (319). That point requires some unpacking. The network is as much a supporter of as a challenge to contemporary notions of structure.

The database, exemplified for now in the online mapping service, gathers spaces of information (streets, routes, places), arranges information (brings them together in an interface), and delivers that information for a given audience for a specific situation (like someone attempting to find the best route to a movie theater). While print-based maps (maps of cities, maps of countries, maps of campuses, maps of shopping centers, and so on) have always done such work, the database-driven map offers some new challenges because the amount of information used to create the map, the amount of information one must navigate, the various positions one can navigate from, and the number of opportunities for arrangement have increased dramatically. Exploring the database as a rhetorical challenge can expand as well as complicate new media expectations of spatial arrangement. Since rhetoric has always been concerned with questions of information organization, spatial arrangement, and place, in the age of new media it has become necessary to consider the role of the database as well. An exploration of the database as rhetoric is both a conceptual gesture (physical spaces like a city or local site are generalized to nonphysical spaces such as idea formations) as well as a theoretical one (what are the possibilities of database driven acts?). Before beginning that exploration, however, I want to place database-driven rhetorics into proximity and context with some of the traditional issues arrangement poses for rhetorical production.

To begin, the database provides a contemporary version of what Richard Enos calls the Ciceronian concern with arrangement, that it "provides a structure, an architecture for the creation of ideas" (109). As Enos argues, the structured arrangement of ideas is central to the invention process. Drawing on Cicero, Enos notes that "ideas must be appropriate not only to the situation but also to the proper place within the discourse" (109) The "ideas" in the *SNL* example—however simplistic they might at first sound—include how to get from one place to another in the most efficient manner as possible. In the definition of invention Enos draws upon, where structure is the dominant feature and every item within that structure has its proper place, "the rhetor examines a preexisting inventory of 'stock arguments' and 'commonplaces' to select those that are most appropriate to the situation at hand" (C. Miller 131). In the Ramist approach to such organizational arrangements—as described by Walter Ong, who acknowledges the Ciceronian influence on Ramus—arrangement is the logical process of navigating categorical places or topoi so that the most efficient way towards understanding an argument or position can be displayed. Ramist arrangement consists of a visual process in which one "sees" how spaces are already ordered and navigated (that is, the mapping of information is already in place; one learns their taxonomies by their visual demonstrations). "One *looks* for things in order to find them; one *comes* upon them" (Ong 114). Again, invention works with what is already in its supposed place. Or, as Ong strongly critiques Ramism for adhering to this principle, "it is a rhetoric which has renounced any possibility of invention" (288).

As Ong describes Ramism, new media affect such spatial movement's influence on invention practices. An analogy might propose that the online mapping service is for twenty-first century culture what the book was for the sixteenth century. "Ramus's notion of method is not only a product of the humanism that sponsors both printing and the topical logics but also is thought of (by Ramus) as an arrangement of material in a book" (Ong 311). This version of arrangement, Ong argues, affected the spatial layout of a page (as opposed to the oral organization of a speech), but it did so in such a way as to create rigid hierarchies and taxonomies. The structuring of the page affected the structuring of ideas, often emphasizing outlines, grids, and tables as arrangement devices. "The origins of Ramism," Ong argues, "are tied up with the increased use of spatial models in dealing with the processes of thought and communication" (314). Through such arrangements, discursive places, physical places, and even one's own place within a given rhetorical structure were seen as separate and distinct. Ramism set a specific standard for invention that required the personal and the so-called objective to be arranged separately. Just as the page's layout divided places, so too, the Ramist argument went, should the rhetorical arrangements of a given topic.

The database, too, structures spatially, but not in the same way as a Ramist or Ciceronian legacy might require. Instead of spatializing place and space in terms of the outline or grid so that items remain in their separate place, the database leaves open how information might be navigated or finally arranged by not dictating the exact structure of the arrangement. It's a vital point because that openness allows for a variety of possible interventions with information, among them the personal investment and involvement that occur in information arrangement. Thus, as the *SNL* example suggests, one might choose between two types of database operations, each of which map the route to the movie theater differently. Or when using an embedded Google map, the site user chooses between the site hosting the map, the embedded map, and the information embedded within the embedded map. Several database operations function in one arrangement. As Aristotle might have noted, each database addresses "how the parts of a speech must be arranged" (*On Rhetoric* 3.1.1). Still, like those who come after him, Aristotle argues, "it is not enough to have a supply of things to say, but it is also necessary to say it in the right way" (3.1.2). In Book 2 of *The Rhetoric*, some of Aristotle's quest for a right ordering sounds very much like someone navigating a database of information. In one discussion regarding how much knowledge one needs to argue a convincing point, for instance, Aristotle poses the following example of needing data. "Or [how could we] praise [the Athenians] if we did not know about the sea battle at Salamis or the fight at Marathon, or [how could we praise the Spartans without knowing] the things done by the Children of Heracles or something of that sort?" (2.22.6). To navigate all of this information as prelude to constructing a solid argument, one would need access to and control of a database of ideas: what kind of forces do the Athenians have; how large or small are such forces; who are their allies? One would need a metaphoric online mapping system to arrange the material and employ it as a "right path" towards some sort of understanding or new rhetorical composition. In the Aristotelian model, that path, however, can only follow one topic (place) at a time because only in one place, Aristotle claims, are ideas to be found. When inventing, Aristotle notes, the rhetor must "have selected statements about what is possible and most suited to the subject" (2.22.10). Because online mapping deals with selecting more than one subject at more than one time, it might not be too far off to propose that finding the "best route" to any given place of information, as Google Maps provides, has become a more complex version of "finding the best argument," identifying the "best delivery of information," or following Aristotle's canonical definition, "[seeing] the available means of persuasion" (1.2.1). I am interested in extending this definition and position to a more contemporary understanding of arrangement that anticipates new media's influence on invention. In that sense, my introduction of the database into traditional Ramist and Aristotelian concepts approaches Carolyn Miller's notion of "novelty" in topos-bound invention. Miller describes the topoi in a manner that resembles what databases do.

> The Aristotelian topos of degree, or of ways and means, suggests a conceptual shape or realm where one may find—or create—a detail, a connection, a pattern that was not anticipated deductively by the topos itself. The topos is conceptual space without fully specified or specifiable contents; it is a region of productive uncertainty. It is a "problem space," but rather than circumscribing or delimiting the problem, rather than being a dosed space or container within which one searches, it is a space, or a located perspective, from which one searches. (141)

The contemporary process is more complex because doing any of this requires a database even more extensive than Aristotle's brief example allows for, a point I will arrive at in more detail shortly. This process also requires a flexible database that is not already set in place and that allows more than one particular subject to be employed. While I will often attempt to move away from topos-bound thinking as I write Digital Detroit, I am also working within what Miller calls a "problem space."

As my introductory *SNL* example suggests, we might consider Aristotle's quasi-recommendation of a database as an initial way around the Ramist preordered divisions of spatial arrangements so that the Google Maps example can be expanded upon. I am, of course, not the first person to make the analogy between places traveled to and places of discussion. Edward Casey's *The Fate of Place* offers an exhaustive study of place and invention, from the fixed moment of invention (thesis) to the deterritorialization of place proposed by Deleuze and Guattari. Early in his study, Casey draws attention to Aristotle's rejection of place's relationship to movement (despite Aristotle's emphasis on accumulating a considerable amount of information to move through). "Since a minimal requirement of place is to be selfsame—to be the *same* place for different things located in it—Aristotle must add to the first definition the rider that place cannot itself be changing or moving: it must be 'unchangeable'" (55). When it comes to arrangement of ideas, the belief in an unchangeability of place, Casey suggests, has had far reaching consequences for rhetorical studies and the pedagogy it practices. "Place is definitely not precedent if by 'place' is meant something like a particular locale or spot: anything of this order of specificity, that is, of the order of *topos* or of *thesis* (position), misses the mark" (43). In addition, Casey offers two points that contrast with Aristotle's notion of place. One of place's "essential properties is its connectivity—its power to link up, from within, diversely situated entities or events" (47–48). And, Casey adds, "From Plato we learn that receptivity is connectivity" (48). In place of the topos (the fixed place), Casey argues for a broader understanding of place that recognizes how various forces coming together (and, we might assume, breaking apart) lead to a place's shifting and moving status. The metaphor, it seems, is one of travel. Place moves.

Regarding pedagogy, Gregory Clark challenges the Aristotelian assumption (which resembles somewhat the Ramist model) by connecting rhetoric and writing to movement as well. In particular, Clark utilizes the metaphor of travel, arguing for

> ways that avoid the theoretical and ethical problems of rhetorical territoriality by exploring the possibility of locating the kinds of collectivities that are formed by interacting writers and readers in a concept of expansive space through which, in their interactions, they travel. My project is to develop terms that describe the act of discursive exchange in ways that avoid the theoretical and ethical problems of rhetorical territoriality by exploring the possibility of locating the kinds of collectivities that are formed by interacting writers and readers in a concept of expansive space through which, in their interactions, they travel. (12)

I see the *SNL* anecdote, then, as an extension of Clark's concerns. Clark's metaphor of travel is an attempt to work around territorializations of space (the ways a writer may fixate too strongly on a concept or body of information). "How can we get our students to write and read, metaphorically at least, on the road?" Clark asks (20). Without limiting the idea of travel, represented here in terms of the database and mapping, to just students, Clarks' question can be situated as one relevant to new media and urban culture. I want to suggest that the types of interactions Clark calls for can be found in a database-driven rhetoric initially suggested by a late night comedy routine. And I suggest that this rhetoric, as the following chapters will show, becomes the vehicle (pun intended) for moving through spaces.

In that way, I am thinking about how ideas are spatialized, how they are put into proximity to one another in ways that a topics-driven rhetorical production does not entirely account for (like limiting physical space to just a street or intersection or to just one discussion on said street or intersection). "In a rhetorical sense, there has to be more commonality than proximity to enable constructive discursive exchange," Clark argues (13). In other words, when writing of the city, for instance, there has to be more to spatial arrangements than just seeing city markers as next to one another. Other forces, emotions, responses have to be included. For place to not be "unchangeable" as Casey's critique of Aristotle highlights, spatial arrangements must allow for movement. Arrangements cannot be spatialized in the Ramist sense—as fixed orderings—but they must, instead, be "interactions." Invention, then, serves to generate interactions among a given arrangement. I imagine this kind of invention as something similar to what Carolyn Miller calls a "problem space." The "search" aspect she focuses on is a type of movement through meanings. There exists a space "from which one searches," but one can also search within one's space. For this reason, Google Maps' embedded map is an appropriate metaphor for Digital Detroit.

Greg Dickinson, too, explores the roles commonality and proximity play in navigating and traveling through space. In his rhetorical analysis of Old Pasadena as a place of nostalgia, Dickinson evokes de Certeau's well-known figure of the rhetorical traveler, whose "walks" generate rhetorical turns and movements. "The walking of passers-by offers a series of turns (tours) and detours that can be compared to 'turns of phrase' or 'stylistic figures.' There is a rhetoric of walking" (de Certeau, *Practice* 100). Dickinson translates this movement as a postmodern gesture where "consumers, grabbing a bit of style from here, a bit from there, can appropriate, even revel in the myriad choices available" (13). In calls like the one Dickinson makes, the traveler is pastiche artist, cutting and pasting, combining, and appropriating. Through such acts, Dickinson writes, the rhetor creates "a stylized invention of the self" (21). Dickinson suggests that spatial recombinations affect a sense of self mostly through an engagement with memory (his example constitutes the places of memory associated with a small, California town, and how nostalgia controls memory). Continuing with the traveling metaphor suggested by both *SNL* and Clark, I wonder, though, how a changing self might not be limited to just the rhetor (speaker or writer) but may include the space itself as well as any number of interactions between the space and the individual. Even in the brief *SNL* anecdote, a similar point is being made: New York is understood by the characters as a shifting self dependent on which Google Maps route a given user follows or sees as indicative of "New York." And Google Maps itself sees New York as a shifting series of spaces and how they may or may not intersect. Both the program and the user generate an object called "New York." In that sense, what I am calling a database rhetoric is not only what may allow a speaker, writer, or rhetor to change or evoke different notions of self; it is also a way for a rhetorical composition (and I use that word broadly) to be "stylized" in a "myriad" number of ways as well. It is a way to stylize a broader concept of rhetoric and writing through one's ability to arrange many spaces at once. And as I will demonstrate shortly, it is a way to rethink how a given space—such as the city one lives and works in—may create various networked, rhetorical possibilities. Nostalgia, therefore, represents just one kind of possibility. Others must exist as well. Arrangement is not supplanted by invention in this process. The two are interacting. The two are networked.

An Economy of Presence

My turn to a mapping program—an online tool that gives directions—may seem like an odd choice for discussing new media and rhetorical production. Yet following Clark's and Dickinson's work on rhetoric, space, and movement, I see an exigence for further exploring how invention situated within a database structure affects a specific kind of identity—whether that identity involves how New York, Detroit, or any other city is organized or even how one conceptualizes a given text as a database. To continue further with this notion, I turn to William Mitchell, whose work, as I noted in the introduction, involves space and digital production "within the framework of a new *economy of presence*" (*e-topia* 129).

Mitchell's phrase foregrounds the difficult choices that are made when navigating online information, choices that have complicated the famous Microsoft slogan "Where do you want to go today?" In the world of online navigation, I may be able to go to more than one place at the same time; I may be able to see a given space as more than one set of data. In the economy of presence, Mitchell writes, we have "the means to interact with one another both locally and remotely, both synchronously and asynchronously, and in all possible combinations of these" (*e-topia* 135). In the economy of presence, we have the means to be both communal and proximal, to shift identities—ours as well as spaces we encounter—as we engage with these types of interactions.

Online mapping makes that presence felt by drawing upon a number of discursive places at once. In *The Postmodern Condition*, Jean-François Lyotard suggested a similar computer-based future (preweb) in which databases would control expression and thus shift how ideas are spatialized. That control comes with a warning regarding how information is arranged and delivered. "Along with the hegemony of computers," Lyotard writes, "comes a certain logic, and therefore a certain set of prescriptions determining which statements are accepted as 'knowledge' statements" (4). Like Clark, Lyotard is concerned with the question of commonality and proximity and how "knowledge" (one kind of identity) is challenged through information shifts (where they are common, proximate, or in some other position in the database). In particular, Lyotard offers a rhetorical caveat regarding how individuals treat information within a given database.

> If education must not only provide for the reproduction of skills, but also for their progress, then it follows that the transmission of knowledge should not be limited to the transmission of information, but should include training in all of the procedures that can increase one's ability to connect the fields jealously guarded from one another by the traditional organization of knowledge. (52)

In the database, Lyotard argues, informational proximity should not be used to keep ideas apart, but rather, to allow their connectivity even when those connections come from different bodies (disciplinary, ideological, compositional), often in unanticipated ways. This connectivity is encouraged by imagination. "This capacity to articulate what used to be separate can be called imagination" (Lyotard 52). In this sense, having an adequate amount of information about Athenian war practices or a California town is not, in itself, enough if it acts to maintain only one kind of identity. Such has often been the case with Detroit. Separate stories or places of information regarding the city (crime, school, the mayor's office, Ford, music) are "jealously guarded" entities. Each is called upon separately in order to explain one aspect of the city or its shortcomings. They are seldom articulated together in what Lyotard might call an imaginative manner, nor are they presented as spaces or places to move through. Following Lyotard's definition of database rhetorics, one must be able to *imagine* ways to connect information that previous set-ups have not yet allowed for. One must, in a metaphoric sense, travel through the information, going "from the territorial to the transient" (Clark 12).

I introduce Lyotard's concept of the database because one of his often-cited claims is that the database replaces narrative constructions, especially "grand narratives" regarding a variety of cultural, ideological, political, and other issues. The grand narrative is the space where information systems are jealously guarded as each narrative attempts to tell only its own story in a sweeping and totalizing way. The grand narrative "determines in a single stroke what one must say in order to be heard, what one must listen to in order to speak, and what role one must play" (Lyotard 21). We recognize these narratives as, among others, literacy, democracy, Marxism, and, in the case of places and cities, urban planning and urban renewal. Like a representational map or a Ramist chart, the grand narrative evokes a totalizing space that does not allow for rhetorical turns, memory associations, spatial searches, or travel metaphors. Place, more or less, is unchangeable (for example, literacy is the fulfillment of certain conventions accepted by school systems and public demand; democracy accommodates only specific activities connected to voting or expression, and so on). A grand narrative is a preset map; it totalizes space much as a Ramist spatial model does or the Ciceronian notion of structure allows. The grand narrative is a master narrative. "Master narratives," Kathleen Stewart writes, "speak a war of positions" (97).

I experience one particular grand narrative in the place I once worked: Detroit, Michigan. In the popular press, conversations, and economic forecasts, Detroit's identity is framed by one particular grand narrative, its status as a city of ruins. The city, this narrative tells us, suffers from a lack of investment, is plagued by racial division, and is perpetually on the verge of an economic revival it can never achieve. We hear that grand narrative in *The Simpsons* episode "How Munched Is That Birdie in the Window," when Moe tells Bart to "lay off Detroit. Them people is living in Mad Max times." We hear that grand narrative in Glenn Beck's 2011 hyperbolic comparison of Detroit to Hiroshima (Battaglia). The rhetorical construction—or we might say, mapping—of Detroit is unchangeable.

Indeed, on any given day, the city's two main newspapers repeat this narrative through unchanging reporting on the city's financial woes. "State Stuck in Stalled Economy," an August 2007 *Detroit News* headline on Metro Detroit failures reads. "Today's Detroit Has Little to Do with 1967," *Free Press* columnist Bill McGraw writes in a July 2007 article. "Michigan loses 12,600 jobs in September," a *Detroit News* October 2010 headline reads. Kwame Kilpatrick's political downfall in the months leading up to his resignation in September 2008, too, belong within this narrative: Local resident rises up through the city's bureaucratic ranks, works against all odds to become the city's youngest mayor, and eventually falls to corruption and perjury.[10]

Detroit decay juxtaposed with the hope of rejuvenation. A mural, Warren Avenue. Photograph by the author.

Economic stagnation. 1967. Political failure. The topoi are still strong. They are still repeated as fixed positions even if a writer or rhetor struggles to argue the opposite. One always experiences—or maps—Detroit via the 1967 narrative. The grand narrative of Detroit prevails. One doesn't metaphorically travel through Detroit via this narrative; one encounters "boundaries that define [a] common territory" (Clark 14). One only needs to say "Detroit," and, despite what may or may not exist in the city or its metro area, the city of ruins is the narrative one typically draws upon in order to visualize or describe the city. One is bound to describe a fixed identity we have communally named "Detroit." In this sense, the city, as it is rhetorically constructed, is nothing more than a description.

"Description," Henri Lefebvre notes, "is unable to explain certain *social relations*—apparently abstract with respect to the given and the 'lived'—which appear concrete but are only immediate" (*Urban Revolution* 46). Lefebvre's argument, similar to Clark's and Dickinson's and in opposition to the grand narrative, is that spaces and places embody relationships that totalizing narratives cannot accommodate. The totalizing narrative—whether it is a Marxist critique of economic disparity or an over-romanticized vision of urban renewal or a gloomy portrayal of a city—can create what Lefebvre calls "the blind field," the moment "we focus attentively on the new field, the urban, but we see it with eyes, with concepts, that were shaped by the practices and theories of industrialization" (*Urban Revolution* 29). The blind field indicates a rhetorical construction of place that—despite the amount of information drawn upon to create that construction—is not allowed to change. In other words, it is the opposite of Mitchell's concept of the economy of presence. While the economy of presence is meant to open up space, the blind field closes space. In Lefebvre's critique of the blind field, he writes,

> The urban (urban space, urban landscape) remains unseen. *We* still don't see it. Is it simply that our eye has been shaped (misshaped) by the earlier landscape so it can no longer see a new space? Is it that our way of seeing has been cultivated by village spaces, by the bulk of factories, by the monuments of past eras? Yes, but there's more to it than that. It's not just a question of lack of education, but of occlusion. We see things incompletely. How many people perceive "perspective," angles and contours, volumes, straight and curved lines, but are unable to perceive or conceive multiple paths, complex spaces? (*Urban Revolution* 29)

One does not have to be blind to realize that Detroit obviously suffers from economic crisis and that its newspaper headlines are not fabricating a very real malaise. Collapsed buildings, empty store fronts, white flight, poor schools, and under-staffed law enforcement are all conditions of that crisis. Traveling down Woodward Avenue from 8 Mile to the city center reveals much of that crisis in the despair of Highland Park or the burnt-out buildings across from the Boston Edison neighborhood. The impoverished conditions topoi that circulate around Detroit are not made up or fake. To speak of a blind field is not to deny the very real material conditions people live in nor the proclaimed desire of city management to fix those conditions. Repeating the narrative of these conditions, however, has done little to change the city's problems since their legitimacy is based on one perspective located in one space. In other words, the rhetorical response to grand narratives of Detroit has been, to date, repetition of the same narratives. It's a vicious rhetorical cycle in which agents (planners, politicians, citizens, observers) want to address real problems, but they do so only by repeating the problems' totalizing position. Some of the best writing on Detroit reflects such limitations; its rhetoric always fixates on perpetual crisis. "Since 1950, Detroit has lost nearly a million people and hundreds of fascinating jobs," Thomas Sugrue begins his detailed history of Detroit and race relationships. "Vast areas of the city, once teeming with life, now stand abandoned" (3). "Nothing fundamental has changed in Detroit because the forces that controlled the city prior to 1967 still control the city and the nation," Dan Georgakas and Marvin Surkin write in their account of labor and race relationships, *Detroit: I Do Mind Dying. A Study in Urban Revolution.* (5–6). "The historical closure of Fordism as a model of socio-economic progress spelled the demise of Detroit, once the proud origin of modern industrial development," Patrik Schumacher and Christian Rogner argue as well (48). In his introduction to *Detroit Lives*, an oral history of Detroit activists, Robert Mast offers a sober portrait of Detroit in 1994.

> Economic decline and population changes have produced astounding contradictions in the everyday life of Detroiters. There are more than 200,000 chronically jobless adults. Nearly half the population lives below the poverty line. Housing activists estimate there are 10,000 public housing units vacant due to corruption and mismanagement all the way up to Washington. In a city that once boasted the highest rate of home ownership in the country, sometimes just one to two permits a year are issued for new single-family homes. About four in ten people have no car in [the] Motor City. (4)

A September 2008 Salon.com feature on Kwame Kilpatrick's resignation due to scandal and perjury framed the affair as yet another example of the decrepit condition Detroit is in. The essay's conclusion has little to do with Kilpatrick or the corruption charges he faced and more to do with the circulated topos of abandonment and neglect. "The fact is, Detroit is hardly a city anymore. The whites have skedaddled to the north, west and south. They took the department stores, the basketball team, the middle-class jobs, the theaters and the concert halls, and prevented the blacks from building a train system to chase after them" (McClelland). I could go on.

Because I am interested in working with an economy of presence, and because I am interested in expanding the understandings of spatial arrangements I introduced earlier, I need to find a way to move out of this fixed place of meaning. The topoi of abandonment, neglect, and devastation have reached their rhetorical limits. Moving out of a fixed place of meaning is not the same as denying that a given meaning like urban blight or racial inequality is real. Instead, it is a move to reposition ourselves in relation to the "blind field" that has failed to alleviate such problems. Thus, along with these fixed topoi that have created a blind field regarding Detroit, I also include Lefebvre's instruction to alter perceptions of space. Further reminding audiences of the grand narrative of Detroit has not changed or altered how we—the supposed audiences—communally map the city. The perspectives we bring to a place, those that we use to frame or create a place, I am arguing, must engage with multiple paths, complexity, and relationships when grand narratives fail to do anything but serve as reminders and, therefore, keep possibilities *unseen*. These perspectives, I learn from Lyotard, are database driven. They should be imaginary and they should be—as the economy of presence suggests—networks. My understanding of the city as network, however, is not entirely the same as the one Henri Lefebvre sketches, for many of his concerns are with physical networks as opposed to rhetorical ones.

> To claim that the city is defined as a network of circulation and communication, as a centre of information and decision-making, is an absolute ideology; this ideology proceeding from a particularly arbitrary and dangerous reduction-extrapolation and using terrorist means, sees itself as total truth and dogma. It leads to a planning of pipes, of roadworks, and accounting, which one claims to impose in the name of science and scientific rigour. Or even Worse! (*Writings on Cities* 98)

I do not deny the ideological gesture I will make throughout this book regarding Detroit and networks (or that I am already making), but the type of network I describe extends the infrastructural network Lefebvre worries over. The pipes and roadworks Lefebvre highlights signify the grand narrative of urban planning. This narrative, as I have noted, is at the heart of the stagnant topos of Detroit, for most of its storytelling draws motivation from the city's failed infrastructure, its collapsed transportation industry, and its lack of public transportation. The planning of pipes is not a rhetorical act to network the city in any way other than infrastructural. A rhetoric of the network, on the other hand, can show the very sociability Lefebvre claims for the urban space.

The network can serve as a metaphoric extension of Clark's writing as travel or Miller's topoi as search because of how it moves information in complex ways, how it shifts perspectives, and how it functions in imaginary ways. Networks, as described by forces as diverse as physics, computer science, and Actor-Network-Theory, are bodies of relationships that shift as new bodies are introduced or subtracted. Networks are found in personal relationships, textual readings, political issues, the web, and elsewhere. "Network is a concept, not a thing out there," Bruno Latour argues (*Reassembling* 131). Latour's point, which I also quote in the introduction, is that the power of networks comes not from the identification of certain "things" and how they connect, but from the process of connections themselves. Generalized to a "thing" like a city space or map, the emphasis shifts from pure analysis or representation to working with the types of connections that may or may not be generated within the space's various processes. The emphasis, in other words, is rhetorical as it teaches another perspective regarding how spaces are organized, arranged, and delivered. Online, networks may be identified in friendship sharing spaces like Facebook, online writing sites like wikis and weblogs, or the web itself. "It's the network," a Verizon advertisement for its cellular phone service declares. Indeed, "it" (a generic qualifier) is the network. That generic "it," which is ubiquitous and unnamed in the Verizon spot, encompasses friends making connections, people writing to online spaces dealing with music, food, or academic life, or people designing and implementing a variety of online applications meant to interact with one another. The "it" is any given space put into relationship with other spaces. Thus, "it," indeed, is the network. Detroit, too, as I will continue to show, is as much a network as any of these other "things."Network "is a tool to help describe something, not what is being described," Latour adds (*Reassembling* 131). As a tool, the network can be employed in ways other rhetorical tools associated with space (memory palaces, outlines, monuments) have been used. And like other new media–motivated database spaces, such as a Google Maps database, networks allow us to arrange information without the requirement that such arrangements remain unchangeable. As Leonardo Madrazo notes, the study of space has recently found the concept of networks relevant to its own work.

> Network, node, flow, information, virtual space, and cyberspace are some of the notions associated with the computer that have found their way into discourses about space, in different ways: metaphorically, when the characteristics of computer networks are transposed to urban space; and literally, when it is argued that electronic networks are structuring the territory. (33)

And for intellectual property advocate Yochai Benkler, networks affect spaces where various types of information management, arrangement, and delivery options come together. In such spaces, networks don't function idyllically. Networks do not solve problems, nor do they offer utopist visions of digital culture. Network spaces may be urban, or they may be something less tangible. Either way, the network poses a communicative challenge for space.

> We see this battle played out at all layers of the information environment: the physical devices and network channels necessary to communicate; the existing information and cultural resources out of which new statements must be made; and the logical resources—the software and standards—necessary to translate what human beings want to say to each other into signals that machines can processes and transmit. (Benkler 23)

A given investment in the network, then, has the potential to be as nefarious as it does to generate a completely different reaction. In economics and in intellectual property cases, the nefarious often is showcased more than the potential. The massive commercial networks that control artistic production (mostly in the entertainment industry) have worked hard to standardize all arrangement and delivery according to their investments. The motion picture industry's history is one of an extended network of production, labor, movie complexes, copyright, and so on, meant to control how products are received and distributed. Yet despite the negative trends witnessed in entertainment industries, the network's potential, Benkler argues, "holds out the possibility of reversing two trends in cultural production central to the project of control: concentration and commercialization" (32). A network may be a tool for commercial production, or, as William Burroughs might have noted regarding media in general, it can be a tool for responding to such situations. A network may consolidate the urban into a topos or it may commercialize it for development. A network may fixate meaning or open it up.

Indeed, covering similar ground as Madrazo and Benkler do, Latour's principle point is that the network is always shifting and changing as new kinds of informational relationships are established (an echo of Lyotard's concerns without the stress on power). To engage with a database rhetoric that begins from the exigence of space and place (as many of my previous examples have done), I need to travel through the various networked spaces that comprise, for me, Detroit so that I might begin to open up the city's network rhetoric (rather than fix its rhetoric as a topos of devastation).

In the next section of this chapter, I apply some of the database ideas I have been working with to Detroit, so that I may begin the process of building Digital Detroit. This brief exercise in database rhetorics will set the stage for the book's following chapters, each of which metaphorically travels through a space and continues this project. Each database entry, noted first in this chapter and then extended through each following chapter, builds the network I call Digital Detroit. First, before I travel through Detroit via its specific spaces, I travel to Detroit.

To Detroit

For some time now, as it should be clear, I've imagined Detroit as a networked city. That statement can partly be explained by following up on my initial interest in the *SNL* skit as well as my interest in Clark's metaphor of travel as a type of rhetoric. Detroit, like any major city, is composed of a variety of institutions, buildings, homes, and other physical entities that make up its urban locale. As I have noted, to understand a specific type of relationship between such places, residents and visitors often turn to digital maps for assistance. I am no different. Like the skit's characters, I can *describe* how I might take out my laptop, pull up Google Maps in my browser, and identify a way I once took to get to work. If I were to replace the *SNL* characters with myself, and if I were to use Google Maps to locate the best route from my home to what was once my place of employment at 5057 Woodward Avenue, Detroit, Michigan, I would be directed to head east on 8 Mile, to follow I-75 south for six miles, and to exit at Warren Avenue. Based on the data Google Maps has collected (traffic, mileage, available highways), this route is determined to be the "best way" to arrive at Wayne State University. Google Maps provides a rhetoric of efficiency. But I didn't take this route when I worked at Wayne State. Instead, I followed the less efficient way to work, down Woodward Avenue and into the New Center. The speed limit is lower. The traffic is slower. Sometimes cars stop in the middle of the road for no reason. People walk across the road without using crosswalks. There are traffic lights along the way. Construction feels like a permanent feature (usually one or two lanes are closed in any given direction). What would take 7 to 10 minutes on I-75 takes 15 to 17 minutes down Woodward.

There is more to this anecdote than the issue of speed. Like the Van de Water family's 1920s road trip Clark describes, how "life lived on the road transformed their conception of America and their own identity within it," I am interested in this road, Woodward, and its ability to affect any number of identities it might generate via a database (Clark 13). The database Google Maps draws upon in order to predict travel is not the same database I encountered nor that would I use as I drove down Woodward. Instead of collecting speed limit markers or the number of traffic lights Woodward hosts into my database, I assembled the sights, sounds, people, places, and other features of the neighborhoods I travel through (Highland Park, Boston Edison, New Center), some of which are appealing (the Temple Beth El synagogue, the Fisher Building), some of which aren't (the impoverished strip of rundown businesses within Highland Park, the various check-cashing storefronts, empty fields, the Normandie flop house). The trip itself can be easy (the right time of day producing fewer cars) or frustrating (traffic congestion, construction, cars stopped in the middle of the street). The route is accompanied by history (the Model T factory, the General Motors Building, Martin Luther King Jr.'s pre-Washington 1963 march) and new construction (various condos, the Youth Center, a new fast-food restaurant). Each item was noted and stored in my database. Each item could be drawn upon to generate meaning.

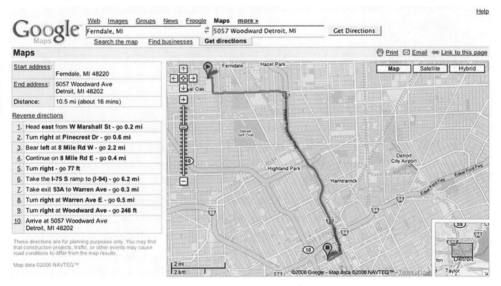

The Google Maps path from Ferndale to Detroit. Reprinted according to Google's permission requirements.

These items comprise the informational scheme I construct to make something called "Detroit." These "physical" places, however, are not all that I assembled as I drove down Woodward. I also assembled communal and proximal places of meaning, most of which build up like a never ending list of moments. In addition to what I saw or noticed, I heard song titles from popular music ("Detroit Rock City" by KISS, "Detroit Bound

Blues" by Blind Arthur Blake, "Cadillac Assembly Line" by Albert King); snippets from fiction (a line from Philip Dick's sci-fi novel *A Scanner Darkly*, "He sat looking at the empty cup; it was a china mug. Turning it over, he discovered printing on the bottom, and cracked glaze. The mug looked old, but it had been made in Detroit"); obscure references (as in Tom Waits's "Spare Parts I": "So I combed back my Detroit, jacked up my pegs, I wiped my Stacy Adams and I jackknifed my legs"); a sudden reminder that Malcolm X's nickname at one point in his life was "Detroit Red"; a boast from the film *Four Brothers* ("This is Detroit; in case you all forgot"); and the mocking of the city's technological legacies (Eminem shouting out in "Without Me": "Nobody listens to techno!"). As I traveled Woodward, I noticed a new retail strip going up or, at times, I paid attention to the arabesque design of the New Center Liquor Store, or I noticed that the grocery store in the Model T Shopping Center had changed names. These moments are emotional as much as they are informational. Am I angry with the destruction of the second Motown building or do I wonder if the Aknartoons Bakery will ever be rebuilt? Do I link the Maccabees Building, wherein I work, with the university's overall plans of expansion (projects like TechTown, new parking structures, or a new dorm), or do I imagine how the recording of *The Lone Ranger*[11] occurred somewhere near where my office now is? What does one choice teach me that the other doesn't? How do I navigate these spaces of imagination, history, space, and other features?

These moments I assemble are a database, a database that is personalized. In some ways, Henri Lefebvre anticipated the need for such personalized networks of information—what he calls "knowledge"—particularly in regards to the problem of how to understand space within a computerized culture. "Should we feed all the data for a given problem to a computer?" he asks (*Urban Revolution* 59). It is not enough only to feed personalized data into this map I am constructing; I must find its relationship to other places, moments, people, and things. Thus, I turn to very specific places as well in order to flesh out my database further, spaces like those that border Woodward and Wayne State University. Engaging with Dickinson's de Certeau-inspired call for "turns" and "detours," my network might require me to *turn* off of Woodward and engage with Detroit and Wayne State University as technological spaces, database entries in a larger network of information. One space I encounter in my turning off is the city and university's own vision of feeding data into a computer: TechTown.[12]

TechTown represents twenty-one businesses concentrated in a twelve-block area surrounding Wayne State University. TechTown is bordered by three major roads: I-94, the Lodge Freeway, and Woodward Avenue. Like many urban renewal projects, TechTown imagines space as a mix of technology, commerce, and urban living. It has been called a "twenty-four-hour neighborhood."[13] TechTown, like many urban renewal projects, tells a narrative of its master plan regarding space and technology. According to the TechTown narrative, its presence in the urban setting tells Detroit's impending technological story in familiar ways: financial improvement, new jobs, new opportunities. "TechTown is creating an entrepreneurial village with global impact. As an incubator, we provide the support and access to capital needed to build high-tech companies. The TechTown organization also serves as a developer, facilitating commercial and residential projects" ("What Is TechTown"). Each entry into the twelve-block neighborhood will supposedly network with other areas and, thus, create a new kind of urban center, a center of technological and entrepreneurial progress. Despite its rhetorical emphasis on technological investment, TechTown does not resemble the database set-ups projected by other technology projects like Google Maps or MapQuest. Indeed, as a rhetorical mapping of space, TechTown's narrative resembles the grand narratives that fail to accommodate intricacies, quirks, details, and personalized knowledge databases offer. TechTown's narrative circulates the same one told in the 1965 promotional film *Detroit: City on the Move*. In the eighteen minute film produced by the city, the narrator speaks of a "new spirit of progress that matches the visions of its people." The new, emerging Detroit, the narrator states as a series of images of new high-rises being built parade across the screen, "reflects planning with a purpose. New office buildings alter the landscape, each, in turn, becoming a bright landmark of progress. Detroit is rebuilding to a master plan of beauty and public service. Detroit is daring to reach up. The inner city is becoming an exciting place to live, convenient to shops, offices, and the most modern of schools." The TechTown narrative, in other words, totalizes. It totalizes a grand narrative of rejuvenation that is mapped onto the city as often as the narrative of ruins. Little in the TechTown narrative, we might add, is drawn from the flexible database one might call "Detroit" (that is, the assemblage of moments and citations like the one I briefly noted for myself). Instead, the narrative draws from a familiar topos.

One of TechTown's main projects is the learning initiative called "Bizdom U,"[14] an entrepreneur boot camp that provides free tuition to students who they hope will become Detroit's investors of tomorrow. Bizdom U, and its general curriculum of leadership courses in management and positive thinking, tell a familiar story regarding investment procedures.

Bizdom U is not a gimmick; it is a real effort to shape an economic identity for Detroit as being financial. Its rhetoric draws upon other familiar tropes of the investment narrative: "innovative ideas," "real world training," "empowerment," and "milestones." These terms are meant to solidify Bizdom U's image as a space of learning. Bizdom U's graduating class of 2008[15] showcases native Detroiters who promise to bring great things to the city because of the financial learning they have acquired. Each graduate, in written profiles featured on the site, promises to "transform" the "economic" and "cultural" landscape of the city. Indeed, *City of Hope: Detroit on the Move* begins with similar language proclaiming Detroit as being "at the threshold of a bright new future" and "rich with the promise of fulfillment." These graduates do not need to have seen the film in order to repeat its language; they only have to be a part of a larger meaning system circulating around them. As they write in their online profiles, each graduate sees an "opportunity" and the value of "hard work" regarding being a future leader of Detroit. Each graduate, in other words, has the keywords of the narrative down well (keywords we hear as well in Chrysler's Super Bowl commercial), but the specifics regarding how to navigate the city as database, how to work within this larger system of meaning that they are located in, are missing.

If these are the best materials available for persuasion (such as how to make Detroit better or how to convince people to invest themselves in the city), their "right ordering" will only result in an already anticipated narrative or blind field. This narrative either dictates that progress is over (as the above narratives claimed) or that progress is on the way. One might even offer the same observation regarding Aristotle's requirements for advising the Athenian war initiative. How much "right ordering," based on grand narratives or anticipated questions, will lead to an eventual blind view and ignore a space's possibilities? Will all the questions Aristotle requires to be answered lead to a progressive state (that is, the appropriate response)? How does a grand narrative of space, of which TechTown is one example, limit database potential? This is not a critique I offer, but a reminder of how such narratives have served as the basis of Detroit's identity (and consequently other spaces' identities) for a long time and still have not changed such an identity. The TechTown-styled narrative, to return to Ramist arrangement, sees and works with what is already there (that is, financial investment) to produce something called Detroit. It does so by excluding, among other things, personal interaction with space; that is, it excludes certain kinds of rhetorical relationships. It excludes a specific way of inventing new relationships. The posted testimonials of recent graduates cannot count as personal interactions; they are canned parts of an already recycled narrative. The distance between these statements and the relationships each graduate maintains with the city is Ramist, if nothing else. The statements encourage distance, not a relationship.

Saying that is also a reminder that identities are comprised of relationships, not empty topoi (like the key phrases TechTown relies upon). A *Detroit News* article quotes TechTown's executive director, Howard Bell, as commenting on the specific relationships the project plans for this strip of land adjacent to Wayne State: "Ultimately we want to build a community where people live, they work and they play" (Bunkley). Bell's comment, as admirable as it is, is a familiar one to urban investment. "A new renaissance is changing the face of the city," *Detroit: City of Hope* declares. "This renaissance is the direct result of considered planning. The applied skills of planners, idea men, organizers, builders." That planning, as we see today, did not materialize in the way its language promised. Its promise, like Bell's regarding shared living/work space, assumes that a series of relationships may be generated by locating a nexus among capital and pleasurable activities. That kind of mapping, however, risks reducing information relationships to preestablished, unchangeable topoi of meaning even when technology is introduced. For *Detroit: City of Hope*, technology is introduced via new types of building methods; for Bizdom U, the technology is introduced via new media–related business practices. These introductions of technology deliver recognizable narratives for how to contribute to urban renewal. Adding "tech" to the mix does not change recognizable meanings void of relationships nor does it recognize the database's role in creating necessary relationships.

Networked Mappings

"Who is going to demonstrate that the 'language of the city,' to the extent that it's a language, coincides with ALGOL, Syntol, or FORTRAN, the languages of machines, and that this translation is not a betrayal? Doesn't the machine risk becoming an instrument in the hands of pressure groups and politicians?" asks Henri Lefebvre (*Urban Revolution* 59). Cities, in general, have already been placed in the hands of specialized groups; housing, investment, and commercial ventures are often dictated by such groups. In Detroit, TechTown is no exception to this process. And such groups, with or without technology (though technology is often at the forefront of their urban planning) fall back upon grand narratives of renewal and rejuvenation in order to map the city's spaces. Neither I, nor anybody else, should reject the call for urban renewal, particularly for cities, like Detroit, which are in need of some kind of change. I do, however, point to the limitations of the call when its database is minimal and fixed. The importance of my driving-to-work anecdote is not that I produce a different representation of Detroit (which I have not yet done here), nor is it that I give Detroit a new identity (which I also haven't yet done). Its importance is that the kind of arrangement the anecdote hints at can allow the rhetor to create a variety of both new representations and identities. That I join the anecdote with the existing narrative of Detroit is also important, for in this network I am not rejecting a relationship with what I find displeasing; instead, I am looking for new types of communal and proximate relationships that do more than provide employment and housing in the same building or that lavish praise on the construction of new buildings. I have only mapped out a small portion of what such a network might entail and what it might produce. My intent, then, is to follow Latour's understanding of the network as a shifting identity. If I were to write a complete version of what I create called "Detroit," it still would not demonstrate the rhetorical potential of the database because that "identity" I create will easily change when I substitute new items in my database (whether driving down Woodward or whether engaging in another kind of activity). My intent is to show the potential of the database for invention, not to totalize it, fix it in one space, nor to create a grand narrative of a given space.

In response to limited databases, I return to my anecdote. Despite the informational overload I feel as I assemble these items (the citations I noted along with the neighborhoods I pass, the histories I recall, the personal moments I experienced, like the time I was at a given restaurant or the recent story I heard about a specific building), they are part of an overall identity I name Detroit; they comprise *my* network. While the network feels egocentric, it is, in fact, a shifting identity based on the individual or individuals who construct it. It is a spatial knowledge made out of the communal relationships between the personal and a given place. This identity is uneasy (I don't know what moment or reference goes where) as well as pleasurable (many of these moments enhance my understanding of Detroit). This identity is not a constant; it is a variable that depends on how I access my database. In what I create, it is difficult to tell what, returning to Enos, is appropriate for what situation. I can assemble these items—and others—in a variety of ways and produce more than one way to get to Detroit as well as more than one kind of Detroit.

Saying that is not a dismissal of Google Maps' services, but an acknowl-edgment of how database driven information takes several forms—from the efficient to the difficult-to-understand, from the impersonal routing of spaces to the highly personalized (and some might argue, eccentric) spaces of encounter and cultural exposure. Reimagining database mapping so that the "digital" mapping popularized by online services also includes other types of databases extends a rhetorical understanding and production of space and creates a vast network of various forces simultaneously working together (online, communal, personal, cultural). "Contemporary urban experience combined with the growth of consumer culture makes the maintenance of stable, coherent identities difficult," Dickinson notes (1). My anecdote about driving down Woodward is meant to highlight just how unstable one simple act (driving to work) can affect a spatial identity (what is Detroit) depending on the type of database I make, draw from, and arrange.

"At every instant," Kevin Lynch begins *The Image of the City*, "there is more than the eye can see, more than the ear can hear, a setting or a view waiting to be explored. Nothing is experienced by itself, but always in relation to its surroundings, the sequences of events leading up to it, the memory of past-experiences." The influence of online mapping takes a fairly familiar position like Lynch's and further pushes us to recognize the relationships that comprise meanings in spaces. "Every citizen has had long associations with some part of his city, and his image is soaked in memories and meanings" (Lynch 1). Gilles Deleuze foregrounded such associations in a great deal of his work; notably, Deleuze and Guattari note how associations and sensations form blocs from which meaning is generated (*What Is Philosophy?* 167). And as I will further explore in chapter 3, Deleuze and Guattari note that meaning exists not just in the thing itself but in the various relationships that connect with or disconnect from a given space. "A map of relations among rubrics," Jennifer Daryl Slack describes Deleuze's concept, "but a map as large as the territory, a map that is the territory, a map that exceeds what habits of representation could conceivably comprehend, a map in which the rubrics fold on to one another to create complexity and possibility" (136). In other words, my Detroit is a map that is more than streets or boulevards. It is more than the accumulation of common places (topoi). It is more than a sweeping narrative of progress or decline. It is more than the best route to a given place or space. It is a complexity and possibility constructed out of, among other things, sensations. It is also, therefore, a metaphoric endeavor as much as it is a project to reimagine a specific city or urban space. What I say about Detroit I could say about any other space: a composition, a rhetoric, a school, a historical moment, a person, a situation, a genre, and so on. The network I call Detroit serves, too, as a moving entity, a concern with Detroit and with mapping space in general. What I learn is that a database map is a network of complex and possible meanings that extends from communal moments as well as personal associations.

And in that acknowledgement, I recognize that when we speak of technology and mapping, we speak of different, yet complimentary, rhetorical systems. Despite its novelty and its convenience, Google Maps still cannot fully accommodate the network I construct. That point doesn't make Google Maps "wrong," but it does ask that I consider networks, space, and navigation further so that personalized data is included. Google Maps' potential is in how we generalize from it, not codify it. The personalization of data extends and complicates traditional applications of rhetorical tools like memory so that other forces and spaces—like sensations, citations, quirky data, and so on—are included as well. In place of retelling narratives of space, particularly those that are largely grand narrative in scope (such as the economic in Detroit's case), I am interested in the complex interchanges of data that make up a given spatial relationship, and how we might engage with those exchanges for urban planning, rhetorical production, and technological applications—areas I see in relationship to one another. I see that complexity in the examples I have briefly described as well as my brief description of traveling to and from Detroit. "The moment of complexity," Marc Taylor writes, "is the point at which self-organizing systems emerge to create new patterns of coherence and structures of relation" (24). My own anecdote about Woodward Avenue is meant as a first step for beginning this process. To go "to Detroit," in my anecdote is not just to leave my home and arrive at a destination in the middle of the city. It is also to share a series of images and moments along the way, which are stored, processed, and eventually used to create a personalized database of space where each element engages another in a variety of ways. Through the sharing of data, these engagements cause me to form a meaning, something akin to what Henri Lefebvre calls "the urban of patterns" (*Writings on Cities* 109). This engagement, I note, is a network directing my understanding and invention of space. This engagement is rhetorical for how it allows my understandings always to be shifting and changing, always to be arranged and delivered in a myriad of ways, in a variety of contexts. This engagement is my first step towards mapping a thing I have started to call Digital Detroit.

That I draw from a very personal experience of one space—Detroit—should not distract from the more easily generalized issues of space, databases, and networks. In fact, personal space, as Lynch notes, is a fundamental component of spatial navigation. Lynch also argues that there is no one way to navigate space. "It now seems unlikely that there is any mystic 'instinct' of way-finding. Rather there is a consistent use and organization of definite sensory cues from the external environment" (3). While Lynch downplays these personal meanings in favor of what he calls "public images," the network requires that public place meanings (like a city's history or the location of a street or the stories told about it) be connected to personal moments as well. Such connections provide the beginning of a new urbanism and a new rhetorical mapping of that urbanism. The next chapter begins that mapping. Woodward Avenue, the first paved highway in America, is an appropriate a place to start this process. I drove down Woodward Avenue every day to get to work when I lived in Detroit. I first began to understand my database because of the Woodward route. For that reason, I take Woodward once again in order to proceed to the next chapter, a discussion of taxonomies and the motorization of space.

2

WOODWARD AVENUE

Never teach any classification, any general law, any taxonomy,
any terminology, for the sake of ensuring that students will
accept it as true, *unless* the truth will serve their further
pursuit of the inexhaustible variety of people and works.
　　　　　　　　—Wayne Booth, "Pluralism in the Classroom"

*M*y mapping of Detroit begun in chapter 1 leads me to a specific
representation (or sensation) along the city's main road, Woodward Avenue. Woodward Avenue is the centerpiece of my mapping route
that I described in the previous chapter; it is the road I would take to and
from work every day. But Woodward, as that mapping also shows me,
possesses meanings in addition to the communal understanding that it
is "just a road." Woodard, the mapping demonstrates, functions like a
database within the network of Detroit. The initial part of that database
that I drew from in chapter 1 was based in popular culture. The historical part of that database shows me that Woodward is named for Judge
Augustus B. Woodward, the early-nineteenth-century city planner of
Detroit. I learn that by 1917, the entire twenty-seven-mile distance of
Woodward Avenue was completely paved. The historical part of this database also shows me that Woodward houses notable landmarks such as
one of the country's remaining movie palaces, the Fox Theater, as well as
more contemporary constructions like the Detroit Tigers' home park of
Comerica and the Detroit Lions' home at Ford Field. These elements all
frame a type of historical database, one that would presumably sit within
a much larger database of spatial information.

Two photographs from David Lee Poremba's collection of nineteenth-
and early-twentieth-century photography, *Detroit: City of Industry*, draw
me another kind of database historical entry related to Woodward. The

first, a photograph of George Miller's "Detroit Hand Made Cigars," and the second, a photograph of the George Moebs and Company Store, depict the manufacture of cigars in Detroit, Michigan, at the end of the nineteenth century. Detroit, Poremba writes, "was once one of the largest producers of cigars and other tobacco products in the country, so much so that Detroit came to be called the 'Havana of the North' by 1901" (50). Moebs's company "employed a force of skilled cigar makers, ranging from 150 to 175 in number, making brands such as 'Flor de Moebs,' 'Ben-Hur,' and 'Detroit Slugger,' among others" (90). Both tobacco operations, Poremba notes, were located on Woodward Avenue. By the mid-nineteenth century, the area where Detroit's tobacco industry was located was also the heart of the city's economic activity. When one spoke of Detroit and commerce at this time period in the city's history, one would have spoken about Woodward Avenue. "In 1865," Sidney Glazer writes in his short history of Detroit,

> commerce centered around the cross-streets of Jefferson and Woodward and the east and west streets south of Jefferson. This area developed as a business section as an outgrowth of the days when business activity was related to river traffic. Very gradually before the close of the century, establishments began to move north and Woodward Avenue became the established "Main Street." The presence of the major retail stores on Woodward indicated that more Detroiters were moving to newly developed northern portions of the city "out Woodward." (76)

With such a promising beginning, one would think that this street would come to symbolize the success of the city, that, as a categorical label, Woodward would mean economic success. Yet Woodward Avenue, a major fairway in the city that runs from the Detroit River to the city of Pontiac, has often been employed as metonymic of Detroit's failures, not as the center piece of a once fledgling American cigar industry. A 1984 *Newsweek* article, "Detroit's Torn Lifeline" posed Woodward accordingly: "Every major American city has a lifeline that reflects its viability and its vulnerability, its history and its hope for the future . . . In the Motor City of Detroit, that lifeline is Woodward Avenue, eight lanes starting at the Detroit River and proceeding for eight unbending miles to the city limits." For the editors of *Newsweek*, such lifelines are typically generated by commerce, retail, and related ventures. And in turn, such lifelines, when they are disconnected, lead to slow deaths. The *Newsweek* article makes that point clear; its author carefully chooses words from a larger lexicon of "devastation- motivated language that will describe the supposedly barren thoroughfare: "a shabby memorial," "weed covered concrete," and "a mere shadow of the past." This image is partly explained by a collapsed auto industry and partly explained by the infamous 1967 riots, which began off of Woodward.

Looking south down Woodward from the Maccabees Building in a 1942 photograph. Library of Congress.

The *Newsweek* image is also partly explained by a romanticized view of the urban, one that frames contemporary urban space as a fallen body ousted from a glorious past. Such representations, like the attribution of nostalgia to space that I briefly encountered in the previous chapter, conclude with laments. This representation of Woodward is the image of what-could-have-been or what-is-no longer. Looking at a series of pictures of Woodward in Jack Schramm, William Henning, and Thomas Dworman's *Detroit's Street Railways*, I see the what-could-have-been lifeline *Newsweek* frames. One photo, taken in the late 1920s, shows Woodward Avenue as if a viewer were looking north from Jefferson Avenue. Streetcars offer public transportation. The streets are alive with shoppers. Model Ts sit alongside the curbs. Stores advertising dental work, dancing lessons, and even cigars are visible (25). Another photograph shows Woodward at Michigan Avenue crowded with Model Ts sitting bumper to bumper in traffic (11). Another image depicts "the first traffic signal n the world" at Jefferson and Woodward; Model Ts, trucks, and other cars compete for space in the crowded lanes (26). Detroit's lifeline, in the 1920s, is commercial, the photographs indicate, not torn. Still, these categorical markers of commerce are also nostalgic markers of a city's past.

To embrace the torn lifeline representation and the rhetorical meaning it projects, one has to situate Woodward with such nostalgic markers as these scenic Woodward photographs do. The photographs populate the street with the Model T, a vehicle that would have been common on Woodward during its heyday, just a little over a decade after the cigar photographs were taken. Like the phoenix image of Detroit I introduced in the previous chapter, Woodward's most famous automobile, the Model T, networks language associated with terms like "lifeline" or "perseverance" with the economic or cultural odds the automobile may have faced. The Model T, as any nostalgic photograph of Woodward attests, offers a rhetoric of hope and possibility where torn lifelines leave the image of despondency and despair. To understand either category as part of a larger meaning (torn and possibility), narratives about Woodward and the Model T are told.

Billy Murray's 1915 whimsical song about the Model T, "The Little Ford Rambled Right Along," is representative of the common tale of being uplifted from the state or feeling of despair. Despite obstacles (they ran over glass/they ran over nails), technical problems ("when it blows out a tire/just wrap it up with wire"), and physical abuse ("smash the top/smash up the seats"), the little Ford will persevere. As the chorus dictates, no matter what may happen, the little Ford rambled right along. In 1936, E. B. White (writing under the pseudonym Lee Strout White) penned a *New Yorker* farewell to the Model T that extended Murray's song by outlining all of the automobile's flaws and susceptibilities to breaking down while still remaining charming. Model T owners, White reminisced, learned how to live with such problems; they learned how to persevere as owners of this special car. And when they couldn't save their automobiles, the car could save itself.

> One reason the Ford anatomy was never reduced to an exact science was that, having "fixed" it, the owner couldn't honestly claim that the treatment had brought about the cure. There were too many authenticated cases of Fords fixing themselves—restored naturally to health after a short rest. Farmers soon discovered this, and it fitted nicely with their draft-horse philosophy: "Let 'er cool off and she'll snap into it again." (White)

While it is common to be attracted to tales of continued determination because of how such stories portray a communal desire for potentiality and success, I'm drawn into narratives like White's and Murray's because of a specific, personal connection. My father briefly owned a Model T.

Where that information fits in a given taxonomy of Woodward, the car itself, and the stories told about both is not clear, nor is it clear why I have this desire to insert myself (or my father's image) into this narrative I am telling. What is even more difficult to understand is how important this point is to me even though I never saw the car. It was bought, driven with great frustration (the expense and burden of transport as it could not be used on just any road), and then sold before I was able to visit and see firsthand the famed automobile. Despite no direct knowledge of the car, one question continues to unsettle me, and I continue to try and resolve it: Why did my father buy that Model T and then sell it so quickly? Without belonging within the larger taxonomy of Detroit, torn lifelines, and the automobile industry, why did he want this car, and why did he quickly no longer want the car? Why did he not follow White's romantic notion of the Model T and uplift himself from whatever disappointments the car may have created?

No matter how many times I pose the question, the answer my father gives me does not satisfy me ("It was too expensive"), for it feels like too quick a gesture for consensus (that is, this one vocal declaration represents a true reason). Social convention (not wanting to share reasons beyond an expected response of cost) does not allow me to fully understand his motivation to sell the car not long after purchasing it. Social convention—an implicit shared agreement regarding the car's taxonomic status as an expense and the difficulty of maintaining it—allows us, the audience for such claims, the ability to "ramble along," to accept the taxonomic understanding, and to move to other matters of importance. In some instances, like my own, we hope to one day persevere with a concrete categorical response.

Still, this anecdote—along with these other references to the Model T— allows me to shape an understanding of the generic category we might call "Woodward." The Model T and Woodward can be placed within the same categorical space regarding Detroit, the automobile, and commerce. The Model T is expensive to maintain. Detroit paid a price for relying too much on automobile manufacturing. *Newsweek*, its article suggests, wants Detroit, too, to fit in this taxonomy of cost, to be like the Model T, to ramble along, to fix itself, to persevere, to rise phoenixlike from its torn lifeline, to move on to more pertinent matters. Yet without the lifeline Woodward once was, *Newsweek* argues, Detroit's spatial history has concluded. It is now a shadow of its past. Without the infusion of the Model T into the atmosphere of its glory days (the metaphoric idyllic, or the nostalgia E. B. White returns to, or the possible historical reason my father bought this car), the city is a shadow of its past. Unlike the 1915 Ford, Detroit, *Newsweek* claims, doesn't ramble right along. It is stuck in a category as well (torn), but a category that cannot move (ramble).

The author's father in his Model T. Photograph by the author's mother.

Critical Taxonomies

The critical gesture associated with a taxonomy, like the one *Newsweek* circulates, argues that Detroit "chose" the wrong path in 1967 when it allowed racial inequality to foster a devastating riot. What the Model T made glorious, the contemporary automobile destroyed. Jobs within the auto industry, as well as those lost, were central to creating the city's inequality. "The combination of persistent discrimination in hiring, technological change, decentralized manufacturing, and urban economic decline had dramatic effects on the employment prospects of blacks in metropolitan Detroit" (Sugrue 261–62). Frustration—economic and racial—is itself a site of meaning, and *Newsweek* emphasizes that point in its analysis in a way that other references to the Model T I assemble don't. The explosion of anger that took place on Twelfth Street in Detroit, the night after a police raid on a "blind pig" drinking establishment, symbolizes the city's economic despair, one that connects commerce, employment, and race as categories of meaning. The African Americans who rose up in anger, the taxonomy tells us, worked in the automobile industry. Woodward is, at times, a space for these meanings to converge.

As with the Billy Murray tune that categorizes the Model T as the everyman car, popular culture, overall, is quick to capitalize on categories such as race and class, and consequently, popular culture places such categories in physical spaces like a street or avenue in order to generate a taxonomy of space. Popular culture also helps shape the meaning of a category like Woodward. These meanings affect our own critical positions regarding various spaces. In "The Motor City Is Burning," the MC5[1] capture the riots as a revolutionary gesture regarding the city's political issues; the song's title equates the city's industrial legacy with the rise of Black Power and with that of the riots themselves. What happened in 1967, the MC5 declare, is something larger than the event itself. The riot is a critical moment. Typically, riots take on larger systems of meaning like government, politics, or commerce.

In the MC5's narrative, Clairmount (where the riots began), not Woodward, contains the various meanings at stake. What the MC5 place at Twelfth and Clairmount is a meaning so intense that the "pigs" walking the street "freak out" and so politically charged that the Black Panther snipers won't let authorities "put it out." The MC5 were not the only ones to localize "riot" as a specific meaning tied to a specific street. In 1967, *Time* magazine placed the center of the riots not at the street where it began, Clairmount, but at Woodward Avenue:

> Rocks and bottles flew. Looting, at first dared by only a few, became a mob delirium as big crowds now gathered, ranging through the West Side, then spilling across Woodward Avenue into the East Side. Arsonists lobbed Molotov cocktails at newly pillaged stores. Fires started in the shops, spread swiftly to homes and apartments. Snipers took up posts in windows and on rooftops. For four days and into the fifth, mobs stole, burned and killed as a force of some 15,000 city and state police, National Guardsmen and federal troops fought to smother the fire. The city was almost completely paralyzed. ("The Fire This Time")

The riots, *Time* reported, marked the city's emptying of space. The riots, too, killed a lifeline. The traditional view, rightly or wrongly devised, is that racial unrest pushed anxious businesses, and car manufacturers, north to the whiter suburbs and metropolitan area. This view locates the recognized street category and ties it to Detroit's malaise. It also utilizes another category, "worker," in order to foreground the first category (racial unrest). The unemployed worker, the Black Panther revolutionary, and the police are all workers (categories of meaning) in a city dominated by automobile workers (yet another category of meaning). These categories help *Newsweek* and *Time* tell one type of story about Detroit and its supposed lifeline, a story obviously different than the one suggested by Murray, White, or my father's purchase, where the worker is a consumer of an automobile. In the two stories of Woodward *Newsweek* and *Time* tell, "worker" functions as more than one category.

If early-twentieth-century Detroit had considered the lifeline of the city to be cigars (as my introduction to this chapter notes), the city's financial and racial meanings might have emerged out of quite a different history than popular publications like *Newsweek* or *Time* believe the city eventually did. A different category might have emerged, a different category regarding both Woodward and the workers employed within its industries and stores. Following that imaginary cigar history Poremba's book elegantly displays, one might imagine, then, *Newsweek* publishing a 1984 article about a cigar industry lifeline along Woodward Avenue that continues to create new jobs, economic success, and significant trade for the state of Michigan. Such a narrative would have settled a different type of meaning about Woodward Avenue, race, and work than the traditional riot narrative provides, albeit one still dependent on the category of "lifeline." Without Fordist divisions of labor or ethnicity (all workers required to learn English, the homogenization of Anglo identity), the cigar industry would not have either fled the 1967 riots nor contributed to the mounting anger that sparked the unrest. Without the massive dependence on the automotive industry, the city would not have found itself constantly looking for a new type of lifeline, one that began breaking apart as early as the 1950s, when, as Thomas Sugrue writes, "auto manufacturers and suppliers permanently reduced their Detroit-area work forces, closed plants, and relocated to other parts of the country" (126). Such a speculation, of course, little resembles the lifeline that was created, a lifeline dependent on the automobile industry stretching from northern Woodward in Detroit at Highland Park all the way to the Detroit River. Such speculation does little to change the reality the city continues to face. Still, speculation has its value.

With my initial speculation, though, I find Poremba's two cigar images among the most striking of all the meanings I have assembled so far in this chapter because they displace a conventional topos regarding Detroit, manufacturing, workers, and more specifically, cigar manufacturing. In the cigar pictures, I don't see automobile workers, disgruntled African American workers, or policemen. In fact, I don't see men at all. In

Woodward's cigar factories, women were the principle workers. A photograph in the *Detroit News*'s online collection shows a group of women workers striking at the Mozier Cressman Cigar Company in 1937, a women worker at a conveyor belt, and a woman worker posing with finished cigars (Jones). While women did work (and still do) in the automobile factories, their presence in this categorical system of Detroit's lifeline complicates the topos of Detroit. Women cigar workers are not usually found within Detroit's topos nor its related topoi like *worker*.

If Woodward Avenue is known at all for manufacturing, as I just noted, it is for the auto industry that arose out of Highland Park (Woodward and close to 6 Mile) and that later positioned its administration at the General Motors Building (Woodward and West Grand Boulevard). In the auto industry, we find a communal topos of the worker. "At one time, around 1917, 23 automobile companies in Detroit, many of them located along Woodward Avenue, assembled more than 1 million vehicles a year" (Schneider 12). Many of these workers were African American men. Along Woodward Avenue, attracted by this corridor of investment and development, many young African American migrants settled just prior to and just after the Second World War. Many resembled the worker described in Blind Arthur Blake's May 1928 recording "Detroit Bound Blues":

> I'm goin' to Detroit, get myself a good job
> I'm goin' to Detroit, get myself a good job
> Tried to stay around here with the starvation mob
> I'm goin' to get a job, up there in Mr. Ford's place
> I'm goin' to get a job, up there in Mr. Ford's place
> Stop these eatless days from starin' me in the face
> When I start to makin' money, she don't need to come around
> When I start to makin' money, she don't need to come around
> 'Cause I don't want her now, Lord. I'm Detroit bound
> Because they got wild women in Detroit, that's all I want to see
> Because they got wild women in Detroit, that's all I want to see
> Wild women and bad whisky would make a fool out of me.

This mythological character who finds salvation on Woodward Avenue has been a staple of Woodward's legacy. Each factory located on or near the avenue attracted workers believing in another mythology, the American Dream produced by assembly-line manufacturing. Blake's worker is the same kind of worker in Philip Levine's poem "What Work Is": "We stand in the rain in a long line / waiting at Ford Highland Park. For work." Most of those dreamers were poor blacks and whites from the rural South.

"Detroit's reputation as a city of unsurpassed economic opportunity, combined with wrenching changes in the southern economy, attracted thousands of new migrants northward to the Motor City" (Sugrue 23). Johnny Cash sings about the southerner who drifted north to Detroit in his song "One Piece at a Time." In Cash's tale, the narrator leaves Kentucky in 1949 to work on a Cadillac assembly line. He watches the cars roll by, hangs his head to cry, and laments that what he really wants is the car he helps manufacture. For Cash, the worker's meaning is built out of the dream to be a consumer of the luxury he helps create.

Indeed, just as the riots mythology is repeated in the MC5 and later in *Newsweek*, Blake's and Cash's immigrants who toil as workers on the assembly line create a mythology as well, repeated as late as 1977 on Blondie's "Detroit 442," a song from the album *Plastic Letters*. The racial and geographical identities may shift; but the worker is still the same. Blondie's worker, who calls Detroit a "concrete factory," spends endless days toiling on the Oldsmobile assembly line. This worker's fantasy is to leave the line in order to "ride with you;" that is, in order to experience some type of life beyond work, some type of excitement beyond being a place on an automated line, some type of life that resembles the symbolism of the Oldsmobile 442's muscle-car prowess. While the assembly line may have proposed one meaning (promise), various narratives representing the worker's experience project a different meaning (dissatisfaction).

Those that searched out success and fortune in Woodward Avenue's automobile plants found themselves replicated in the very machines they worked on; in other words, their lives and notions of self became generated by the automotive industry that attracted them to Detroit. Cadillac, Oldsmobile, these, too, served as sites of meaning that produced identity. Such categories of worker are replicated like an assembly line's production (one worker is exchangeable with the next), but the meaning located in one space (Detroit is a worker's town, Detroit is itself a "concrete factory") is repeated as well. Even more important, to find the same figure in 1928 again in 1967 and again in 1977 signifies how such repetitions stretch into popular culture vocabulary, as well as how a general understanding of the city that depends on one fixed meaning ("Detroit's lifeline is Woodward and the automotive industry"; "Detroit's worker is the automobile worker") creates the types of impressions circulated by publications like *Newsweek* and *Time*, and not by a once nascent cigar industry.

What these references show me is that despite what *Newsweek* claims, Woodward is not a mere shadow of its past nor is it simply a weed-covered concrete. It is a space that maintains various meanings that move along its lanes, meanings like the repetitive image of a specific category in several very different musical scores. The worker, as one example of this process, is repeated in separate temporal moments differentiated by distinct racial and gendered identities. These repetitions suggest a different kind of lifeline than either a failed industry or even a speculated industry can support. These repetitions suggest that a given space holds multiple approaches towards generating one or more meanings. That these repetitions exist in popular culture spaces motivated by the technologies of electronic distribution is a point I will return to in the beginning of chapter 5.

Thus, Woodward teaches much about categories and their repetition as well as their circulation. Woodward is a road of repetitions, a point emphasized in the worker example but also found elsewhere. There are two Model Ts, the long-abandoned factory in Highland Park and the shopping plaza of the same name that sits adjacent to the factory. There are two Temple Beth Els, one close to the New Center at Gladstone, one farther south and now owned by Wayne State University. And, as noted, there are (at least) two images of a Woodward worker (cigar and auto). These repetitions suggest the duality of meaning that a given space, particularly one allowed to stress movement like an avenue does, maintains when it functions as a network. That words may contain more than one meaning in a given institutional, rhetorical, or disciplinary vocabulary is not a new concept to rhetorical studies. The entire keywords enterprise—begun with Raymond Williams's text of the same name—breaks down terms' etymological, social, and cultural meanings (Williams's project begins with the duality of the word "culture") in order to reveal the complexity of language at social and cultural levels. Elsewhere, Derridian deconstruction evokes homonyms and puns to highlight the "differance" (defer, different) meanings always participate in. These are familiar rhetorical gestures. Still, the rhetoric that surrounds urban affairs—from development to critique— seldom takes seriously how and where multiple meanings within one or more categories may move in a given rhetorical situation or space. The topos of Detroit typically is not allowed to move nor to be dual; it is posed *as is* (that is, torn). The category is required to remain singular and in one place: Detroit *is* ruins. A worker *is* male and in the automotive industry.

Woodward, then, is as appropriate a metaphor for moving space as it actually is a space that transports meanings as material, people, and cars but also as conceptual things and ideas. The narrative of "the factory worker" is but one topos that moves meaning down Woodward (as these songs demonstrate). This "street" (in a generic definition that mixes the names "street," "avenue," and "road") moves much more as well. In the *Urban Revolution*, Henri Lefebvre emphasizes the role of movement within streets, writing that the street is a conduit beyond the transportation of material goods and people. He notes that "the street is more than just a place for movement and circulation" (18). Lefebvre continues:

> It serves as a meeting place (topos), for without it no other designated encounters are possible (cafes, theaters, halls). These places animate the street and are served by its animation, or they cease to exist. In the street, a form of spontaneous theater, I become spectacle and spectator, and something an actor. The street is where movement takes place, the interaction without which urban life would not exist, leaving only separation, a forced and fixed segregation. (18)

While such descriptions of the street might feel as romantic or hyperbolic as de Certeau's "walking," they also position a specific space as functioning on dual levels: place to meet; place to move. We might expand that definition to include: Meanings meet up; meanings move on. Lefebvre's notion of "the street" could easily be a portrait of how meaning repetitions on Woodward Avenue lead to specific types of movement. Those movements are the focus of this chapter, particularly for the way they shape taxonomies in a given networked rhetoric. I begin with Woodward Avenue as a space of movements—rhetorical and physical—so that I can discuss how this movement informs a very specific kind of new media practice that suggests meanings move when located within the digital space or the network in general. This taxonomic space has come to be called *folksonomy*. Before I discuss folksonomy, however, I need to address the motorization of a space like Woodward and its early implications for digital meaning.

Motorized Space

In *The Art of the Motor*, Paul Virilio argues that digital technology's effect on space is leaning to a moment where we "motorize the reality of space" (151). Virilio, whose other work draws connections between technology and speed, is not optimistic about this technological shift, arguing that in the supposed motorization of space, faith lets "itself be abused, it would seem, by the virtuality generator" (151). Communal beliefs in fixed meanings are exposed as vulnerable, malleable, and impermanent. For Virilio, communicative space is deeply tied to the question of speed, how quickly or slowly information is received and produced. Virilio, like many other critics of digital culture, connects obsolescence with the history of sped-up communicative innovations, for meanings that are not fixed can easily be eliminated from our cultural or institutional vocabularies. "The communications industry would never have got where it is today had it not started out as an art of the motor capable of orchestrating the perpetual shift of appearances" (23). These shifts to obsolescence become hyperextended in the digital age so that perceptions alter, notions of real and unreal are always under question, and fixed beliefs are destabilized. Hypermobility, which Virilio pessimistically attributes to how we access information as well as the delivery of such information, generates a crisis as critical distance (we don't know what means what) vanishes. That crisis sounds like a rhetorical one, for its concerns are with how ideas, people, and moments are positioned, and thus, understood. "With confusion setting in between the *real space* of action and the *virtual space* of retroaction, all *positioning* is, in fact, beginning to find itself in an impasse, causing a crisis in all position forecasting" (*Art of the Motor* 155). In other words, hypermobility dislocates comfortable or accepted meaning systems, and because of that displacement, information is at an impasse. What a given space means now, Virilio argues, hypermobility causes quickly to mean something else (as my worker example demonstrates). Instead of an affirmative "yes" to the Verizon call across mobile networks, "Can you hear me now?" we might imagine Virilio responding "no, we cannot hear because there is too much information delivered too quickly, in too many spaces. I cannot hear anything but the rush of information." Too many meanings at once, Virilio might add, produces too much displacement where "the thing described takes over from the real thing" (*Art of the Motor* 43).

Unlike Virilio, I am not afraid of such a condition. As I've already argued, the flexibility of space is central to networked rhetorics. This point becomes somewhat evident as the "worker" category is positioned in such a way that several meanings occupy the same space on Woodward Avenue. Worker is a mobile meaning when each usage is brought into that space and allowed to connect to the next. These meanings are positioned and repositioned. Instead of reading the mobility of the network as a crisis (or, for that matter, as a utopia), I want to extend Virilio's observation as a point of departure for this chapter. Under the rubric of "positioning," we can consider how spaces dislocate meaning systems in productive as well as counterproductive ways when the metadata (the label or name) becomes mobile. While the database aspect of networked rhetorics already suggests mobility, the motorization of space might contribute further in this line of thought. Accordingly, I want to push Virilio's insights away from either a pessimistic/optimistic binary that plagues much technology writings and to move his work towards his own concerns with information navigation.

In *Everyware: The Dawning Age of Ubiquitous Computing*, Adam Green-field coins the neologism "everyware" to describe a networked state where mobile meanings created by RFID tags, the web, GPS, and wearable computing create a "language of interaction suited to a world where information processing would be everywhere in the human environment" (14). Everyware is a mobile condition of acquiring and producing information. Everyware promises a type of "motorized" system of positioning. Everyware extends the definition or category of what kind of space produces information (a memo, a report, a webpage, a newscast, a shirt) to include less accepted, or yet to be used, devices: "clothing, furniture, walls, and doorways" (19). Under this definition, any space—physical or conceptual—can be "motorized" to produce meaning. Any space can move meanings. Such is the very condition Virilio fears, one in which information consumption becomes overtly hectic and confusing because a vast number of material and immaterial objects are producing information, and no one space can be localized. "To navigate space, Cyberspace" he writes, as one formerly steered a motor vehicle: this is indeed the great aesthetic mutation of information" (*Art of the Motor* 145). Virilio draws an analogy between navigating two media: the road (motor vehicle) and the digital (cyberspace). Our current media, Virilio notes, have mutated, or dislocated, the former media used to convey information. The motorization of space, then, is a negative act for how it positions information in unseemingly ways. Motorized space makes a previous system obsolete.

Instead of accepting this premise, I want to take up both Virilio's initial metaphor of the "motorization of space" and Greenfield's assumption about ubiquitous computing so that motorization is a productive, folksonomic gesture, not an act that makes other systems obsolete or that makes obsolescence a negative rhetorical act. Greenfield argues that positioning, or ubiquitous computing, actualizes objects to transfer information. We can also call this process "motorization." "When everyday things are endowed with the ability to sense their environment, store metadata reflecting their own provenance, location, status, and use history, and share that information with other such objects, this cannot help but redefine our relationship with such things" (Greenfield 23). If, indeed, all material objects may one day project information within larger networks of things, people, places, and various objects, they would then be motorizing each other through the network. The network, therefore, acts like a road, a street, or an avenue; it transports. What might it mean to "motorize" an already automotive-based space like Woodward Avenue? Towards what type of information systems might we steer ourselves and the meanings we work with and among? How have I already seen Wood-ward motorize "worker"?

To begin to answer these questions, I turn to Marshall McLuhan. Like Virilio, McLuhan identified speed, travel, and electronic communication as related entities indicative of contemporary communicative practices. The road, McLuhan writes, is tied to the development of information distribution. "It was not until the advent of the telegraph that messages could travel faster than a messenger. Before this, roads and the written word were closely interrelated" (*Understanding Media* 90). For McLuhan, the road serves as both physical entity (that which actually played a role in information distribution by allowing people to transport themselves and the ideas they carried) and as metaphor (a concept regarding in-formation delivery). This duality of meaning allows him to play with the idea of the road so that it is one of many media that participate in communication. The road, like other media, affects our sense of what generates meaning as well as what carries that meaning from space to space. "Each form of transport not only carries, but translates and trans-forms, the sender, the receiver, and the message. The use of any kind of medium or extension of man alters the patterns of interdependence among people, as it alters the rations among our senses" (*Understand-ing Media* 91). That a road "translates" and "transforms" also suggests a sense of movement already within this media, one explained by Latour as a characteristic of networks. Translation, in this context, means that information affects (changes) other information upon a meet-up or con-nection. The importance of the network is not that information con-nects, but rather that the connections affect other connections. Under the name Actor-Network-Theory (ANT), Latour explains this process: "We don't know yet how all those actors are connected, but we can state as the new default position before the study starts that all the actors we are going to deploy might be associated in such a way that they *make others do things*" (*Reassembling* 107). Such is McLuhan's contention when he notes that the "speed up" of information partly generated by the road "causes a change of organization" (*Understanding Media* 91). Indeed, as I will argue throughout each chapter of this book, networks move and are moved; they transform and translate experiences and ideas as they form and break connections. They *do things*.

Despite the implied emphasis that transformation generates improve-ments or an expanded presence, McLuhan also notes that while it led to increased proliferation of print culture by serving as a conduit for mer-cantilism and the distribution of ideas, the road emptied out the city of its residents. "Great improvements in roads brought the city more and more to the country" (*Understanding Media* 94). Ed Hustoles, former Detroit deputy director for planning at the Southeast Council for Governments, blames the bringing of the city to the country (or to the suburbs) on the privatization of transportation, another type of motorizing of space. Hustoles extends McLuhan's observation to Detroit's collapse, an observation that begins with the expansion of the city's highways, like I-75. After all, I-75 changed the city's dependence on Woodward by shifting the bulk of its automotive transportation away from Woodward to the massive interstate highway. "A lot of things happened that I wished hadn't happened," Hustoles notes.

> It turned out that we helped empty out the city of Detroit. We didn't expect to do that. We didn't anticipate the almost complete elimination of public transportation. Everyone was going to have to drive a car. We laid out 120-foot rights of way for the mile roads in the middle of nowhere because they may end up being four-lane roads. We anticipated a lot of traffic. (qtd. in Mast 157)

The emptiness of Detroit space is a familiar topos. What Hustoles claims might be described as the popular image *Newsweek* clings to in its lament over Detroit. Or it might be the type of emptiness Marc Augé focuses on as a principle feature of the non-place. "Motorway travel is thus doubly remarkable: it avoids, for functional reasons, all the principal places to which it takes us, and it makes comments on them" (*Non-Places* 97). Or this emptiness might be indicative of the postmodern melancholy Jerry Heron romantically attaches to Detroit in his book *Afterculture*. "In the postindustrial era of 'service' or 'information' this classic city no longer refers to anything real; or else the reality of things has so altered as to render the representational surface of the city a failed, aphasic relic: more an artifact than a practical text" (*Afterculture* 124). Hustoles's comments network with a number of topos-driven beliefs and statements about the emptying of the city and, thus, repeat yet another familiar category: emptiness. These categories as I list them here, of course, are not networked positions that translate or transform; they are fixed definitions of a space that do not enter into relationships with other spaces. As I write this chapter, I begin putting them into relationship with one another, but on their own—and as they tend to see themselves—these statements are not yet networks or part of networks. They have not been made mobile or motorized. They remain as static taxonomies. The network changes that final point.

While each category may offer some focus on the road, they differ dramatically from the type of role McLuhan imagines the road playing in information creation and distribution, as well as its emptying. McLuhan, unlike these views or those who convey them, portrays this emptying out as a power shift, as a transformative process, arguing that "any new means of moving information will alter any power structure whatever" (*Understanding Media* 92). That power, this chapter shows, is in how we categorize information, whether it be the name of a road, the name of a city, or the traits and characteristics associated with taxonomies in general. I will expand upon this point shortly, but for now I note that the power shift is one of agency regarding what or who is an agent in this network of categories. An early feature of this agency or power shift, I understand, is the informational shifting of fixed categories (worker, road, empty).

Woodward Avenue, Highland Park. Photograph by the author.

Instead of these nonrelational views of space and roads I briefly highlight, I am more inclined to see McLuhan's emptied meaning in terms of information organization. The one system that both filled in Detroit's meaning, including Woodward Avenue, as well as emptied it was Fordism. As the songs I begin this chapter with attest, Ford brought industry and the category of "industrial city" to Detroit. But when the automotive industry needed to extend, change, and transform its own category of "production," its failures to do so contributed to the city's dwindling revenue and, eventually, its number of inhabitants. Repetition offers some insight into this activity as the speed attributed to the road contributes to repetitive meanings (acceleration pushing overlaps in shortened time spans). McLuhan calls this process the "total field of inclusive awareness," the point when "in electronic technology, the principle of specialism and division as a factor of speed no longer applies" (*Understanding Media* 103). Detroit's first major center of specialization and division may not have been in the cigar factories on Woodward as I wanted to speculate early in this chapter, but in Highland Park, home of the Model T, designed by Albert Kahn.

Highland Park's position on Woodward Avenue, in particular, represents the role organization systems like Fordism play in the production and dissemination of information and products, as well as how it has shaped the individual. In Fordism, the individual becomes replicated much in the way that an automobile is or a series of meanings along a major road like Woodward. Replication becomes an all encompassing system. In addition to the replication of the category called "the worker," Highland Park popularized organizational systems on larger scales, mechanisms that contributed to other structurings of society. In fact, that one architect can claim the design of two major automobile centers (yet another duality) along Woodward (Highland Park and the General Motors Building) speaks to this repetitive activity: the repetition of one designer, Albert Kahn (even as each building's design differs) and the repetition of a space's story regarding its creation and its success (the legacy attributed to Ford). In his discussion of Modernism, Terry Smith emphasizes this point. Despite Kahn's differing designs (the General Motors Building doesn't look like Highland Park), "the fundamental organizational form remains the same as that of Ford—the tendency toward 'one man, one product, one process'" (Smith 87). The same worker represented in Blake's music reappears in Blondie's. The same designer of one building reappears in another. The same concern over emptiness in one person's remarks (Hustoles) reappears as romantic emptiness in a writer's work (Herron). Unlike the transformation of information McLuhan, and later Virilio, attributes to speed, the speed of factory production maintained levels of conformity via division (each worker represents the same category of Ford). There are larger implications to this replication regarding communicative practices. "The entire tendency of Kahn's practice is in this sort of direction, as would be expected by an architecture of mass production. Indeed, much of the buildings' power, their clarity as structures, depends on their total disregard of human scale, anthropo-morphic reference, and workers' needs, and on local or regional relation-ships" (Smith 88). The obvious relationship found in early-twentieth-century Detroit is the production of automobiles and the overall project of efficiency. In rhetorical production, the relationship involves maintaining semblance in categorical organization. To disregard "needs," as Smith writes about Fordist production, is to disregard categorical difference within one meaning in the hope of maintaining efficiency. From Aris-totelian rhetoric to contemporary argumentation, categories serve the production of meaning. One such category is the worker. Another is the city itself. Mastering such categories, one might think, produces efficient rhetorical expression. Steven Mailloux defines rhetoric: "A production or performance model of rhetoric gives advice to rhetors concerning probable effects on their intended audiences" (40). That advice comes by knowing which audiences will respond to which categories.

Though the category of Detroit often replicates as a fixed meaning equating the city with automobiles, the initial images that spark this chapter suggest something otherwise. At some point in the city's his-tory, its image, its categorical reference point, could have been the cigar, not the automobile. Posing that historical possibility would, no doubt, produce anything but a "probable" effect. Detroit and cigars? How could that be? Posing that possibility is also to pose the likelihood of a differ-ent kind of categorical replication. It asks if Detroit could have come to be associated with, of all things, cigars? What odder category can one imagine than Detroit as an American Havana or Tampa? How does this imaginative gesture *expand* the image of Detroit and, in particular, of Woodward? How does this gesture alter probable effects on a given au-dience? How does this gesture alter a Fordist legacy or create another type of repetition? Even more important than tying the city to cigar production and distribution, what other categorical spaces might we situate Detroit within?

To get at those questions, I want to spend the rest of this chapter fur-ther exploring the role of categories, information distribution, and Wood-ward Avenue. My purpose is not to reimagine Detroit as cigar capital per se, but to engage with the kinds of imagings the convolution of taxono-mies allows for in the network. What I am interested in via Woodward is the question of information organization and the expansion of taxono-mies. While the Fordist assembly-line-driven, organizational project is still present in the remainder of this chapter, I will explore these issues through the more contemporary new-media practice called folksonomy. The move from Fordism at Woodward to folksonomy at Woodward will teach me how Digital Detroit creates other types of informational relationships at the level of categorical organization when such organization is motorized. This motorization of names and spaces, I will show, marks another characteristic of network rhetoric.

An early hint at this mobility comes to me via the Detroit Public Library, located at Woodward Avenue in the New Center, adjacent to the Maccabees Building, where the Department of English at Wayne State University is housed. Among the many murals the library hosts is John S. Coppin's *Man's Mobility 1965*. In this painting, a bare-chested man looks upward through the archway of what might be the library and sees rockets firing into outer space. In the age of information delivery, the mural suggests, technology and man unite to create a mobile body, a motorized body, a moving folk blasting out of earth, who search out new meanings in new spaces (outer space as opposed to earth). One can assume that this "man" the mural boldly depicts represents the larger folk, or people, of Detroit.

The mural provides an exigence for exploring this relationship between the folk and movement. To do so, I first focus on 1965, the year the mural imaginatively illustrates, and the concept of the "folk." I also do so by discussing, of all people, the folk's relationship to the non-Detroiter Bob Dylan, who performed at Detroit's Cobo Hall in 1965. One reason for doing so is that Dylan appears in the beginning of William Mitchell's *Placing Words*, a text I name in the introduction as motivating my discussion of Digital Detroit. Mitchell's network of Dylan and a place previously visited arises out of a later connection I will add to that network (a passage in Dylan's *Chronicles*). Another reason stems from my desire to extend the musical reference points of the Woodward mapping I introduced in the beginning of this chapter. As a category, music is often used to reference Detroit. Dylan may be one of the least likely markers of that category since his origins are in Minnesota, not Michigan. But as I will show in the next section of this chapter, my connecting Dylan and Woodward comes from not just the temporal overlap with the mural, but also from appearances he makes at Cobo Hall, both in 1965 and more recently, and how these appearances extend his notion of the folk. As a category, the folk moves music into this next section. My first move before clarifying that point, however, is to revisit Newport, Rhode Island, in 1965, just prior to the Detroit appearance in the same year.

Motorized Meaning Systems: Folksonomies

"This is a folk song," Bob Dylan insisted as American and English crowds booed during his 1965 and 1966 tours. Between those two years of touring and presenting new material, the concert at Newport in 1965 became the centerpiece of that angry response. In a brief fifteen-minute set, the annual concert of folk and standard blues had been transformed by Dylan's new rock outfit. Dylan had gone electric, and the folk world was in shock. Fans wanted him to return to the inward looking, folk-based protest songs that comprised albums like *The Freewheelin' Bob Dylan* or *The Times They Are A-Changin'*. Contrary to the crowd's negative judgment, Dylan was, however, singing a folk song. Whether he performed the raucous, electric "Leopard Skin Pill Box Hat," the odd piano-led "Ballad of a Thin Man," the raunchy and loud "Like a Rolling Stone," or the more popular, acoustic "A Hard Rain's A-Gonna Fall," the music was still "folk." It still encompassed the sense of a collective identity; it still held connection to the category of folk even as it bent that category for technological innovation (electric guitars). "Folk" is a type of classification, and classifications are always ideological, as well as rhetorical. Groups classify information as well as identifications along ideological positions. Kenneth Burke tied this sense of identification to group mentality, or the corporal (that is bodily) apparatus that shapes thought and meaning. One area this occurs, Burke notes, is in music. "We see this process in its simplest form, when the music-lover clamorously admires a particular composer, and so 'shares vicariously' in the composer's attainments" (*Attitudes toward History* 267). Dylan's history pre-1965 was no exception to this notion. Songs like "When the Ship Comes In" and "Only a Pawn in Their Game" were indicative of how this folk sensibility shared in-common identification. These songs spoke to a collective identity organized around grass-roots activism, civil rights, and social justice. When Dylan played in Detroit on October 17, 1964, prior to going electric, he appeared on a bill that also advertised appearances by fellow folk singers Booker Bradshaw and Ellen Stekert. The concert was held at the Masonic Scottish Rite Cathedral, a theater founded by a nineteenth-century secret society that stressed the shared identification of national rituals such as using the same trowel George Washington used to lay the first cornerstone of the Capitol in Washington, DC. Dylan played folk in a space that argued for a specific type of folk.

Even though the crowd's hostile responses in 1965 and 1966 argued otherwise, the new media of electric guitars and amplified sound did not alter the sharing of identification the folk promotes. At Bob Dylan's 1965 appearance at Cobo Hall in downtown Detroit, audiences, we can imagine, reacted as they did elsewhere; they recognized the communal sharing of meaning even as they hated the electronic delivery of that meaning. The folk was no longer the same *kind* of classification system it had been.

That alternative classification system I draw attention to was remembered in Dylan's 2004 pseudoautobiography *Chronicles* (the text Mitchell draws from). "Gutenberg could have been some guy who stepped out of an old folk song," Dylan writes as he recalls this time period (27). In some ways, Dylan became the symbolic point of Gutenberg technology updated for a new kind of classification or folk. Whereas the pre-1965 folk represented a very specific type of classificatory system whose categories included "protest," "civil rights," "labor," "equality," "antiwar," and other related tropes, the new electric folk introduced confusion, allusiveness, and bravado into a scheme that demands accurate representation of the thing named and the category it represents. With that point, it isn't hard to understand why the audiences booed Dylan. This "in your face" electric performance was hard for audiences to rationalize outside of the traditional, fixed boundaries that had previously defined folk music. "Innumerable confusions and a profound feeling of despair invariably emerge in periods of great technological and cultural transitions," Marshall McLuhan wrote two years after Dylan's tour. "Our 'Age of Anxiety' is, in great part, the result of trying to do today's job with yesterday's tools—with yesterday's concepts" (McLuhan and Fiore 8). One such concept in 1965 and 1966 was information classification. That same concept came to Detroit the same year.

Thus, there is a metaphor for rhetoric and digital composing in the booing Dylan heard at Newport and eventually Cobo Hall in 1965. What is unfamiliar, or whatever rhetorically combines items that don't seem to belong together, often induces anxiety, anger and hostility. Dylan's decision to plug in offers important insight into my examination of Woodward Avenue and some of the categories it projects. This examination, when reduced to the singular category of economic failure, focuses on anxiety; popular accounts of Woodward treat it as a torn lifeline. Where there once was (or even, could have been) financial success, there now is devastation, this account claims. In *Chronicles*, anxiety carries over into taxonomies and how such taxonomies are used for a variety of purposes, some of which include the narration of a city's failure or the narration of a life's story. When Dylan recalls his signing at Columbia Records at the beginning of his career (just a few years before he went electric), for instance, the taxonomy of this narration became mixed-up and anxious. As Dylan narrates his story, he tells the head of publicity at Columbia he is from Illinois (he was from Minnesota) and that he worked a number of odd jobs he never had held.

> He asked me if I ever did any other work and I told him that I had a dozen jobs, drove a bakery truck once. He wrote that down and asked me if there was anything else. I said I'd worked construction and he asked me where.
> "Detroit." (Dylan 7)

Whether or not Dylan's tagging of Detroit in this narrative reflects a reality or is a lie is unimportant. The accuracy of his narration evokes some sense of anxiety (then how can we believe him if his ethos is suspect) or it generates a feature of networked writing best understood as a generic confusion regarding classification systems in general. Does it matter if Dylan worked in Detroit or not? Can we utilize his diegesis regardless of its validity? Can we tag Dylan as yet another former Detroit "worker" without evidence he did this work? This confusion, as the beginning of this chapter showed, makes a site like Woodward Avenue contain more than one possible meaning (such as cigar or car manufacturer) in one space. This confusion allows a spatial story of Detroit and Woodward Avenue to reference Bob Dylan's 1965 Newport tour even though Newport is not in or near Detroit. This confusion, as I will explain in more detail shortly, is a primary feature of new-media classification systems.

This confusion regarding classification is highlighted further in a telling moment in D. A. Pennebaker's documentary *Don't Look Back*. Filmed during the same time period as Dylan's turn to the electric, *Don't Look Back* documents Dylan as performer, celebrity, and writer working to understand the emerging technological culture he is situated within. In a canonical scene, Dylan flips cue cards to the fast-paced, almost raplike "Subterranean Homesick Blues." Each cue card either mirrors or plays off of the lyrics. When the song is over, Dylan reveals a final cue card that reads "What?" In that final moment of visual confusion, we hear the overall confusion of the folk I have begun mapping out with both my initial discussion of Woodward and Dylan's work. What to do with technology? What am I doing, Dylan might be saying, merging visual displays, aural performance, and the electronic? What kind of idea am I now producing? What else? What more? What the hell? When I see that final "What?" Dylan flashes, I ask a question as well: Does there have to be a meaning here beyond the exasperation of "What?" Do I have to know what Dylan means when he says "What?" How would a "What?" fit with the rhetorical production generated by traditional classificatory design that networks either support or alter?

Bob Dylan flipping cue cards to "Subterranean Homesick Blues" in D. A. Pennebaker's *Don't Look Back* (1967).

These Dylan-esque moments are a lesson for networked rhetorics. They are emphasized even more in the title of Martin Scorsese's 2005 documentary on Dylan, *No Direction Home*. Its title a line from one of Dylan's most influential hits "Like a Rolling Stone," *No Direction Home* resonates as a generic response rhetorical studies might make when it feels the pressure technology and digital culture place on practices like classification. "How does it feel to encounter the digital in a particular taxonomy?" we can imagine rhetorical studies asking. "Like no direction home." Home signifies the familiar. We have come to find our dwelling places (our ethos) in rhetorical production to be the most useful when they utilize familiar categories. When these dwelling places demand meaning, when they provide neatly arranged classification schemes like those Aristotle details in *The Rhetoric*, when they can be conveyed in tidy ways, we are part of the folk. To do that kind of work, one might assume that the places where such work occurs need to be scaffolded as well so that relationships are foregrounded along with physical and ideological places of information production. The folk, therefore, would become a more complex place of meaning and not only a set of common beliefs, accepted reference points, or familiar practices. Woodward Avenue would be, then, more than a torn lifeline.

The lesson Dylan shows is that any kind of technological change may put familiar places (folks), like Woodward Avenue, under question. When change evokes the exclamation "WHAT?" we might wonder, in fact, what to do next, where to go next, what to say next, where to dwell next. Our familiar places where meaning resides, our metaphoric homes, become disrupted by the confusion of "What?" To accommodate the "What?" we must add to, delete from, or build anew our homes, that is, our familiar meanings. Edward Casey emphasizes that point when he writes that in dwelling, "*bodies build places.* Such building is not just a matter of literal fabrication but occurs through inhabiting and even by traveling between already built places" (*Getting Back* 116). The traveling metaphor Casey suggests (like the one I explore in the previous chapter) implies a movement between bodies (topoi) of information even when that movement is not completely understood. The metaphor also suggests that this activity will build something else, that it will establish other kinds of relationships, other kinds of folks not yet accounted for in current dwellings. Yet despite the potential of this movement, rhetors are often too concerned with making sure a move is tied closely to one body (or one meaning) or will be understood as belonging to an already established system of information. Roland Barthes posed a similar dilemma when he considered how common classification systems based on identity, like the autobiography, are too dependent on the acquisition of meaning as well as the classification of the genre itself.

> Constant (and illusory) passion for applying to every phenomenon, even the merest, not the child's question: *Why?* but the ancient Greek's question, the question of meaning, as if things shuddered with meaning: *What does this mean?* The fact must be transformed at all costs into idea, into description, into interpretation, in short, there must be found for it *a name other than its own.* (*Roland Barthes* 151)

Beyond Dylan's taxonomically confused autobiography, I am interested both in Dylan's settlement on something that resists *What does this mean?* and in Barthes's acknowledgment that meaning is itself illusory when it is subjected to only its own fixed name or place. The rhetorical implications for this observation have not yet been fully considered regarding Detroit, particularly for how they relate to the city's relationship to new media and organization. In what follows, I explore this issue in more detail, beginning with the overall question of classification and then moving towards the question of how the folk generates classification schemes from networked, rhetorical production.

Taxonomies

Much contemporary rhetorical theory still depends on the classification schemes Aristotle outlined as necessary for establishing ethos or for recognizing audience. In pedagogy, the classifications of current-traditional rhetoric—narration, classification, definition, argument, compare and contrast—may be the best known, exemplified as organizational schemes within numerous textbooks and syllabi. These schemes are hierarchical and fixed in meaning; they typically progress through a numbered or ordered state of affairs and are not meant to be broken up or altered in any significant manner. When Aristotle writes of the importance of the "law," for example, we can also hear a commentary on the nature of how hierarchies overall are generated.

> It is highly appropriate for well-enacted laws to define everything as exactly as possible and for as little as possible to be left to the judges: first because it is easier to find one or a few than [to find] many who are prudent and capable of framing laws and judging; second, legislation results from consideration over much time, while judgments are made at the moment [of a trial or debate], so it is difficult for the judges to determine justice and benefits fairly. (1.7)

In this system, orders are preestablished and deliberated but are also created through the power of one or a few individuals. These individuals ("prudent" and "capable") are empowered to establish the necessary standards for rhetorical exchange. As Casey argues, "the limiting power" of this scheme "is *already in place*; it is of the essence of place itself to provide this delimitation by its capacity to contain and to surround: to contain by surrounding" (*Fate of Place* 55). Such a model—putting information in its place—is recognizable to users of encyclopedias, those who study within university curricula, those who belong to a given discipline, and those who come into contact with any other selectively structured system of thought. *The Rhetoric*, as predecessor to these structures, is complete with ordered systems created by Aristotle (some of which preceded Aristotle as well) and which are meant to be exemplary for others. An early example of this method comes by way of Aristotle's discussion of Happiness.

Let us, then, for the sake of giving an example [of what might be more fully explored], grasp what happiness is, simply stated, and the source of its parts; for all forms of exhortation and dissuasion are concerned with this and with the things that contribute, or are opposed, to it; for one would do things that provide happiness or one of its parts or that make it greater rather than less, and not do things that destroy it or impede it or effect its opposites. (1.5.2)

The category of Happiness is then established through minor categories: wealth, friends, honor, strength, health, and so on. One could move down this order and understand each part's overall relationship to the larger term because of logical structure. There is little to argue with here; you accept the system and apply it when needed.

This, therefore, is a taxonomy of a state, or a topos, that a writer or rhetor can draw upon depending on rhetorical context. Knowing this taxonomy allows a rhetor a certain privilege in constructing meaning, what Burke calls "frames of acceptance." "By 'frames of acceptance' we mean the more or less organized system of meaning by which a thinking man gauges the historical situation and adopts a role with relation to it" (*Attitudes toward History* 5). The writer adopts her role—or as Wayne Booth might write, her rhetorical stance—through her relationship to a given organization taxonomy. Burke locates the practice in the literary writings of William James, Walt Whitman, and Ralph Waldo Emerson, noting how frames shift under various pressures. "As any given historical frame nears the point of cracking, strained by the rise of new factors it had not originally taken into account, its adherents employ its genius casuistically to extend it as far as possible" (*Attitudes toward History* 23). Jack Goody details how taxonomies become framed through the construction of factors that are at some point new: economics, mythology, and literacy. The invention of movable type (that is, Gutenberg) pushed this process into pedagogical domains as well, creating practices like the Ramist outline, which I describe in chapter 1 as the distancing of the rhetor from the objects to be arranged in a given writing or speech.

This order was set out in schematic form in which the "general" or inclusive aspects of the subject came first, descending thence through a series of dichotomized classifications to the "specials" or individual aspects. Once a subject was set out in its dialectical order it was memorized in this order from the schematic presentation—the famous Ramist epitome. (Goody 71)

As I noted in the previous chapter, Walter Ong describes the pedagogical and ideological consequences of Ramist thought. Whereas information organization—despite its structure—is still conceptual in the Aristotelian model, the Ramist model (a onetime response to "new factors") stretches the conceptual into being purely visual and diagrammatic. Ong writes that Ramism "was a movement away from a concept of knowledge as it had been enveloped in disputation and teaching (both forms of dialogue belonging to a personalist, existentialist world of sound) toward a concept of knowledge which associated it with a silent object world, conceived in visualist, diagrammatic terms" (151).

Scholastic practices institutionalized Ramus's taxonomic system at the disciplinary level—division of school subjects—and at the practical level—what one writes or speaks about. In my discussion of databases, I noted that the personal relationship to taxonomic knowledge—which Ong traces to Socratic dialogue—yielded to a method that views relationships as outside of one's self (that is, a thesis or an outline). The Socratic diegesis (dialogue) divides ideas into pairs (dialectic) in which argumentation occurs. In the Ramist update, the dialogue, and with it the personal interaction dialogue supports, is removed so that uniform information structures are sustained. Ong quotes Ramus as writing, "For it is foolish for a philosopher to look to human opinion rather than to the thing known" (43). Opinion, or what we might more generally categorize as "personal," is inferior to a supposedly more stable category called "fact" or the thing known.

To understand the distance between writer/rhetor/student and a given taxonomy, Ramism not only encouraged distance between the individual and the object of study but also proposed employing a visual display so this extensive structure could be supported. As Francis Yates notes, however, this visualization occurred not in the display of images (as a more contemporary understanding might allow for), but rather in the spatialization of the printed page: columns, outlines, lists. This spatialization was a "transformation which keeps and intensifies the principle of order but does away with the 'artificial' side, the side which cultivated the imagination as the chief instrument of memory" (236). The moment when Dylan flashes a visual "What?" cue card, then, is important for networks. It is one moment when the visual challenges a tradition of Ramist organization via the imagination (that is, Dylan imagines a response to organizational questions like, what is folk music, or what does this film sequence mean, through this elusive display and projects that response via cue cards that don't match their referents). Because Ramism is a pedagogical belief system, and because I will discuss education and Detroit in the next chapter, I note that despite Dylan's "What?" classification still resists the elusive in a number of pedagogical practices. In particular, visually based pedagogy that focuses on order and discounts imagination or personal interaction (Ramus's "human opinion") in the organization of meaning is evident in many contemporary, media-oriented textbooks. One notable example can be found in Bedford St. Martin's digitally influenced *Seeing and Writing*.

Warren Avenue, Twenty-Third Street

To think further about folks, networks, pedagogy, and this initial discussion of organization and Woodward I have begun, I first draw attention to one particular assignment in *Seeing and Writing*, an examination of Joel Sternfeld's photograph "Warren Avenue at 23rd Street, Detroit, Michigan." Warren Avenue and Woodward meet at their intersection almost in front of the Maccabees Building, my previous place of employment at Wayne State. The Maccabees, the former home of the Detroit public school system, marks pedagogy's place within the city. *Seeing and Writing* taps into that place by framing Detroit as a rhetorical exigence for writing. Early in the textbook, the Detroit image is given along with a writing prompt. The assignment for this image asks students to compare the photograph with their "observations." The example of an expected student response is a brief list that includes: "I notice that there are flowers on the sidewalk in front of the building." "I notice that a brightly colored image of a person has been painted on the wall." "I notice that there is an orange cone on the sidewalk in front of the building" (xxxvi). Through this ordered noticing, the student is asked to create a basic taxonomy of experience. There is the building. There is the photo. There is me. A student who writes within this scheme of meaning always engages with separate categories at separate moments of experience. The "folks" are distinct, and their visualization is meant to be distinct as well. The same kind of pedagogy can be found in the similar media-oriented textbook *Convergences*. In this textbook, one set of prompts asks students to work with the autobiography genre by examining Norman Rockwell's *Triple Self Portrait*. Rockwell signifies one of the most admired artists associated with twentieth-century representational art and thus is positioned as a specific type of taxonomy. The prompts that follow the image's introduction ask: "What does the elaborately framed mirror resemble? How does it feature the symbol of an American Eagle?" "What do you think Rockwell is saying about the art of portraiture?" (Atwan 72). These kinds of questions pose visuality and identity as an ordered, reference system of exchange, a taxonomy that suggests that the image and the response to the image are always paired as being in exact reference of one another. That the painting they are framed around is a self-portrait is important; the textbook asks the student to see the self-portrait as a distant experience.

Despite the Ramist influence of visual categorization evident in these two textbooks, I have come to realize that referentiality and the self are not two terms easily divorced, particularly in terms of "noticing." When the student completing the *Seeing and Writing* assignment "notices" Warren Avenue, she fills in a preset category base much as "the torn lifeline" discussion does. That sense of categorization tells her that Warren Avenue is in the New Center, in Detroit, in Michigan. These are the topoi (places) of Warren Avenue. While all of this is true, these are not the only parameters one *might* engage with when "noticing" Warren Avenue. Noticing might, therefore, stand for a limited method of knowing, particularly when it is limited to its Ramist legacy. Since Warren Avenue is a prominent avenue in Detroit, I have been to it many times. I have stood at Warren Avenue just outside of what was once my office, and I have walked along it further to the east on the way to Dearborn. And when I take my own picture of the same Warren Avenue site located in Sternfeld's photograph, I find another kind of meaning occurring, another kind of knowing.

Malice Green memorial, Warren Avenue. Photograph by the author.

When I take this photograph, what I notice, what I encounter, is activated by a series of events, moments, and feelings that a textbook prompt cannot account for. What I visualize is based on something more than what Ramist pedagogy dictates, for Ramism, as Ong argues, reduces "the personalist, dialoguing element in knowledge to a minimum in favor of an element which made knowledge something a corporation could traffic in, a-personal and abstract" (152). That a popular writing textbook like *Seeing and Writing* includes an image located near my place of employment is meaningful to me in a way set categorization cannot account for, and nor could the publishers of this textbook understand, not only because Bedford St. Martin's is a "corporation" in an economic sense, but because it is *a corporation*, as Burke writes regarding identity. It is a corporation like other corporate bodies: industry, religion, publishing, government, and, of course, education. It is a "*body of thought* matched by a *collective organization*" (*Attitudes toward History* 268). That body of thought has been taught in, of all places, the Wayne State English department located near Warren Avenue (and on Woodward). It has been taught in classes by instructors I taught. It has been taught by me. The collective organization of a specific kind of *Seeing and Writing* media-based pedagogy, however, does not appeal to the body of sensations Warren or Woodward evoke in me. When the authors of *Seeing and Writing* opted to include the image of Warren Avenue at Twenty-Third Street, they framed it as one kind of corporate body, institutionalized pedagogy. And just as the publishers pose the self-portrait as a system of categorical questions dictated by the corporate body of institutionalized pedagogy ("what does this represent"), the publishers propose space as outside of another kind of corporate body, me and my encounters.

These authors and their textbook publisher were not aware of my encounters when they chose to focus on this location near Woodward Avenue because they are working from a specific type of taxonomic scheme. Missing in many of these taxonomic schemes, either directly inherited from Aristotle and Ramus (even as the two are opposing figures) or pedagogically instituted through textbooks like *Seeing and Writing* and *Convergences*, are the affective dimensions of meaning, the ways taste, desire, interest, moments, encounters, or something else play into the choices we make when we organize and when we imagine ideas. Randall Collins taps into that dimension when he notes how much of our ability to categorize is based not on logic or hierarchical reasoning, but rather on emotional response and personal investment in such imaginative spaces. "Now if we trace individual human bodies moving from one encounter to the next, we see that the history of their chains—what sociologists have conventionally referred to as their positions in the social structure—is carried along in emotions and emotion-laden cognitions that become the ingredients for the upcoming encounter" (105). When I identify Bob Dylan's challenge to the corporate body of folk as an important moment, I notice how the encounter of Newport '65 reworked a specific kind of meaning structure by shifting organizational schemes so that such affective dimensions, too, could play a role (like a crowd booing). Dylan's moment is an emotionally charged one for how the bodies—the actual people, but also the bodies of meaning engaged—moved from an aural to an electronic state while still existing within a generic category called "folk." I, too, feel that moment when I consider the Sternfeld assignment's relationship to me and where I have worked. I recognize a "folk" category we might identity as Detroit, one that includes all of the communal meanings I have already brought forth: the 1967 riots, the city's racial divisions, and the collapse of the automotive industry. It also includes pedagogy, music, and visuality. In addition, I feel my own encounters as part of these references. That a category remains, but that its contained meanings shift as new possibilities are imagined, has become the focus of a great deal of network rhetorics. It is also the spirit of what on the web researchers and theorists are calling folksonomy.

Folksonomy

Folksonomy is a neologism for new-media taxonomy, a method of categorizing information according to desire, taste, personal interest, communal knowledge, imagination, and so on. The December 11, 2005, "Year in Ideas" section of the *New York Times Magazine* placed folksonomy as one of the year's most innovative practices. In his short definition included in the section, David Pinker commented about folksonomy: "Grass-roots categorization, by its very nature, is idiosyncratic rather than systematic. That sacrifices taxonomic perfection but lowers the barrier to entry. Nobody needs a degree in library science to participate." Folksonomies, David Weinberger writes, "are characterized by ambiguity, multiple classification, and sort-of-kind-of relationships" (*Everything Is Miscellaneous* 196). Thomas Vander Wal, the originator of the term, describes folksonomy accordingly: "The value in this external tagging is derived from people using their own vocabulary and adding explicit meaning, which may come from inferred understanding of the information/object. People are not so much categorizing, as providing a means to connect items (placing hooks) to provide their meaning in their own understanding."

Folksonomy's basic principle is the tag—the mark-up attributed to a site, name, or image in order to establish one or more corresponding categories. The open nature of folksonomy—anyone can name anything any name—is a direct challenge to referentiality because tagging does not require direct reference. Folksonomy is experienced and employed on the web via bookmarking sites like del.icio.us, image-sharing sites like Flickr, and website lists like Metafilter and Digg, and in posts on common weblogs. On such sites, users rename and redefine the placement of ideas and places according to an ever-shifting degree of categorization. Folksonomies provide reference systems, as any taxonomy does, but in digital spaces, they do so by challenging various assumptions about classifications and how such classifications generate meaning. As David Weinberger writes in "The New Is," in folksonomy, "Meaning is no longer attached firmly to being: It often works better to assign meaning after the fact." While the "people" aspect related to folksonomy (allowing people with similar reference points to connect via tagging) is popular on social networking websites like Facebook or MySpace, folksonomies suggest broader applications for organizing spaces, information, and ideas.[2]

In folksonomy, references are not based on what something is, as Aristotle details taxonomic knowledge in *The Rhetoric*, but rather they are based on the relationships that emerge out of interactions and connections. As I write in the introduction, Bruno Latour calls this process "the social," "the heterogeneous nature of the ingredients making up social ties" *Reassembling the Social* 43). Latour draws attention to how taxonomic relations are processes connecting diverse things.[3] "What lies *in between* these connections?" Latour asks. "What's the extent of our ignorance concerning the social?" (221). One response to Latour's question is folksonomy's association of different names (tags) for different places of meaning (words, images, sites), which users, in turn, apply in order to create relationships that didn't already exist in any pretaxonomic order. Folksonomy, thus, continues communal referencing (as, for example, what folk music might entail or mean; what an autobiography might entail or mean; what a worker might entail or mean) while also allowing such references to be flexible so that they may be reimagined at given moments (the folk, then, becomes the social). The process greatly intrigues me for how it moves networked rhetorics out of a topos-based space and into a non-space, a choral[4] place of movement. In this choral space, meanings are not fixed to any other meaning but are always in flux. Thus, folksonomy places meaning in an ever-shifting network of relationships. "Multiple tags, not single meanings," Weinberger notes.

"A thing gains more meaning by having multiple local meanings" ("The New Is"). For writers like Weinberger, the web provides a space to conceptually and practically engage with this type of rhetorical activity that stresses the social relationships among meanings.

The web, Clay Shirky writes, "is actually a radical break with previous categorization strategies, rather than an extension of them." That previous system, which Shirky calls "the constraints of the shelf," insists that one name be given to one "thing" at one place. Information studies scholar Elaine Svenonius stresses this practice as the foundation of bibliographic organization. Bibliographies, like any kind of system, carry ideological positions into sites of exchange. As Svenonius notes, the ideology of the modern organization of information was meant to reduce random association or happenstance findings.

> Walking through library stacks (a microcosm of the bibliographic universe) and browsing, a user may suddenly come across just the right book and credit this luck to serendipity. But such a finding would be serendipitous only if the books were shelved in random order, whereas in fact they are ordered according to a rigorous system of semantic relationships, which like an invisible hand guides the seeker to his "lucky" find. (Svenonius 19)

Shirky contrasts this organizational rigor with the idea of linking. "If you've got enough links, you don't need the hierarchy anymore. There is no shelf. There is no file system. The links alone are enough." Links are enacted not by filing them away, Shirky tells us, but by browsing them, a browsing based on relationships encountered or imagined (whether they have been preestablished or not), and not, as Svenonius critiques, on the accident. Like Collins's interest in ritual chains, links are not categories we turn to in the browsing Shirky foregrounds, but moments we come across. In networks, links may be hyperlinks, but more broadly, they reflect the complex connections forged as meaning is made and classified.

To return to the Sternfeld photograph and accompanying assignment, I *notice* that the meaning I attribute to this scene connects to the moment I go to the site and I snap the photograph. But it also connects to other Detroit moments and places as well, some that I may foreground at the moment I encounter the scene, some I may not be aware of until later (or not at all), some I began this chapter with. Ash Amin and Nigel Thrift state that places are "moments of encounter, not so much as 'presents,' fixed in space and time, but as variable events, twists and fluxes of interrelation" (30). Amin and Thrift describe how those items we encounter—

a place, a concert, a street, a meaning—interrelate in obvious and less-than-obvious ways. For Amin and Thrift, cities mark a place where such encounters occur. Drawing from Deleuze and Guattari, Amin and Thrift call cities and their various spaces "flows" that "are best described, there-fore, in terms of a language of forces, densities, intensities, potentialities, virtualities" (81). Thus, when *Newsweek* encounters Woodward, it does so not as a flow, but as the communal, taxonomic reference point: 1967, racial tension, economic hardship, devastation. A folksonomic approach, on the other hand, can shift that reference point to a type of flow by allowing for other types of meanings to promote the point's potential.

A communal reference point such as "torn lifeline" is not a flow. It does not have virtuality or potentiality; it merely offers an accepted category. I know the *Newsweek* references, too. I visualize them. They are well-circulated topoi. But after working at Woodward for five years, I found myself at the avenue in ways these reference points do not account for. I found myself within a series of encounters the taxonomy doesn't allow for because the spaces I occupied were virtual or intense (they flow) as much as they might have been a reference. Because of these flows I moved within, I found myself, as Roland Barthes writes in *Camera Lucida*, the reference point of every image I encountered.

Detroit Day. Reprinted with permission from the Walter P. Reuther Library, Wayne State University.

Such encounters occur in physical and virtual spaces. To further my thinking regarding the encounter, I draw from another visual example. The photograph[5] in figure 2.6 foregrounds an event called "Detroit Day." In my research, I can find no place where "Detroit Day" is referenced, catalogued, or indexed. I can find no place where it is communal knowledge. "Detroit Day" is no longer observed nor is it physically encountered. There does not exist a referential bibliography of "Detroit Day." The image I isolate looks as if "Detroit Day" is taking place alongside Woodward Avenue, but whatever activity or event that may have occurred at that moment eludes me. "Detroit Day" is a type of flow; it is virtual. The concept of "Detroit Day" is, to me, "fantasmatic," as Roland Barthes writes. It carries me back to "somewhere in myself" even if I cannot initially explain how or why (*Camera Lucida* 40). In this image, I *feel* referenced. In this moment of being referenced, I identify the relationship between visuality and new media, between encounters and rhetorical expression, between networks and classification systems. The image in figure 2.6 returns me to the pedagogical examples I offered earlier because when I see this other image of Detroit and referentially, my initial response is to imagine "Detroit Day" in terms of my own self-referencing system (itself generated by the logic of networks). This response is pedagogical; its purpose to teach me "something" about the encounter between myself and Detroit. This response also teaches me how folksonomies work within network rhetorics. The value of folksonomies is more than attributing a name or tag to a website or an image. Folksonomies are valuable for how they might teach us to compose or communicate. That I see myself as the generator of a folksonomy indicates that I am the reference of every image I make; I am an agent within the folksonomy as well. I am as much a part of the social fabric of meaning as is a given taxonomy. I am within the network I construct. Folksonomy, then, can also be a folksono(me).

Folksono(me)

Bruce Sterling writes that folksonomy is "a new way to crowd-surf." I understand Sterling's comment to mean that in folksonomy, writers surf through a variety of meanings in order to demonstrate an image, a point, a place, or some other moment or event. The act of surfing also involves the formation of connections and relationships among the material surfed. The "crowd" aspect of surfing reflects the multiple agents and forces that come together in any given surf. Surfing the web, of course, is the process of following links; it echoes Shirky's understanding of folksonomy as browsing and refocuses Svenonius's dismissal of accidental encounter so that relationships encountered in a given folksonomy are not the result of avant-garde-inspired "accidents" but are, in fact, new kinds of meanings formed. When I surf the categorical meanings my encounters provide, I navigate a series of visual reference points linked by the ways I browse them. These reference points are communal (they are known as belonging to something called "Detroit"), but they are also not a part of the influential taxonomy that names Detroit or Woodward for most people. They are part of me. In one of the Web's most popular folksonomic spaces, the image-sharing site Flickr, "me" has been credited as an organizing principle of information sharing. "Some such tags," Axle Bruns remarks, "(such as 'me') may be filtered out as anomalies already when large numbers are engaged in a decentralized effort to tag content" (184). Or, as I would rather imagine, instead of being filtered out, the "me" tag of a space like Woodward might become a dominant way to sort images, text, and ideas about this aspect of Digital Detroit (as much as tags like "cigar" or "car" would do as well). The first part of this chapter allowed me to explore a variety of tags one might use to explain or identify Woodward Avenue to a given audience. However novel some of the tags might appear at first (like "cigar"), they are still fairly communal. Missing is the role the "me" of a folksono(me) might play in a network. The "me," I note, is a way to browse.

Two places in particular that I browse along Woodward Avenue have the same name, Temple Beth El. Designed by Albert Kahn in 1902, Temple Beth El is a place I would encounter daily to and from work. In fact, Temple Beth El is the name of two synagogues; the first (located at Woodward and Eliot) serves as the Bonstelle Theater. The second one is today a church (the Lighthouse Tabernacle) and sits at Woodward and Gladstone. The people (folk) who moved from the first Beth El to the second Beth El struggled to find their place in Detroit (eventually Beth El was moved outside of Detroit to West Bloomfield). Jew, city resident, and Detroiter are all categories Temple Beth El congregants manipulated as they moved from space to space. In what I identify as a struggle of multiple meanings in multiple places, I can begin to flesh out a type of folksono(me) rhetoric within the network.

Between the two synagogues is the Maccabees Building, my former place of work. "The forming of work sets constitutes the prototypical act of information organization," Svenonius writes regarding the clustering or gathering of information into accessible places. "Defining a work operationally amounts to specifying what two documents must have in common to be included in the same work set. Specification is not easy"

(36). My encounters with the two Temple Beth Els foregrounds that point. Specification, indeed, is not easy, particularly when we attempt to specify particular places. The Maccabees Building, one such place on Woodward, was built in 1927 as the world headquarters of the Order of the Maccabees (this point will be the focus of the next chapter). This secret order took its name from the Jewish fighters who are memorialized in the holiday of Hanukkah. At one secret society building (the Masonic), a Jew performed in 1964 (Dylan). At another secret society building (Maccabees), another Jew taught and did research from 2004 to 2007 (me).

Kahn, a Jew, designed both the two synagogues and the Maccabees. Kahn's signature is all over Detroit; in addition to these buildings, he designed many others including the Highland Park Factory at Woodward where the Model T was first produced by Ford. Fordism has come to mean for many the ideology of work responsible for a specific way of thinking in terms of economics and globalization, but also for how institutions, like education, have been structured. Many have argued that we are moving into the post-Fordist economy, a system outside of the hierarchies and belief in equal parts in the system that marked Fordism as a type of classification system. Ford believed in a different kind of folk (volk), which placed ethnic unity at the center of modern economics and industry. Only by being the same, Ford required, would people (volk) be equal (like the Model T itself, which came in any color as long as it was black). While he admired Kahn's work, Ford, the anti-Semite, never considered Kahn, a Jew, an equal. In fact, of all the ethnic groups Ford hired at Highland Park and that he "equalized" within the category of Fordist worker, Jews were one of two absent groups.

> Members of the two minority groups most reviled by the ignorant and prejudiced in America remained virtually absent from the car making business. African Americans were hired at only a few auto factories, most notably Packard, until the labor crunch caused by the First World War. Jews were similarly discouraged from seeking employment in the automobile industry—and they were almost nonexistent at Ford Motor Company. (Brinkley 159)

As a Jew and as an educator, I find Fordist volk-systems of classification intriguing. Regardless of who Ford's anger was directed at, in this particular classification system, I see myself named in the multiple and overlapping categories: educator, Jew, worker, Detroit, Woodward. James Berlin drew sharp connections between Fordism and the educational system and pointed out the failure of Fordism as the ideological basis of contemporary teaching for how it classified students as a future manage-rial class. Berlin instead argued for a post-Fordist education that would

> require preparation in dealing with the abstract and systemic think-ing needed for the dispersed conditions of postmodern economic and cultural developments, in distinct contrast to the atomistic, linear, and narrowly empirical mode often encouraged by modern conditions. Students need a conception of the abstract organizational patterns that affect their work lives—indeed, comprehensive conceptions of the patterns that influence all their experiences. (54)

This lack of "postmodern" thinking is evident in the Detroit public school system's collapse, its failure marked by economic, political, and, of course, pedagogical issues, many of which are tied to either Ford the company or Fordism the ideology. Assembly-line educational practices (instead of "the patterns" Berlin associates with post-Fordism) can be found in the model of education progression (adding one part of an education at a time through grades), the categorization of distinct educational pieces (differ-ent subjects), and the emphasis on standardization (outcomes, testing).

My office was previously part of the Detroit public school system's headquarters in Detroit. By accident, Berlin connects me to Fordism. For three years, in my Wayne State office, I was responsible for the depart-ment's "Digital Literacy Initiative," a plan to integrate technology into the teaching of writing. The potential failure of any kind of digital initiative is there from the start when we hear the generic first critiques, warnings, and decisions that most digital initiatives or programs face: computers can't teach writing; let's standardize how we teach with computers; ev-erybody make a webpage. These, too, are taxonomic markers, and they rely heavily on communal meanings. One might initially assume that a digital literacy initiative is part of the post-Fordist situation we are in—the very system Berlin associated with the logics of cultural studies and poststructuralism (of which Roland Barthes's work is often identified). Before accepting such an assumption, however, it might be prudent to question how a digital literacy is organized or named in the post-Fordist situation, as well as whether or not a digital literacy is, in fact, still Fordist. The first step towards that questioning is recognizing that the overlaps I have outlined here suggest an organizational shift in the places meaning is stored: Judaism, education, and technology. These places of meaning name me as well, a Jewish professor who works in education and deals with issues of technology. These categories overlap and name one another in ways a traditional taxonomy does not allow for. If one "noticed" Detroit based on taxonomic reference, one would miss all of these categories not bound to a communal meaning called Woodward; one would miss the folksonomic overlaps. These overlaps name a meaning system not evident in a precategorical assumption regarding what a digital literacy might entail. I don't know yet what the overlaps mean, but I encounter them. At their merger, at this moment of encounter, I am looking for a feature of networked rhetorics; that is, I am looking for a response to the question of meaning and digital literacy. I am looking for my metaphoric equivalent of Dylan's Newport appearance.

The encounter I have with these two places (topoi) called Temple Beth El is emotional. "Just because I feel named, is this me?" I ask. "You are the only one who can never see yourself as an image," Roland Barthes writes (*Roland Barthes* 36). But I do. I see myself as an encounter of images (and not just as a representational self-portrait—as the Rockwell image and the pedagogy surrounding it suggests). These images stir emotions. They are affective. Collins argues that the representations we use to generate meaning are bound by such emotional linkages. "One symbolic representation leads to another, not merely because of similarity but because they have been charged up with similar kinds of membership significance, and because they are weighted emotionally by recent interactional usage, and by past interactions that were especially emotionally intense" (Collins 203). I, therefore, can only classify these places in terms of the encounters they evoke in me. I do so through these patterns I outline here as well as through my initial virtual encounter with "Detroit Day."

Folksono(me) 2: Detroit Day

In *Geographies of Writing*, Nedra Reynolds writes: "Geography gives us the metaphorical and methodological tools to change our ways of imagining writing through both movement and dwelling—to see writing as a set of spatial practices informed by everyday negotiations of space" (6). "Detroit Day," however, is a different kind of geographic metaphor than the one Reynolds employs in her ethnographic research into place. "Detroit Day" is the emotional connection *I* make to place. To say that is not to deny the communal "we" that categorizes space (or that folksonomies depend on), but it is to recognize a need to return what Ramism removed and what the Dylan anecdote frames: the additional personal connections that make up information organization. I visualize the "Detroit Day" connection as a series of metaphoric moves that are my method for writing; these moves capture what Casey calls *implacement*. Implacement is "occasion-bound; or more exactly, it binds actual occasions into unique collocations of space and time" (*Getting Back* 23). The metaphor that makes "Detroit Day" possible as an occasion is the diegesis. "In Greek, narration is called 'diegesis': it establishes an itinerary (it 'guides') and it passes through (it 'transgresses'). The space of operations it travels in is made of movements: it is topological, concerning the deformations of figures, rather than topical, defining places" (de Certeau 129). Gregory Ulmer notes that a digital diegesis occurs in the imaginary space or the remake and functions by the logic of dreamwork, association (*Heuretics* 48). In the digital diegesis, the movements are those activities that move from spaces or topoi of discussion. A digital diegesis is not an actual new media artifact; it is the imaginary space a writer or rhetor creates in order to think through a given issue or problem. It is the space Ramus rejected in favor of diagrams and outlines. It is the space I mapped briefly in chapter 1. It is the space I will return to in the final chapter's conclusion when I discuss decision-making. It is the space Dylan invents in the cue-card scenario (and, one might argue, in the Newport appearance). The logic of the digital diegesis extends from Casey's argument that place is based on three key terms: "imagination, memory, and place." (*Getting Back* xvii). These are important terms that comprise my interest in visuality and taxonomies: The occasion of the imaginative. A fictive place of enactment. A myth. Association. Linkages. The imaginative asks: What if Woodward Avenue became the site of cigar manufacturing? The imaginative asks: How is Bob Dylan a taxonomic space for Detroit and Woodward Avenue? The imaginative asks: How am I or any other body the reference point of a meaning? As a reference point, as a folksonomic tag, "Detroit Day" is mythological to me, fantasmic.

Was there ever such a thing as "Detroit Day?" Can I find it on the web? Where was it? Did someone experience it? Is it a category? Asking such questions is like yelling "What?" in exasperation at Newport, 1965. Asking such questions is like trying to understand Norman Rockwell's self-portrait as a kind of visual truth. Asking such questions is like trying to understand Woodward from a purely communal reference point like 1967, racial tension, or economic failure. Asking such questions is like trying to prove a digital literacy or visual literacy. The questions depend on how evidence fits a category. I am, however, looking for evidence that fits more than one category at more than one time. I'm looking for mythology or fantasmic writing. I'm looking for the imaginative Lyotard stresses as relevant to database logic. In a mythological-associative writing that the network supports, the need for proof is replaced with the production of an imaginary, folksonomic space that forms the linkages within a given network.

The diegesis allows me the chance to visualize "Detroit Day" in terms of folksonomy as me, not category as proof. That process begins with the "folk." Detroit and Woodward Avenue often reference music; this "folk" or group identity is frequently associated with hip-hop. Along Woodward, the Majestic Theater in Detroit and the Magic Bag in Ferndale host various hip-hop performances. The Hip-Hop Summit (a mix of entrepreneurial thinking and hip-hop) has taken place at several venues along Woodward Avenue; most recently it took place in 2006 at the Bonstelle Theater (formerly Temple Beth El) and in 2007 at the Max Fisher Music Center (after Max Fisher, a prominent Jewish Detroit philanthropist). Hip-hop is one category for the folk. Another category, and maybe one of the best markers of "folk" music, is, as I noted in the beginning of this section, Bob Dylan. During that famous 1965 tour, Bob Dylan played Cobo Hall. On April 12, 2005, Bob Dylan played Cobo Hall once again. His 2005 playlist included the 1963 song "Masters of War." "Masters of War" is emblematic of typical 1960s folk music. It deals with common tropes of the movement: antiwar attitudes, civil liberties, counter-culture feelings. When Dylan played the Cobo Hall in 1965, "Masters of War" was the kind of song audiences expected to hear. Instead, they heard a newly electric Dylan ("Maggie's Farm") and, like other audiences on the tour, booed in response. The lack of acceptance of Dylan's newly shaped folk is revealing. The matching of an emerging meaning to an established category often results in failure when logical reasoning is used to determine the match's legitimacy. That match is often what is asked of taxonomies that must first prove their value (either as vocational or pedagogical objective) before being attempted. The lack of acceptance teaches a lesson for how to work within digital culture and networks: Don't ask what a digital moment means or try to prove its value (syllogistic reasoning). Instead, enact the change through encounter (like audiences encountering Dylan, or Dylan encountering Newport, or me encountering a city I worked in). Such was my initial response to Warren Avenue and to Temple Beth El. This, too, is a gesture I extend to "Detroit Day." The encounter stands, therefore, for a kind of pedagogy within the network.

In my digital diegesis called "Detroit Day," Dylan enacts a moment of change when he plugs his guitar into one of the stage outlets at Cobo Hall. This time, when he plays "Masters of War," the lyrics sound different. Dylan accuses his audience of having "never done nothin'" except building "to destroy." The lyrics echo the dilemma of the Woodward Avenue that *Newsweek* describes: building to destroy. The city's circulated and communal meaning (its taxonomy) revolves around destruction and ruins.

In Dylan's lyrics, we might also hear: "You [Detroit] build to destroy." I don't hear this as a condemnation (a typical categorical response that focuses on Detroit's ruins) but rather as an acknowledgement that in this process of destruction, there is always the opportunity for rebuilding; that is, for rebuilding meanings, relationships, and representations. "Detroit Day"—as demonstrated in Dylan's diegetic appearance—is a declaration for a digital taxonomy based on destruction. In that destruction, I compose a new taxonomy—a folksono(me)—through a mix. Detroit's reference point of hip-hop as folk teaches me to mix (the mix a basic principle of sampling); and in that mix, I alter Woodward's folk. In other words, the open nature of folksonomy encourages the mix of meanings and reference points. In this rhetorical move, I mix Dylan, Albert Kahn, and the Cobo's designer, Gino Rossetti. These are three names, three categories, I merge with my own image. Rossetti also designed Wayne State University's Welcome Center, which sits adjacent to what was my office, which is on Woodward, which is between the two Temple Beth Els (the old and then the new place of worship). To move among these spaces and meanings is to sample a remixed Dylan playing the Cobo. In my mix, is Newport the same as the New Center (the area where the university is located in Detroit)? Is the "newness" of digitality we work to generate in university settings the same as Dylan appearing before "folk music" crowds at Newport? Is the "Welcome" of the welcome center the category of invitation ("We encourage a digital literacy.") or rejection ("Your efforts are not welcome here.")? Are these places the points of categorical convergence? Are their emergences explanation for why our digital initiatives in so many departments, on so many university campuses, discussed with so many colleagues, are metaphorically booed?

These questions are not meant to generate fixed responses but rather are meant to evoke the feeling of "What?" as new encounters are sought out and as folksono(me)s are constructed in order to engage such encounters. The lyrics, therefore, echo my own digital-visual invention that Digital Detroit encourages: I build to destroy. I am destroying a specific framework—one whose focus is often on communal meaning observed from the distant representation—to consider folksonomic remixes centered around an individual's encounters as alternatives. The alternatives appear more as suggestions or speculations than as statements of truths. Folksono(me) is more a rhetoric of query or conjecture within the network than it is of set reference, and that, I know produces anxiety ("Then why do it!"). In this rhetorical gesture, I take apart the meanings and referents that comprise Woodward and my own self-image to build something else in its place. I create new kinds of categories while destroying established practices. I do so through my own place within this system. My folksonomic gesture is imaginative and data driven. "One's 'I' is called forth in varying strengths by present interactions and past symbolic residues, magnetically attracted to some situations and repelled by others. And this dynamic operates, as I have tried to suggest, in the inner chains of situations that make up sequences of thought" (Collins 205). What I produce is another piece of the networked rhetoric within what I am calling Digital Detroit. But what kind of rhetorical act is this that blends association, taxonomies, fictive reenactment, personal interest, and theoretical speculation? Where is its claim, its support, its evidence, its organization, its audience, its purpose? Such are the demands of a specific taxonomy of rhetorical expression, and in particular, of writing about cities. Henri Lefebvre demands that there be a philosophy of the city, "a project of synthesis and totality which philosophy as such cannot accomplish" (*Writings on Cities* 86). Neither, though, can writing. Writing may be the most inadequate of all rhetorical terms to apply to a folksonomic or folksono(me) communicative act because of its own taxonomies, but it is one I use for now. Claims, supports, evidence do, in fact, exist in a folksono(me), but the ways we visualize or name those moments shift from the categories we are accustomed to using. In those shifts are pedagogical challenges we are still attempting to understand.

Dylan as folksono(me): The Cobo Digital Diegesis. Remix by the author.

A writing like my example is part of a larger visually motivated digital composition built out of an emerging networked taxonomy. It attempts to work within a logic of digital culture that alters our sense of referentiality and representation. This type of writing generates a collective identity built out of links and browsing, an identity situated within new media. My efforts resemble Bruno Latour's: "I don't want to confuse the assembling of the collective with the mere review of the entities already assembled or with a bundle of homogenous social ties" (*Reassembling the Social* 103). I don't want to present that confusion because linkages do not always (or often) reflect homogeneity. The folksonomic linkage that also includes the "me" works to avoid such homogeneity as it generates a nonpermanent classification system (What is it to be digital? What is composition? What is an encounter? What is a space—physical, conceptual, or other—that I inhabit?). That lack of permanence can, at times, evoke the overall sense of "What?" as a meaningful gesture.

The linkages I follow in this brief example of a digital diegesis do not reveal a code, meaning, or discourse.[6] They can't. In "Detroit Day," I have not found resolution to the question "What is Detroit Day" or "What is Detroit" or "Who am I" or "Why did Detroit come to be a set of ruins?" or "What does it mean to teach digitality?" Or "Why is Dylan in a story about Woodward?" Instead, "Detroit Day" complicates the nature of referentiality and writing in digital culture by not rushing to answer the questions, even if the questions remain for us to further consider. Even in this brief example, "Detroit Day" settles on the question of "What?" rather than "What is?" To respond to "Detroit Day" with a "What?" I contend, is more appropriate in terms of the open nature of folksonomy than a response that tells me what this day is or what it signifies. The "What?" allows me to browse the links. Rather than fear the "What?" it might be preferable to remember that Dylan's standoff with the booing crowds at Newport did not end in disaster nor in the death of one folk type (folk music) for the survival of another folk type (rock and roll). Folksono(me) is not the end of communal meaning or current classification, just as Newport wasn't the end of folk music. The blending of categories generates other kinds of encounters. In that blending, we notice challenges for how we teach information organization in networks, how we allow categories to shift both in the composing we do as well as in the way we label and tag such composing. Our challenge is to build folksonomic linkages that are communal, personal, affective, and broad. The links I find and demonstrate here, then, are beginning points; they allude to further connections I can flesh out and develop in other compositions, in other encounters, in other moments of rhetorical invention, in other chapters in this book.

Because these links settle initially on the Welcome Center of the Wayne State campus, which is adjacent to my former office in the Maccabees building, and because the Maccabees was designed by Albert Kahn, who I began this chapter with, and because there is a sense of unsettledness to this example I conclude here with, a sense of a remaining "secret" I have not entirely revealed, I turn in the next chapter to the Maccabees Building itself. The Maccabees continues with folksonomic linkages while also teaching me how networks embody a specific type of interface for navigating and working with these linkages.

3

THE MACCABEES

The city can be read because it writes, because it was writing.
—Henri Lefebvre, *Writings on Cities*

The English department at Wayne State University, in Detroit, Michigan, is housed at 5057 Woodward Avenue in the Maccabees Building, a 1927 building designed by the famed Detroit architect Albert Kahn. The Maccabees were a secret order whose origins are traced to both the Masons and the Jewish fighters whose revolt against the Seleucids has been historically and religiously remembered in the holiday of Hanukkah. The Maccabees Building was founded by the insurance-oriented secret society of the same name, but it later became the hub for the Detroit public school system (DPS). In *The Rise and Fall of an Urban School System*, Jeffrey Mirel traces the history of Detroit's public school system in excruciating detail as a series of political and economic struggles among various state and city constituencies. The school system, Mirel argues, fell into disorder as the result of longstanding labor and political conflicts that crippled Detroit schools' educational mission. Mirel's analysis is relevant today. According to a January 2007 *Detroit News* story, approximately fifty-one thousand Detroit students opted out of the city's public school system in favor of suburban education or charter schools. As the article makes clear, such loses have economic consequences. "That's either a $1 million drop or $1 million bump in state aid," reporter Mike Wilkinson remarks. "It could mean hiring teachers—or laying them off." By May 2008, the *Detroit News* upped its dire forecast by predicting a $45 million deficit for the city's schools. Tied to students abandoning the city's public schools, the windfall created a loss of "$11.3 million in state funding" after "3,000 students went missing from the 33 schools closed" (Mrozowski).

When students leave a school district, school buildings suffer as much as the economy does; the structures are closed, emptied, abandoned, or sold to other interests. The buildings are forgotten in physical (no longer used) and cultural (no longer thought about) senses. "An empty building rots fast and attracts trouble," Stewart Brand writes (112). "This issue is core and absolute: no maintenance, no building" (110). Buildings, when not paid attention to, slowly deteriorate in both physical and conceptual ways. A similar history led to the eventual purchase of the Maccabees by Wayne State University. At some point, the public school system gave up on the Maccabees, let the building sit abandoned for some time, and eventually passed it along to higher education. Despite the faded "Detroit Public Schools" lettering that is still visible on the building's entrance marquee and that still announces its presence to all who enter the building, the legacy of abandonment holds. Most who visit the Maccabees today have forgotten the building's educational past (even as they encounter the different educational present now present). Visitors to the Maccabees forget that the building once housed the city's public school system. As a façade or display of education, the Maccabees succeeds in only representing one aspect of its educational history. Its interface, like its marquee, is faded.

Fading school marquee in the Maccabees entrance. Photograph by the author.

The Maccabees. Photograph by the author.

The building's particular meaning (as former hub of the DPS), and the many other meanings I've already hinted at, however, don't really vanish, though they may fade a bit like marquee lettering. In the space of transfer, where the Maccabees moves from insurance society to public school system to higher education, we see several folksonomic meanings come together: fighters, secret society, public school, and university. These meanings house the building as much as it houses them. While these meanings will be fleshed out in this chapter, the overall goal is to recapture them from their current state of abandonment. The key, in network production, is to not treat the building like a space that merely holds meanings for temporary periods of time and then fades into neglect. The key is to engage the meanings for their rhetorical potential, much as folksonom(me) allowed me to engage certain areas of Woodward Avenue in order to explore classification within the network. As Henri Lefebvre writes, "To picture space as a 'frame' or container into which nothing can be put unless it is smaller than the recipient, and to imagine that this container has no other purpose than to preserve what has been put in it—this is probably the initial error" (*Production of Space* 94). The Maccabees, in the network I am calling Digital Detroit, is more than a container that houses a university's various offices. The Maccabees contains physical objects (desks, books, hallways) as well as concepts (education, secrecy, and more). What it contains exceeds the space of that which holds it within.

And yet, as complex and detailed as Mirel's history of the city's public school system is and as much information as it contains, missing is any mention of the Maccabees Building or other names the building has housed. For Mirel, the building is not even a container; it does not appear to belong in a spatial history of education and Detroit. Thus, even an exhaustive and detailed history like the one Mirel poses may not be as complete as it should be when it is not placed within the context of networked meanings or the spaces that hold those meanings (like buildings). Mirel's treatment of Detroit education, as massive as it is, is too much like a container. It works hard to preserve certain kinds of meanings while others, like the Maccabees, are left outside of the container. Mirel's history, though, is not unique; it mirrors contemporary discussions regarding education in Detroit. These discussions are limited in their container-like approaches to education; what is larger than the topos of education (though not necessarily physically larger), such narratives argue, cannot be allowed to share its space.

Taken over in 1960 by the DPS, the Maccabees Building foregrounds its school meaning by signifying an educational presence in the heart of the city even as that presence engages in a long-standing conflict over the role of education in the Motor City (public or private; government regulated or free market; print or digital). In more recent years, the conflict surrounding urban education has led to the establishment and eventual abandonment of a CEO position to head the DPS (the position was meant to replace the traditional role of "superintendent"), the mass firings of teachers and closings of schools, the emergence of a chain of suburban charter schools luring away Detroit students, and the premature declaration by then mayor Kwame Kilpatrick to take over the school system himself. By April 2, 2009, the *Detroit Free Press* reported that the DPS "will have to cut thousands of jobs and close as many as 50 schools over the next two years because the district has accumulated a $305 million deficit" ("Up to 50 Schools"). On May 19, 2010, the *Detroit Free Press* updated earlier reporting, claiming a projected DPS deficit of $332 million ("DPS Budget"). And in 2011, the *Detroit News* reported plans to cut half of the district's schools in order to restructure the DPS's financial situation and solve a $327 million deficit (Chambers).

The DPS's downward collapse, as recent events demonstrate, does not end with Mirel's history. The collapse continues today as if there were no other meanings to connect with and to. That is, even though the container may have been filled in by Mirel's historical overview, more information can still be piled in because the metaphoric container is large enough to house a continuing topos of education's demise. What has not been allowed to be housed in the container as well is the building itself are other types of meanings connected to education, the Maccabees, and Detroit. Yet, as this chapter will explore in more detail, even if it is no longer based in the Maccabees, the DPS still belongs within the building's narrative. The DPS, now headquartered elsewhere, is a part of the building's spatial story. There are spaces within this one specific space that network with each other (spaces within the building, within the DPS, within other spaces). The container, in effect, is not really a container at all.

If I were to return to the mapping I began with in chapter 1 and map the Maccabees and its relationship to Detroit and education, I might begin with such observations regarding a building's narrative, its topos, cultural references, education, and technology. The map I construct would note the absence of the Maccabees in a popular conceptual map like Mirel's (one based on timelines, political pressure, and economic fallout, and not on physical space) and its central presence in the geographic locale known as New Center. This map would also extend to another folksonomic space, me and the office I once occupied on the tenth floor of the Maccabees, a space now owned by Wayne State University. In that space, as I noted in chapter 2, I worked on the Department of English's "Digital Literacy Initiative," an attempt to integrate technology into the teaching of writing. Begun by the chair of the department, the Digital Literacy Initiative imagined a digital future for Wayne State undergraduate students, who would learn relevant skills for the highly technological society they would inevitably join. The Digital Literacy Initiative, unlike Mirel's history of Detroit education, whose focus is on politics and financial matters, posed technology as central to students' lives. The rise and fall of the Digital Literacy Initiative, I might egotistically add as an aside, seemed to peak with various projects I began and seemed to falter when I left behind those projects for a position elsewhere. Thus, like Mirel's history, the success of educational initiatives sometimes owes more to issues outside of education than to education itself (internal politics, opportunities elsewhere, frustration, and so on). The perception of educational success can be too tied to one figure or body, as much of Mirel's narrative argues regarding the forces that could not sustain educational policy. Educational meaning can be too tied, at times, to one meaning.

The rise and fall of Detroit education, I also note, can be mapped to include my past office space even if that connection seems only superficial at first. Educational policy in Detroit meets up with educational policy in the Maccabees. The connection on this map that I imagine joins technology to space. It is, as I argued earlier, a database-driven map (one set of data joined with another). Its representation, though, does not depend on literal navigation. Maps, Katharine Harmon writes, "find their essence in some other goal than just taking us from point A to point B. They are a vehicle for the imagination" (10). Based on this preliminary map I draw, then, I want to *imagine* my connection to the Maccabees as a technological one; I want to imagine a space where Mirel's history meets up with the history of education in the space I once worked. This imaginative gesture is a continuance of the mapping and folksonomic gestures I have already begun with. It is the gesture I discovered with Lyotard's concept of the database. The imagination, Harmon as well shows me, is a vital component of the networked map.

The focus of contemporary work on technology and space, and one that fuels my imagination, is (as I claim earlier in this book) the network. Networks draw expected connections (A to B) and unexpected connections (the imaginative). In his work on intellectual and social networks, Randall Collins writes that in networks, "ideas are created out of the distribution of symbols already available at a moment in time, by being reshaped for anticipated audiences" (190). The Maccabees, a symbol of secrecy, institutional foundation, education, and now technology, is being reshaped as the city itself (an enduring symbol of economic decline) stands also to be reshaped conceptually. The Maccabees, I want to show, can be shaped as the hub of a different part of the network I have begun with mapping and folksonomies. Its status as "building" might allow for a building of other sorts once the network it resides in is engaged more fully; that is, its place will build off of the mapping and folksonomic network characteristics I've already outlined. Its status of being a building will allow for more building to occur.

In that sense, the Maccabees as building inherits rhetorical thinking laid out by Aristotle in *The Metaphysics*. In a discussion of being and existence, Aristotle argues that "a thing may exist in actuality only, or potentially, or potentially and in actuality, and it may be a this, or a quantity, or any of the others. But motion does not exist apart from things; for that which changes does so always with respect to the categories of being, and there is nothing common to these which is any one category" (K.9.5). Categories, Aristotle tells us, maintain relationships to being.

The most prominent category of the Maccabees, to date, has been as a site of educational learning. My own experience as a faculty member at Wayne State University confirms this category. We, the Department of English, conducted our teaching and research out of this building. Our structure (our pedagogical mission) was tied to the physical structure (the building). The question of being a thing or a potential thing of any kind of body is, then, attributed to structures.

> For each [such] thing may sometimes be in actuality and sometimes not, as in the case of the buildable qua buildable; and it is the actuality of the buildable qua buildable that is [the process of] building. For this actuality is either the [process of] building or the house. But when the house exists, it is no longer buildable; and it is the buildable that is being built. This actuality, then, must be [the process] of building and [the process of] building is a motion. (K.9.35).

While the initial history of the Maccabees and the experience I had in that structure suggests an already-built edifice, the preliminary history I've begun to sketch simultaneously performs a type of motion, a folksonomic drift from one term to the other (much as the previous chapter demonstrates early on with "worker" and concludes with "folk"). When I note in the first paragraph of this chapter that the building's name stems from a secret organization, I hear a hint of that drift. Aristotle's *Metaphysics* suggests that a building contains such drifts, what he refers to as "substance," that which "is neither element nor does it consist of elements. From our inquiry it appears that the constituents of a syllable are not its letters plus their combination, nor, in the case of a house, are they bricks and combination. And this is right; for a combination or blend does not consist of those objects of which it is the combination or blend" (H.3.5). Secrecy. Education. These are motions. They are elements that are not elements. They do not combine or blend as much as they network or build *if they are allowed to do so*. These elements perform what Latour calls "constructivism." "To bring constructivism back to its feet, it's enough to see that once social means again association, the whole idea of a building made of social stuff vanishes" (*Reassembling the Social* 92). The idea of stuff vanishes (desks, tables, signs, plaster) so that the building may build associations, so that it may become social (a collective or assemblage, as Latour argues), so that the network of a given space can be traced. A building builds, as Aristotle would say. In this observation there is, therefore, an initial connection to networked structures. That point will become clearer shortly.

Virtual Buildings

A discussion of structures as always in motion or always building themselves resembles a discussion of the virtual. "What have we been assuming about the nature of 'real' society, against which its 'virtual' counterpart constitutes a significant change?" Steve Woolgar asks (3). In the virtual, bodies and objects continuously form and change. They build. They form connections without the burden of representation. "Our network connections are becoming as important to us as our bodily locations," William Mitchell writes (*City of Bits* 166). An initial, potential, connection I see in the Maccabees unites education with secrecy and starts the process of forming something other than what these two initial bodies represent on their own. This connection feels as important as *my* bodily presence in the building once did. It feels virtual (buildable qua buildable) and digital (the Digital Literacy Initiative).

In the age of the network, Mitchell writes regarding his concept of "recombinant architecture" that education and buildings become digitalized and made virtual in profound ways. "The idea of a virtual campus," Mitchell notes, "paralleling or perhaps replacing the physical one—seems increasingly plausible" (*City of Bits* 70). Virtual education seems plausible to Mitchell because of the proliferation of communicative technologies that reshape pedagogy such as online chat, networked computers, and large virtual library holdings. "School and university libraries become less like document warehouses and dispensaries and more like online information-brokering services. Reserve desks are supplanted by online document collections, and slide libraries by huge image and video-on-demand servers" (*City of Bits* 69–70). Mitchell describes an alternative interface for how users of specific buildings—in this case, libraries—interact with virtual and digital information. While the Digital Literacy Initiative never explored virtuality as central to its cause, Wayne State University's library has, as Mitchell predicts, done so to some extent. The library's virtual holdings (such as Digital Dress: Two Hundred Years of Urban Style; the Herman Miller Furniture Consortium; and Virtual Motor City)[1] collect, digitize, index, and display a virtual educational site for students and faculty. Detroit is amassed within the library as not a physical place to visit, but a series of images, images featuring places, possessions, activities, and people. This database projects the city and its heritage as virtual. A student of Detroit, therefore, is not required to be in Detroit in order to study the city and its culture. One can imagine space's physicality via its virtuality, and in particular, for the way this virtual space collects and assembles a variety of artifacts into a usable interface. This kind of virtuality, I might assume, encompasses some of what Mitchell imagines, though I doubt he would stop with collections as a totalizing representation of the virtual. While it relies on a database, the library collection is not a networked collection since it is assembled once (with room for some additions) and its contents have minimal effect on each other. For the most part, it resembles the traditional library or museum collection, but with a digital interface. While a considerable amount of Mitchell's argument is devoted to innovations in software and hardware, he draws specific attention to how individuals might continue to *imagine* digital spaces, educational and otherwise. And he places that imagination within an educational context.

> The most crucial task before us is not one of putting in place the digital plumbing of broadband communications links and associated electronic appliances (which we will certainly get anyway), nor even of producing electronically deliverable "content," but rather one of imagining and creating digitally mediated environments for the kinds of lives that we will want to lead and the sorts of communities that we will want to have. (*City of Bits* 5)

I can *imagine* a Virtual Motor City, but as I do so, what I imagine does not entirely reflect the fairly commonplace setup established by the Wayne State library. That particular digital building does not yet perform *buildings building buildings*.

Perhaps Mitchell's focus on the importance of imagining digital space is itself a pedagogical gesture meant to demonstrate how virtuality is often actualized through very specific physical locations—as opposed to the generality of a library that does not (currently) hold meaning for me. By that, I mean that in order to imagine a digital reality, one may not have to look farther than one's own physical location, which already holds some kind of relational meaning, assuming the location represents the places where we want to live and work, as Mitchell claims. While the building does not hold a relational meaning to me, Wayne State's library system imagined its own location as something beyond the physical space of Purdy/Kresge (the building's name) without abandoning the attachment to the Purdy/Kresge Building itself (it remains as a metatag on the virtual holding website). And even more so, the library system in general imagined the broad category of Detroit as something beyond the city's limit; it created an interface for the city that could be engaged by people not living in the city. "An interface is humane if it is responsive to human needs and considerate of human frailties," Jef Raskin writes (6). Wayne

State imagined the need to access information globally, not locally, and thus, we might assume, created a responsive interface. Jeffrey Mirel, too, performs such an imagining; he frames the school system's failure as beyond the physical building that housed it and thus creates a textual interface that responds to the need to know why Detroit education collapsed. Another interfacial need might be to imagine a digital education (whether that education is within the liberal arts, architecture, science, or other categories). One could begin this imagining in a very physical (as opposed to virtual) educational space.

One such location that intrigues *me* is the Maccabees, for it is the site of two educational missions: the DPS and Wayne State University. That duality, like the ones I note in chapter 2 regarding Woodward, prompts me to think of space, technology, and pedagogy in ways not yet imagined, but that appear relevant to network rhetorics. That duality prompts me to extend Aristotle's understanding of the motion-oriented category so that it motivates my introduction of the Maccabees into the network I am constructing. What is the relationship between my physical location and technology? I ask. Following Mitchell and Harmon, I first have to imagine it. Thus, not just any building will do for any kind of educational mission or any kind of imaginative gesture. One begins with a specific—and likely personal—building interface. "The least advanced, most neglected area of electronic culture is interface design" (Ulmer, *Electronic Monuments* 40). Beginning with a *pedagogical* building interface situates this chapter as being about pedagogy as much as it is about the interface. Beginning with a building I have worked in returns the (me) characteristic of categorization I have found important to network rhetoric.

In the age of the network, Mitchell claims, "Buildings will become computer interfaces, and computer interfaces will become buildings" (*City of Bits* 105). The interface, Mitchell argues, is at the basis of informational relationships. "Screens typically function as electronic protagonists in social interactions" *e-topia* 34). He adds: "As the [computer] evolution unfolds, the distinction between building and computer interface will effectively disappear. Inhabitation and computer interaction will be simultaneous and inseparable" *e-topia* 60). The obvious response to Mitchell's conjecture regarding buildings, digital culture, and the interface—and a test case for the relationship between buildings, motion, and networks—would be to ask what kind of interface my location, the Maccabees, produces. This is not an instrumental question (that is, using a building to make computations) but instead is a theoretical one that asks how interfaces are constructed, the role they place in networked rhetorics, and what it might mean to speculate on a given structure's potential to serve as an interface. In essence, I am asking the question Aristotle asks regarding structure. If I understand the Maccabees as the site of educational struggle, as Mirel's history implies, then I understand its structure, its building-ness (the quality of being a building), as that of education. In *The Metaphysics*, Aristotle poses the question "'Why is the matter some one thing?'; for example, 'Why are these materials a house?'" His response to his own question is one of structure and thing-ness (the symptom of fulfilling categorical expectation). "Because to them belong this, which is the essence of the house; and because a man is this, or, this body has this" (Z.17.5). Aristotle's response is that a building (or anything) has its own enclosed essence or categorical quality. Every "thing" resides in a container. Education, for instance, would be one category. Digital literacy would be another. Networks might be another. A secret social organization would be yet another. Each reflects a separate purpose users of the building interface with even if they are not initially joined or unified. There are no limitations regarding how many items a user might interface with. "An interface should have few, if any, fixed-length limits," Raskin notes (117). While such a statement may suggest anarchy, the interface unites these elements together based on the role or purpose of each within the system. How these items interact and affect one another within the interface, though, remains unanswered.

"How is the building unified?" David Kolb asks in his breakdown of "systems" and "places" (88). His response balances the question of purpose so that overall operational systems are included in any discussion of structure or physical essence.

> Although the office building has a current purpose, buildings can last a long time and their purposes can be changed. The office building could become an apartment house, and in that conversion some elements of the building would not change: the walls would still support the roof, the windows let in light, and the heating system warm the spaces. These elements, and others, make up what I call the operative form of the building, which includes the physical systems that move air, resist gravity and wind, provide heat, and do other tasks of this sort. (Kolb 88)

In this discussion of the generic building, Kolb argues that the building "would still need an operative form that would be a kind of whole" (88). Operative forms are exchangeable. Heating systems can be replaced without changing the building's purpose. Operative forms can be exposed.

Pillars and pipes can be shown for aesthetic reasons. What changes, Kolb insists, is the relationship between "system and aesthetics" (89). What changes, he appears to suggest, is the interface.

Therefore, a discussion of the Maccabees as interface would involve the alteration, at least conceptually, of the building's networked relationship between aesthetic and system and the ways the two affect one another. What would change would be the already-established interfaces of education, digitality, or any other categorical reference point treated separately and not as part of a larger, networked system. What would change is the operative form. In the opening pages of *Designing Interfaces*, Jennifer Tidwell proposes that interfaces and their operative forms function according to patterns. Patterns, she notes, are the features of a variety of interfaces, from websites to buildings. "Patterns are structural and behavioral features that improve the 'habitability' of something—a user interface, a web site, an object-oriented program, or even a building. They make things easier to understand or more beautiful; they make tools more useful and usable" (xiv). Raskin calls patterns "habits," and he frames them as the repetitive activity associated with interface design. "We must design interfaces that (1) deliberatively take advantage of the human trait of habit development and (2) allow users to develop habits that smooth the flow of their work. *The ideal humane interface would reduce the interface component of a user's work to benign habituation*" (20; emphasis in original). Habits can be critical gestures (to always find fault with a city's past or failures) or they can be hyperbolic gestures (to imagine city buildings as utopian technological artifacts). These are conceptual interfaces. To design an interface, Tidwell recommends, "you need to take many 'softer' factors into account: gut reactions, preferences, social context, beliefs, and values" (5). In other words, one must connect a variety of affective experiences within a specific space and cannot rely on the so-called essence a space might project (as critique or praise might generate). Paul Dourish poses a similar notion of interface in his definition of "direct manipulation," "in which the elements are combined and extended. The fundamental principle in direct manipulation interfaces is to represent explicitly the objects that users will deal with and to allow users to operate on these objects direction" (13). Again, what makes up a space is not its essence, but its mobility or the mobility of the features that give a space meaning. Manuel DeLanda notes that the history of building construction—including its interfacial designs, facades, and exteriors—reveals interests in connectivity motivated by direct manipulation of such mobile features.

> Other components [in building construction] playing a material role are those determining the *connectivity* of the regions of a building. If locales are stations where the daily paths of individual persons converge, the regions that subdivided them must be connected to each other to allow for the circulation of human bodies and a variety of other material entities. (96)

An interface connects; it does not act only as a conduit between user and information. As Matthew Fuller and Florian Cramer write, "'Interfaces are the point of juncture between different bodies, hardware, software, users, and what they connect to or are part of. Interfaces describe, hide, and condition the asymmetry between the elements conjoined" (150). And without using the term "interface," Lefebvre highlights the role connection plays as we study and navigate the complex issue of space in general. Indeed, as I am examining the role of the interface within the network in this chapter, Lefebvre calls for a methodology of space (or we might add, spatial interfaces) at the level of connection. "A comparable approach is called for today, an approach which would analyze not things in space but space itself, with a view to uncovering the social relationships embedded in it (*Production of Space* 89).

Testing Mitchell's claim that buildings will become interfaces by exploring the connectivity within my own building is relevant to calls like those Lefebvre makes. Such a test relates as well to my work with "digital literacy," the assumption that meaning-making and the interfaces we engage with to make meaning change in digital environments. These interfaces, particularly at the level of metaphor, softer factors, and direct manipulation, generate different ways for users to connect with information. The Maccabees as an interface, therefore, can be both metaphorical as well as a system of connectivity. We are already familiar with similar metaphoric usages of the interface. In desktop computing, the business interface serves instrumental reasoning by directing how users interact with technology and eventually make connections between writing operations. This is the interface most familiar to those who work in university workplaces and in the classrooms where digital literacies are taught. The desktop metaphor is "supposed to assimilate the computer to the physical desktop and to the materials (file folders, sheets of paper, in-box, trash basket, etc.) familiar to office workers" (Grusin and Bolter 23). A building interface, one would assume, behaves similarly, though like the computer interface, it can be imagined differently. The office space may function to facilitate "the exchange of information—as it occurs among brokers, bankers, couriers, and other traffickers of knowledge—and its shops with the office space sought out by these service providers" (DeLanda 103). In that sense, a specific ideology of work is also facilitated. But just as alternative computer interfaces challenge the desktop metaphors (Linux's operating system and interface is one of the most recognizable to the computer; others are found on PDAs and cell phones), the building's interface as digital interface can be made not to assimilate users into an ideological state (like joining a workforce), but instead to serve as a metaphor for rethinking the relationships between space and technology, rhetoric and networks. "The forces of production and technology now permit of intervention at every level of space: local, regional, national, worldwide" (Henri Lefebvre, *Production of Space* 90). Whatever metaphor I arrive at regarding the Maccabees should take into account the soft factors and direct manipulation aspects of the interface others have highlighted. In other words, the interface's purpose can be rhetorical, and not just symbolic of one kind of experience (work) in favor of other experiences. "Another name for 'rhetoric' in a computer context," Gregory Ulmer writes, "is 'interface.'" The need to invent new interfaces, Ulmer argues, arises out of the problem of working with new metaphors in emerging technological experiences that "function as a model of the system" (*Heuretics* 28).

For this reason, Mitchell queries the building interface. But as Adam Greenfield writes regarding his concept of ubiquitous computing and its relationship to architecture, "The idea of a building whose program, circulation, and even structure are deeply modeled by flows of digital information is nothing new" (59). Such a concept is not new when its focus is on constructing interfaces that are instrumental and not conceptual (as Mitchell's building interfaces appear to be). Greenfield notes that buildings that merely reproduce digital scenes through wraparound surfaces or projected imagery still are not situated within networked culture. "For all the lovely renderings, we have yet to see the appearance of buildings structurally modified in any significant way by the provision of real-time, networked information" (Greenfield 59). Such buildings—like those one may encounter in Manhattan or Tokyo—have yet to make their way to Detroit.[2] One reason is that such buildings evoke the essence of the consumer economy that they help support; large, wraparound digital displays speak to the economic and technological status of the buildings who project them. The digital skylines of Manhattan and Tokyo interface wealth, prosperity, and consumption for those who look up to read them. Detroit cannot project the same message. Wraparounds are imaginative interfaces for how they display given information, but they do not do what

I think a networked interface might be capable of doing. Still, following Greenfield's concerns, I want to use an imaginative map of the Maccabees to invent an interface not structurally designed for the network (like a wraparound display), but conceptually designed. This design I am going to imagine here is based on patterns and connectivity similar to what Tidwell suggests, one that is buildable qua buildable because of its material, emotional, and technological features. This interface encourages a type of direct manipulation. It is also metaphorical, but its metaphorical status does not interpellate users to be workers in the building environment.

Tunnel between terminals in Detroit Metro Airport. The interface is meant to reflect Detroit's techno heritage. The city imagines passengers interpellated as techno-residents. Photograph by the author.

Can a building, like the Maccabees, serve as a computer metaphor for enacting digital work within the network? If the Maccabees is a computer interface, and if we are, indeed, in the age of the network (as Mitchell also argues), how do we enact that interface to conceptualize the city as network? In the *Phaedrus*, Plato conceptualized a response to the emergence of writing and the role of rhetoric by making Socrates leave the city before the argument could begin. Socrates, the narrative explains, had to be out of place; his interface with the topos under discussion had to shift. Socrates says in the Phaedrus,

Forgive me, my friend. I am devoted to learning; landscapes and trees have nothing to teach me—only the people in the city can do that. But you, I think, have found a potion to charm me into leaving. For just as people lead hungry animals forward by shaking branches of fruit before them, you can lead me all over Attica or anywhere else you like simply by waving in front of me the leaves of a book containing a speech. (6–7)

The topos, in this case the speech, demands a change in positioning within the container (the city). A building, the Maccabees, requires similar movement. You can lead the building out of its container by waving a number of items at it, and then by tracing their movements. Before I trace out that movement, I follow the pedagogical narrative of the *Phaedrus* as well as the building's historical connection to educational work, and I examine the building's spatial grammar.

Spatial Grammar

In *Home Rules*, an exploration of the kinds of rules generated out of space and spatial things, Denis Wood and Robert Beck write "Do not the things of the room (of the house, of the world) comprise a lexicon?" (45). Generalizing from their interest in homes and rooms, I, as a teacher embedded in literacy practices, ask the same question of the city and its buildings. Do cities have lexicons? Are not cities also part of discourse? And what does that discourse look like when imagined in a digital space? Such questions are relevant to constructing digital interfaces and to the overall project of rhetorical production. "Unlike literacy, which was one size fits all, the interface giving access to the electrate datasphere may be specific to each user" (Ulmer, *Electronic Monuments* 102). If the Maccabees can function as a computer interface, the ways we utilize that interface stem from rhetorical choices and moves we make, and those choices—despite various communal understandings—are specific to users of the interface.

The merger of rhetoric and the computer has come to be known generally as information technology. Alan Liu offers a useful definition of information technology, one employed as the spatial metaphor of architecture. "In terms of information architectures, first of all, the networking paradigm arose through a twofold rhythm of *convergence* in underlying technologies and *divergence* in understanding what might be called the 'philosophy' of those technologies" (141). This juxtaposition of ideas and things (the computer itself) introduces a new type of grammar (a lexicon) whose basis is no longer alphabetic, but instead is alphabetic plus something else. The "plus something else" is the convergence and divergence from what we already know as well as what we explore and investigate as we discover what information technology does to our perceptions of place and idea formation. That something else consists of the various network characteristics Digital Detroit teaches.

A grammar of the network requires a mapping of places and technology so that the physical places we inhabit generate new kinds of meaning systems that display innovative kinds of thinking. Information technology, Albert Borgmann notes, "has a plausible claim to representing the fundamental and universal alphabet and grammar of information" (166). Borgmann continues: "The genius of information technology consists in making information pliable by digitizing it, making it abundantly available by collecting and storing astronomical amounts of it, and putting it at our disposal through powerful processing and display devices" (170–71). Indeed, most of Borgmann's overview of information technology is about a specific contextualization of display, one always filtered through relationships to place. In Borgmann's analysis, that place is Missoula, Montana, site of the University of Montana, Borgmann's place of employment. For Gregory Ulmer, the merger of place and digital culture occurs in a different spatial display, Gainesville, Florida, site of the University of Florida, where Ulmer teaches. Ulmer's *Electronic Monuments* is a book-length exploration of space and digital culture, an investigation into how space and technology might inform public policy (a different approach than Mirel's query into how public policy shapes educational practices). Ulmer proposes "one possible response that education might make, taking up the democratic spirit of the [Lower Manhattan Development Corporation] mission statement by calling attention to an experiment in progress at the University of Florida" (xi). The experiment is to map space outside of the barriers of logical or instrumental thinking, for such thinking limits our abilities to conceptualize space as a possible response to various issues and problems. No matter how logical Mirel's tale maps the DPS, the DPS will fail (and as we currently see, it remains in a state of failure). In my own, location, instrumental logic will not help me generate an interface.

The mergers of space and technology Borgmann and Ulmer situate in their respective spaces occur for me in my former place of work as well: Detroit, Michigan, the Maccabees Building, the Department of English, site of Wayne State University. Unfortunately, that listing pushes me, at first, towards a logical response regarding education, one similar to Mirel's. That listing prompts a conclusion that these categories define education and Detroit. In other words, these categories immediately situate me within the individualized—not networked—meaning a city building might project. Instead of interacting with only this listing, I need the imaginative, nonlogical, patterned interface informational technology alludes to.

Making that gesture is also the first step towards thinking about buildings as computer interfaces; I begin with where I have worked. For me to imagine a spatially based information technology, I turn to the Maccabees. William Mitchell extends the kind of gesture I start to make to the general category of "cities." But Mitchell's exploration of the "bits" that make up digital space more closely resembles the logical progression of Mirel's examination of the DPS's failures. Mitchell wants to argue for a logical development of digital culture and space, one that is prophetic but also practical. "If we understand what is happing, and if we can conceive and explore alternative futures, we can find opportunities to intervene, sometimes to resist, to organize, to legislate, to plan, and to design" (*City of Bits* 5). Thomas Horan writes similarly when he notes that "Digital place design at the community level is concerned with developing electronic space in a manner that aids and is abetted by more traditional public places, with widespread access a top priority" (60). Resistance, legislation, access: These are keywords of instrumental logic. They are argumentative positions (topoi) regarding space and digital culture; they argue for better, more efficient, more equal futures. If there is any fault in this kind of structuring, it becomes apparent when we realize that an interface constructed solely from this type of thinking has limitations since it seldom lives up to the promises it proposes. Fixed topoi, as I have already argued in this book, do not lend themselves to the kind of digital interfaces writers like Dourish, Tidwell, and others imagine. These fixed topoi depend too strongly on one of two outcomes: success or failure.

In the case of the Maccabees, and in the larger context of Detroit, logical reasoning has proven to be a failed method of mapping space and related issues. The kind of conceptual (and sometimes physical) maps used to project and explain the financial, racial, construction, and related problems Detroit faces yearly never solve the problems the city grows ever too familiar with. A December 2005 *Detroit Free Press* headline reads, "$17 Million a Sign of Faith in Detroit," regarding recent Ford and Kellogg Foundation grants for city development. The headline is but one of countless promises of economic investment in a city (dating back, at least, to the Renaissance Center's development in the 1970s) where economic investment (a focal point of logical reasoning) has never eliminated physical malaise. In his 2002 inaugural mayoral speech, Kwame Kilpatrick kept this type of promissory rhetoric at the forefront of the city's mission.

> We already have the largest foreign trade zone and designated area for international trade and a port. It's time to maximize that resource. We already have the world's largest corporation downtown—General Motors—that invested a half-billion dollars in a building and is now standing ready to do more. We already have a nationally traded technology company that just invested over $400 million right in downtown Detroit. (Kilpatrick, "State of the City Address")

Mayor Dave Bing's 2010 inaugural speech does not stray too far from Kilpatrick's promise of a better future, a future not to be defined by past categories or meanings. "We will no longer be defined by the failures, divisiveness and self-serving actions of the past. We are turning the page to a new time in Detroit, focused not just on the challenges we face, but the opportunities we have to rebuild and renew our city . . . and the Spirit of Detroit." Even more so, Bing argued, whatever challenges Detroit faces, capital investment will solve the problems that lie ahead. "We must also repair the image and perception of Detroit. By changing the way we do our business, by improving our tone, and by sharing in the progress I know we will make, we will be better positioned to attract the investment and jobs we need."

Despite such gestures to change space through economic investment or even through hope, the overall maps of Detroit's spaces remain the same. The city is populated by ruins, racial division, and undeveloped zones. These familiar maps confirm what we know about investment and despair; they do little to change how one imagines space in the age of the network; they do little to alter the interface the city operates within. Instead, they reenforce a print based model of mapping dependent on referentiality (money equates renewal) and causality (investment will lead to salvation) or even spirituality (we have to believe in the future). When Horan and Mitchell map out digital places of the future, they make similar rhetorical moves by claiming that future spaces will make our lives more productive and more enjoyable.

These kinds of maps ask readers to see the interfacial features of a city as either economically impoverished (as in Detroit's case) or as utopian fantasies (as Mitchell and Horan proclaim). These maps pose space as a rational problem (money or technology serve as logical end pieces to a puzzle). Ulmer asks about this tendency to solve public problems solely through logical reasoning. "Why does the community insist on treating public and private crises on a case-by-case, individualized basis? Is it possible to grasp the frame, bring into perceptibility, make recognizable for a public consciousness the cumulative significance of a quantify of dispersed, private acts?" (*Electronic Monuments* 35). The logical map has been the traditional answer for such work because of its focus on one private act affecting one private place at a time: Introduce capital or introduce a physical computing device. If the logical map worked, the Maccabees would have remained the DPS. All the city needed, after all, was more capital.

Instead of a logical map, like Mitchell's or Mirel's, my interest in the Maccabees as computer interface returns to the database mapping I outlined in chapter 1. I take my cue from the "maps of the imagination" Katharine Harmon collects in *You Are Here: Personal Geographies*. These maps—drawings, cut-outs, computer generations, personal stories—are imaginative in that they propose alternative methods for organizing space based on both private and public connections. Their imaginative responses do not argue for concrete or economic solutions to spatial conflicts, problems, or issues but rather map out ideas, iconic gestures, disputed historical points, fantasies, and other nonreferential features of a given space. From Howard Finster's *All Roads One Road Headed the Same Way* (a 1978 mapping of physical and spiritual paths to heaven) to Simon Patterson's 1992 *The Great Bear* (a remapping of the London Underground as a series of celebrity and personality stops), these imaginative maps provide alternative interfaces for interacting with space and cultural issues. As one of the volume's contributors, Stephen Hall writes regarding the complexity of mapping, space, and the imagination, "To orientate is to hop back and forth between landscape and time, geography and emotion, knowledge and behavior" (15). In Hall's remarks, I hear a methodology for the building as computer interface. Rather than adapt an already-existing interfacial, and logical, metaphor (like desktop computing or investment), we have to imagine a new type of interface based on landscape, geography, emotion, and knowledge. This mix may prove to be anything but logical, since the connections among each trait are not predicated on a logos-oriented position. What follows in the remainder of this chapter, then, is meant to be one kind of personal map, an exploration of the Maccabees as computer interface. The rationale for doing this mapping is to introduce another aspect of the network relevant for the digital rhetoric I am pursuing. My interest is in allowing this building to build.

Computer Buildings

Since the principle of the map, as noted earlier in this book, is navigation—how to get from one space to the next—the methodology I begin with challenges our perceptions of order and space. While housed in the Maccabees, Detroit's educational mission, Mirel contends, overemphasized order and structure at the expense of pedagogy. "As important as changing urban educational politics and economics surely are, our preoccupation with these efforts tends to overwhelm discussions of what goes on in classrooms" (436). One might think that the dependence on order the DPS found so valuable was inherited from the city's automobile heritage. That heritage stressed an order based on an object's or space's functionality. As designer of both the Maccabees and Highland Park, Albert Kahn, as I discussed in chapter 2, optimized order as a Detroit logic, or what Terry Smith calls the concept of "functionalism" central to Kahn's work. "Functionalism is essential to modernity, not just as a design expression of the rhetoric of rationality, efficiency, and simplicity, but as the bottom-line materialization of the organization of the productive process itself" (Smith 72). The productive process in this sense, educational or architectural, is always ordered. An ordered environment, Kevin Lynch writes in *The Image of the City*, "may serve as a broad frame of reference, an organizer of activity or belief or knowledge" (4). The very nature of the Maccabees speaks to the question of order: how we order space, information, ideas, and related materials in a networked environment. Mirel's argument is that order prevented the DPS from learning how to teach *and* succeed within cultural change. The city's state of thinking and rhetoric for engaging policy was too ordered. Smith's argument is that Kahn's design techniques, visible in the Maccabees, used order for the "exclusion of other possibility" and the "commitment to infinite mass-reproduction of a single type" (77). Only one order, what we have come to term Fordism, could capture Ford production. It did so via a specific type of logic but also in the physical space where such thinking was enacted.

The assumption that order is a known or a logical progression deserves scrutiny when the Maccabees Building is employed as an interface. The Maccabees were a *secret* order; members often went by the mysterious rank of the Mystic Circle Degree. Secret orders in general, as Albert Stevens noted in the 1907 *Cyclopaedia of Fraternities*, are secret to their members as well as to the general public. "Very few among the six million members of nearly three hundred secret societies, fraternities, and sisterhoods in the United States are familiar with the origin, history, or function of these organizations" (Stevens xv). According to Michele Valerie Ronnick, most of Detroit's founding fathers were members of the Masons, a secret society (whose theater once served as the location of a 1964 Bob Dylan concert in Detroit). As she writes about the modern city's founder Augustus Woodward, after whom is named the street the

Maccabees is located on, Valerie Ronnick states, "It can be argued that the star-shaped and radial pattern of streets, which puzzles modern Detroiters, is a reflection of [Augustus] Woodward's association with the Masons" (15). The presence of the Maccabees in the heart of Detroit, on Woodward Avenue, is itself a mystery. Why was this city chosen over London, Ontario, the initial location of the Maccabees? Why the biblical and Jewish connections for a group that was white and Christian? Why are these religious and ethnic connections made prominently visible in the interior mosaics in the building's entryway, including images of the Garden of Eden and other Christian metaphoric imagery that covers the foyers ceiling? How did a secret order's headquarters become the center of Detroit education?

The interior of the Maccabees. Photograph by Derek Risse; reprinted with permission.

The challenge of secrecy, and not only the reference point, to both cities and technology, therefore, commands attention. Michael Maffesoli names secrecy as an organizational principle relevant to networks. "One of the characteristics," he notes, "and by no means the least, of the modern mass is surely the law of secrecy." Secrecy, Maffesoli writes, is a characteristic of the tribe, a type of network formation he calls "the growing massification and the development of micro-groups" (6). Secrecy, Maffesoli writes, is also an urban projection. "We can say that the multitude and the aggressiveness of urban images, resembling the Mafia's *borsalino*, is the clearest sign of the secret and dense life of contemporary micro-groups" (90). Secrecy, as Maffesoli highlights the concept, plays a role in the development and sustainability of communicative practices. "The reflection on secrecy and its effects, even if anomic, leads to two conclusions that may appear paradoxical: on the other hand, we are witness to a saturation of the principle of individuation, with the attendant economic-political consequences and, on the other, we can see the increasing development of communication" (Maffesoli 95). While the secret should encourage individuation (as Detroit's problems and most public policy dictates), secrecy is also a group affair. Groups (networks) share and disseminate secrets. The paradox could be deemed unproductive (the contradiction means that we shouldn't produce the role of secrecy) or itself essential for continuing an investigation into secrecy's role in the building of an interface (the motivating heuristic that asks, what could this *possibly* mean?). The building, the Maccabees, is an individual entity in a larger system, but I sense its role in a larger secretive communication practice in a way that its individuation changes. In the tribe (or network) secrecy allows individual members, the micro-group, to contribute to the network while they "are free to move from one to the other" (Maffesoli 6). Such groups, like the Maccabees, extend secrecy to the city, as the "tribe" is a metaphor generalizable to a number of spaces and conditions.

Cities, and their buildings, often encompass a sense of secrecy. As Jane Jacobs notes, "A city's very structure consists of mixture of uses, and we get close to its structural *secrets* when we deal with the conditions that generate diversity" (376). One such condition generating diversity is technology. Technology, particularly when computers are engaged, is typically considered to be a secret mastered by a select few. That sense of secrecy depends on instrumental logic, typically how a machine physically operates. "How does this work?" "How did you do that"? "How do you get online?" "How do you save an image?" "How do you make a link?" The web, the force that drives much of current technology and that gives the ever expanding, computer network shape, constitutes most of this secret. What the web means to commerce, privacy, and writing still provokes debate as forces argue over what sounds like a secret meaning behind this massive network of communication. "We're worried, we're giddy, we're confused," David Weinberger writes of the web. "The Web is putting us into positions where the lines are not just blurry but have been redrawn according to a new set of rules that don't make sense to us" (*Small Pieces* 12). How is a given relationship to a building or place ordered when the digital rules (its grammar or lexicon) regarding how to generate order are not yet known or don't even make sense? If the web doesn't make sense, how could a digital interface based on a building make sense? How can a city's own order (how it came to be within pre- and posttechnology waves) make sense?

In its almost forty-year search for economic revival (dating in the public imagination to the canonical 1967 riots I have noted in previous chapters), Detroit has asked the same question about itself. Detroit, too, suffers from the burden of secrets: What is the secret that will save the city from its economic despair? What is the secret of an "alternative to neo-traditional models of planning and urban design and their naïve revisionist strategies for the recuperation of the pre-industrial city," as the editors of *Stalking Detroit* call for (Young 12)? These generic questions, floated in academic queries, on Internet message boards, on weblogs, in newspaper columns, and in political campaigns, relate to what Henri Lefebvre calls the "urban illusion": "Like classical philosophy, urbanism claims to be a system. It pretends to embrace, enclose, possess a new totality. It wants to be the modern philosophy of the city, justified by (liberal) humanism while justifying a technocratic utopia" (*Urban Revolution* 153). The secret of urban illusions, Lefebvre points out, is the quest of a humanistic order, an objective not removed from the Maccabees, who worked for humanistic aims by creating an insurance system for its membership. "The Order of the Maccabees is quite comprehensive as to the relief it extends. It not only pays benefits at the deaths of members, both men and women, but for disability, during extreme old age and sickness, for accidents, and to meet funeral expenses" (Stevens 154). In *The Death and Life of Great American Cities*, Jane Jacobs stresses the humanistic importance of maintaining order in city planning (as opposed to yielding to the lack of order artistic drives encourage). "City designers should return to a strategy ennobling both to art and to life: a strategy of illuminating and clarifying life and helping to explain to us its meanings and order—in this case, helping to illuminate, clarify and explain the order of cities" (375). Jacobs, as opposed to Lefebvre, stresses the rhetoric of urban illusion, the desire that only order will save a city's demise (it is a claim echoed by city planners and government officials). Yet Jacobs recognizes that even complexity generates order. Still, the notion that complexity is based on a *known* and not a secret is where I find difference. What is the complexity of networks? I don't know; it is not a known variable. In networks, while it is possible to trace the connections and how they form relationships, a fundamental feature of the network is its randomness, its dependence on unknown variables.

Albert-László Barabási explains that within the largely unknown space of a network, complexity is tied to the concept of clustering. Clustering is the process of gathering connections together. "The discovery that clustering is ubiquitous has rapidly elevated it from a unique feature of society to a generic property of complex networks and posed the first serious challenge to the view that real networks are fundamentally random" (51). Indeed, despite the presence of the urban illusion in parts of her argument, a significant aspect of Jacobs's analysis is to shift urban planning away from seeing the parts of a given city as known, independent entities (a building here, a park there), and instead to see these parts as interconnected in ways initially and not initially realized, almost as clusters—though she doesn't use that term. The secret of the cluster, therefore, is not always knowing how connections form or will form. The illusion is in believing that the knowledge is readily available, that it encompasses a totality. The concept applies to Detroit, to the New Center, and to the position of the Maccabees at Wayne State University. "In parts of cities which are working well in some respects and badly in others (as is often the case), we cannot even analyze the virtues and the faults, diagnose the trouble or consider helpful changes, without going at them as problems of organized complexity" (Jacobs 434). What is the secret of urban planning, then, in the age of the network? Complexity itself. Clustering. Gathering connections. Understanding connections. "We live in a moment of unprecedented complexity," Marc Taylor writes, "when things are changing faster than our ability to comprehend them" (3). Physical space is no exception. The Maccabees, as a fraternal secret order, metaphorically emphasizes this point through the complex arrangements of its members (the mystery regarding who belongs where within the secret society) and how dues (as part of the business of the Maccabees of making insurance payments) were collected and paid out. To sort through the secret order of the Maccabees would be to understand the network of relationships its members maintained; the sorting would unravel the organization's rhetoric of organized complexity and reveal the points at which clustering occurred. Yet where does such a sorting of the Maccabees exist? Nowhere. And that is a vital point. There is no place to pinpoint as the answer to this secret. The metaphor teaches me something about the Maccabees interface and the role the network, especially regarding how "the secret," plays in Detroit. We don't unravel the secret to organize complexity. Instead, we "anticipate more complex structures of psychological, social, and cultural organization" (Taylor 15). We do that through clustering, and we do that through media.

Media

This sense of secrecy and networking extends the building as interface metaphor. In does so through the generic category of media, a category, folksonomies show, that can include radio, film, print, and, of course, the web, among other elements. The secret of the network is the way messages are routed, or not routed, from one node to another as they make their way through these various media. "The Web," Albert-László Barabási notes, "is full of such disjointed directed paths. They fundamentally determine the Web's navigability" (167). Navigating a networked space involves following disjointed paths as much as it involves following carefully ordered and routed paths. In the Maccabees Building, messages were eventually sent through ordered and disjointed paths; not via the web, but through radio transmissions. Atop the Maccabees, the call letters WXYZ once stood. The WXYZ radio station (whose television affiliation is today a part of ABC), broadcast at FM 101.1. Its call letters were supposed to have stood for the "Last Word in Radio." WXYZ was a member of the Mutual Broadcasting System, a network of radio stations founded in 1934. WXZY lasted only one year in the network. Its initial relationship to the networking of early communicative technologies (the radio) was disjointed.

The call letters the final letters of the alphabet) also indicate the moment when space becomes unordered. "Under conditions of high technology, the work of putting things in order (this structural activity) becomes as old fashioned as it is inescapable," Friedrich Kittler notes (371–72). WXYZ's movement out of the ordered financial structure of the Mutual Broadcasting network may be indicative of this process as well. Radio, as Marshall McLuhan writes, participates in the unstructuring of order because of how it traverses distances and travels through broken and reassembled frequencies. The appeal to the masses—the broadcast—can be an appeal to the lone individual, or even the isolated micro-group. Radio "affects most people intimately, person to person, offering a world of unspoken communication between writer-speaker and listener. That is the immediate aspect of radio. A private experience." (*Understanding Media* 401). In the secrecy of the Maccabees, privacy (as noted in the previous section) is not unique. Still, why did WXYZ eventually opt for the private experience (outside the network) as opposed to the networked experience Mutual offered (the belonging to a larger social order)? The logical answer might be an economic one; WXYZ experienced a lack of profitable return when based in Mutual. But the secretive answer speaks more to the question of order.

This secret involves the reason individuals (whether we mean people, things, places, ideas, bodies of power) understand information as separate and private rather than as belonging to a larger network of connections. McLuhan understood this tension as a negotiation between the two major forces of privacy and group identification: "radio gives privacy, and at the same time it provides the tight tribal bond of the world of the common market, of song and of resonance" (*Understanding Media* 405). At WXYZ, the secret of individual and group identification materialized in "the Log," an overly structured record of the station's broadcast that bound the individual (listener and DJ) to the group (WXYZ). "If radio ever had a Bible of its own, it was that inviolable document known as—The Log," remembers Dick Osgood in his narrative of WXYZ's history. "The Log told to the second when every sound was to be broadcast. The studio was to treat it as the law of Moses. No announcer, director, engineer, newscaster, sportscaster, singer, pianist, or orchestra leader dared stray one second from its dictates" (117). The Log explained a philosophy of private order, the adherence to a single point of view. A structured plan—whether how a city is laid out or how a program is followed—can lead to a fixed perspective on space, a sense of one thing having its one place in a system. The Log served as both institutional practice (WXYZ) and ideology (how to organize). The idea of the Log is still felt in Detroit urban planning. Detroit's city planners often see, for example, its building plans as motivated by the strict dictates of financial investment. The secret to planning, this position claims, is economic. This dedication to the narrative of financial order, in turn, views the city's buildings as distinct entities renovated one by one, not as a series of interlinking spaces affecting one another. Such organization assumes a centralized, organizational power. Radio, McLuhan argues, and I note, via WXYZ, works against centralization for how it aurally decentralizes a fixed space (the aural allowing for associative logics formed by decentralization of sound, that is, "sounding out"). "Radio is not only a mighty awakener of archaic memories, forces, animosities, but a decentralizing, pluralistic force, as is really the case with all electric power and media" (*Understanding Media* 409). Radio, in other words, breaks up blocks of information at various levels that affect and involve one another. "News bulletins, time signals, traffic data, and, above all, weather reports now serve to enhance the native power of radio to involve people in one another" (*Understanding Media* 400).

Urban planning is built by blocks (blocks of economic zones, blocks of streets, concrete blocks of construction), but these blocks do not shape one another. Whether the building is Compuware, the Detroit Public

Library, the Book-Cadillac, or the Maccabees, each project is treated as a separate link, not as a link connected to a network. Projects may be described by city planners as hubs—the Lower Woodward Plan, the Detroit Riverfront Conservancy—but the hubs are not connected. And even if connected, the complexity of networks demonstrates—as opposed to the principles of urban planning—that when hubs are joined, connections are not stable, nor are they ordered. They shift. Encounters or interactions with such places affect those shifts and challenge ordered viewpoints or perspectives on place.

The interface of order is learned from the overall project and influence of literacy, a position that affects reading and writing practices, but also how institutions and cities are structured. "The full-blown city coincides with the development of writing," McLuhan argues (*Understanding Media* 138). McLuhan notes how fixed perspective is a literate phenomenon tied to print's emphasis on single authorial presence (one author/one view—one reader at a time/one reading). The mass adoption of block-printing through moveable type "intensified perspective and the fixed point of view" (*Understanding Media* 235). Literacy established the regulations (the grammar/lexicon) we utilize to organize space, both in literal terms (the setting of language grammar) and conceptual terms (a fixed perspective on how to organize information). The interface for writing, the page, reflects that organization by requiring a writer's and reader's perspective to settle into one block of information at a time (the paragraph). In manuscript culture, Walter Ong writes, the paragraph as one such block allowed the writer to interface with information organization. "A favorite sign was the 'paragraph' which originally meant this mark ⁋, not a unit of discourse at all" (*Orality and Literacy* 122). Visual markers organize space; discursive meaning, on the other hand, plays a lesser role. City development, McLuhan and Fiore write, results from such organizational inventions. "The hand that filled the parchment page built a city" (48). As is often the case, each part of the city is understood as a visual "block": street or city block, but also, following the logic of print, individual buildings that mark a given space (as a paragraph once did). Thus, Henri Lefebvre critiques the urban illusion, an experience of only recognizing the "blocks," of having a limited perception regarding informational organization whose focus is limited to the visual marker and the force that connects and links. "Though a *product* to be used, to be consumed, [space] is also a *means of production*; networks of exchange and flows of raw materials and energy fashion space and are determined by it" (*Production of Space* 85). Lefebvre, like McLuhan and Fiore (though for different reasons) preaches the rhetoric of involvement. Lefebvre's involvement functions by way of network exchanges that alter the perception of space, that is, it may alter how we interface with a given space so that a "practice" might emerge. McLuhan and Fiore's involvement counters print organizational schemes dependent solely on a visual observation (distance between viewer and object) and that McLuhan and Fiore trace to the advent of print during the Renaissance.

> The viewer of Renaissance art is systematically placed outside the frame of experience. A piazza for everything and everything in its piazza.
> The instantaneous world of electric informational media involves all of us, all at once. No detachment of frame is possible. (53)

The print-block organizational scheme that favors unified perspective (one block at a time) over the more complex sense of involvement (which McLuhan and Fiore tie to the birth of printing in the Renaissance) is in opposition to the overall structure of new media space, like that which gave rise to the Internet and contemporary needs for new interfaces. Perspective, in a variety of new media, is often not limited to one block of information at a time as hyperlinks and other new media features deliver information at once within a number of perspectives. "No detachment of frame is possible" since information fills all frames of experience at once, often in pieces or blocks that are connected via different kinds of relationships. The Internet's structure, as well, is based on this notion. Its concept of packet switching, as devised by Paul Baran in 1964, distributes blocks of information as broken pieces and not stable structures. The blocks are assembled later, after they are routed through the web, not beforehand as unified markers. "Each block carried its address as well as other control information. Each block that made up a message was routed independently, and the message could be reconstructed at the local switching node so as to be comprehensible to the receiver" (Rasmussen 450). The metaphoric lesson-packet-switching teaches literacy conventions to not begin with already-structured and distinct sequences (set blocks), but to work with unassembled sets of meaning (broken blocks). In other words, the interface for this type of work acts a series of disjointed messages. This type of interface is different than the one print enables, an interface that stresses continued structure from the beginning, what McLuhan and Fiore call the "dominance of the vertical and the horizontal-of symmetry-as an absolute condition of order" (57). With the proliferation of disjointed delivery comes noninstrumental reasoning regarding space. What also arrives is a space (or interface) not dependent on vertical and horizontal organization.

In terms of the Maccabees, this addition to my query offers one type of response to the question of secrecy that motivates this chapter and section of Digital Detroit. Members of a given information environment often feel that the interface they will employ to do work has already been regulated (put in place) for them (as the Log shows) by literate conventions. "When users say that an interface is intuitive, they mean that it operates just like some other software or method with which they are familiar" (Raskin 150). Familiarity and regulation can be treated as synonyms in the network. In the age of the network, literacy is the most recognizable regulatory practice for generating meaning. Literacy, whether in new media or print, is understood by individuals as a structured form—both a physical and an ideological structure. The familiarity of a literate convention (WXYZ) can be made to structure a new media practice (radio). The challenge is to rethink or reimagine the role within the Maccabees interface. "Radio's section of the electromagnetic spectrum was born regulated," Matthew Fuller writes (20). The same might be said of the Maccabees and its communication history. WXYZ, an alphabetic ordering within the radio frequencies that structure telecommunications, is the dictation of literacy-bound practices. The "Last Word in Radio" might, then, be read as "The Last Word in Literacy." Literacy, McLuhan argues, fashioned the private individual. The age of new media challenges that image by demonstrating how all subjects (individuals and subject matter) are interconnected through disconnected and disjoined meanings. Thus, while the call letters plead the case for a specific type of structured literacy, the very medium they worked through, radio, suggested otherwise. It offered a way to respond to, challenge, or, at the least, amend, the literate regulation of communication already circulating. That the Maccabees failed to listen to that suggestion is another matter completely.

Still, I don't want to dismiss the private entirely by drawing a binary division between perspectives. Despite the presence of the Log, WXYZ's programming evoked much of the imaginative, nonregulated activity I highlighted early in this chapter as related to the private. While radio committed ideologically to the Log, within the television network it belonged, WXYZ's sister television station (also located in the Maccabees) seemed to drift into less regulated forms of rhetorical production. The station earned a reputation as a pioneer in the highly imaginative world of children's television programming. Contemporary children's programs may stick closely to set scripts and logistics (often motivated by the tight connection between advertising and the content of the programming). Early children's programs on WXYZ, however, functioned differently.

Two of the station's most popular programs, *Lunch with Soupy Sales* and Johnny Ginger's *Curtain Time Theater*, positioned the individual within the interface in unique ways, often showcasing the odd, off-beat moment as an imaginative gesture within a larger communicative moment. *Lunch with Soupy Sales*, for instance, was rumored to film without a script; Soupy and crew would work off of each other's unregulated antics and hi-jinks and create a nonunified sense of involvement (riffing off each other) that strayed from a prescribed focus. In one 1959 episode, such straying is evident in a routine that poses Soupy speaking to someone off camera about dancing, and the off-camera voice responding by comparing Soupy's dancing to a chicken that is also shown to dance. The skit strays from dancing to egg production to Soupy saying hello to the children viewing by introducing the sponsor, Jello, to a dog puppet licking Soupy's face. Nothing in the skit is unified; it is obviously disjointed.

Two *Curtain Time Theater* examples demonstrate such straying. While I cannot locate where they were filmed exactly in the Maccabees (My former office? The floor I worked on?), I can build these shows into the structure I am assembling. In one episode's feature, Ginger plays himself, speaking to himself on an adjacent TV. In a moment one might call early multimedia, Ginger's image appears both as live actor and as televised image. The two images perform together; the televised image frustrates the live one by showing him up with elaborate dancing and piano playing. In another feature. Ginger repeats the dual image gesture; this time he is both the presenter of a sweepstakes contest and the televised image of the winner. A cheap effect for contemporary new media, it still serves as an early instance of the secrecy of the media image that would perplex 1950s and 1960s audiences: how can one person act both live and on the TV at the same time? How can someone project their image into another space? These questions also pose disjointed representations as a compositional gesture. The main image is disjointed and disassembled as separate blocks of information. Its interface is the disjointedness itself.

When faced with disjointed information, one must fill in the details. McLuhan's concept of "cool media" derives from that point; cool media are media low in resolution; hot media are high in resolution. "Hot media are, therefore, low in participation, and cool media are high in participation or completion by the audience" (*Understanding Media* 36). Viewers or listeners fill in what is missing (for example, Charlie Brown does not look like a real kid; a reader fills in the details mentally to see Charlie Brown, the drawing, as a kid). TV and radio personalities can evoke the cool image. "Another way of explaining the acceptable, as opposed to the unacceptable, TV personality is to say that anybody whose appearance strongly declares his role and status in life is wrong for TV" (McLuhan, *Understanding Media* 288). There is something elusive, not declared, in the Johnny Ginger dual images because of the type of information viewers had to complete. Which is really him? How can he speak with himself? "The cool TV medium cannot abide the typical because it leaves the viewer frustrated of his job of 'closure'" (*Understanding Media* 288). Part of the secret of the interface, then, involves not achieving closure, not figuring out the so-called answer that would provide a unified perspective. This secret asks us to fill in details, but not to achieve closure (space is always left for more filling in). "Not even the most lucid understanding of the peculiar force of a medium can head off the ordinary 'closure' of the senses that causes us to conform to the pattern of experience presented" (*Understanding Media* 286). The literalness associated with a building (it has fifteen floors; it is on Woodward Avenue) or of an interface's function (this icon is where deleted files are; this icon is a document) has long been a project of closure. The project of fixed representation ("The Maccabees is a building," "Detroit's schools face collapse") is concerned with closure. Understanding such representations, however, is not in itself an act of closure, for the very nature of what, following McLuhan, we might deem cool rejects that possibility. Cool media are not literal representations; they leave open details for further participation and involvement. In fact, the literalness literacy advocates—represented in the call letters of WXYZ—claims a sense of closure focused on knowing how to read and write, knowing how to understand, and knowing how to translate such skills into a profession. To put such thinking into a cool interface would be to look for a response other than that of closure. It would be to work with the secrecy I have been following throughout this chapter.

The coolness I find in Johnny Ginger is different than that of the station's literate call letters. Cool's imaginative play on the interface Ginger demonstrates is both local and virtual. A viewer of *Curtain Time Theater* would find the image cool for the lack of representational value ("I have to imagine how he can be in two places at once"). I, on the other hand, fill in parts of Ginger's performance as part of a larger project this chapter seeks to fulfill regarding networks and interfaces, and which has its own cool implications. "TV is above all a medium that demands a creatively participant response" (McLuhan, *Understanding Media* 293). *Curtain Time Theater* demonstrates the role of participation in the Maccabees. Mitchell's call for a virtual space might be actualized not through an abstract notion but one's very specific, localized space. One has to imagine, however, how that space might become digital or virtual. One has to fill in the details. One has to participate. This participation, McLuhan argues, comes from a feeling or sense. This participation is, to stretch the meaning a bit, as *sensational* as seeing an actor appear as a dual image on a 1950s TV program. "This feeling does not have its basis in concepts or ideas, but seems to creep in uninvited and unexplained" (*Understanding Media* 293). As an interface, the Maccabees is not based in the representational idea but in the sensation or set of sensations it generates. Another example of the building's TV broadcasts assists me further.

The localized studio in the Maccabees broadcast imaginative content like *Curtain Time Theater* or *Lunch with Soupy Sales* as well as radio programming not aimed at children, including *The Lone Ranger*, which from 1933 to 1955 was included in WXYZ's format. A show about justice and revenge, *The Lone Ranger* is imaginative, though not in the way children's programming is; its imaginative gestures are not based on media play but rather on identity. The Lone Ranger, with mask, is not identifiable. His coolness is the result of a viewer's desire to be that figure, to have one's eyes where the masked heroes are hidden. While Johnny Ginger was televised, *The Lone Ranger* was broadcast over radio. Both television and radio are identified by McLuhan as cool media.

Possibly, though, one could have heard this Western on WXYZ's radio while also viewing the show on the TV station's Sunday lineup of kids' shows, which would include commercials for Detroit-manufactured Faygo soda. The Faygo Kid, hero of the animated spot, exemplified the Sunday lineup's Western figure. With large cowboy hat, black vest, and boots, he embodied the same visual traits as the Lone Ranger. In the commercial, the Faygo Kid saves a stagecoach of Faygo Old Fashioned Root Beer from being robbed by archenemy Black Bart. The commercial concluded with the song:

> The Faygo kid.
> Which Way did he go?
> Which way did he go?
> He went for Faygo!
> (Kiska 9)

The Western is the prototypical child's dream, to save someone in distress, to save the day, to rescue, to be the hero. That it is difficult or impossible to live out that fantasy is unimportant. The notion of being a cowboy, despite its lack of literal relevance, is still repeated in various media, at various times. On WXYZ, Western fantasy and children-oriented fantasy focused around individual adventures (one of a cowboy, the other of a goofy host). Despite the near impossibility of living any of that fantasy out, listeners and viewers tuned in to these programs in order to follow these adventures, these wanderings, these reroutings of visual space, which are always narratives disconnected from the viewer and any immediate experience. Why would a viewer want to do this? That, too, marks another moment of the secretive, the question of why other, unknown lives spark imaginative rhetorics in viewers. It is also a place where the interface's relationship to cool media is more pronounced, or indicates what McLuhan calls a shift in meaning organization. "It is precisely this imaginative organization that has occurred via the TV image" (*Understanding Media* 290). While we may "relate" or "identify" with a host or character, a continued interest in disjointed narrative (viewer's narrative/character's narrative) is never completely understood; it's a type of media secret that depends on the imaginative. "'Identification' is hardly other than a name for the *function of sociality*" (Burke, *Attitudes* 266; emphasis in original). We cannot completely fill in the host's image with our own, but we can maintain a type of media sociality with it. Like the two Johnny Ginger images or the two cowboy images, some portion of this sociality is disjointed. Yet, there still exists a type of relationship with the image. I sense this relationship even it if it not wholly representational. With these two broadcasts, I note how the sense of the imaginative, which inspires my inquiry into a new type of building interface (drawn from Harmon's collection), is always secretive (what does another's imaginative query mean when it is not *my imagination*) and yet also rhetorical (when a text, like a TV show, is produced, it generates meaning). As media-based, WXYZ presents networks in terms of an imaginative rhetoric that refigures a social relationship.

In other words, in the WXZY call letters atop the Maccabees, I find the literate order reconfigured. In the Maccabees, *The Lone Ranger*, *Curtain Time Theater*, and *Lunch with Soupy Sales* stand for a new kind of spatial literacy, one structured by media and which interacts with viewers/readers at an imaginative level through a McLuhan-esque cool narrative, not through fixed geometric space as basic architecture or urban planning might require. Nor is this narrative as intricate and detailed as Mirel's history of the Detroit school system. To repeat that narrative would be to embrace "hot" media and the lower levels of participation (as well as the structured Logs) they encourage. Buildings, I discover, like TV shows, have cool narratives. As an element of media literacy (motivated by the network it is in), the Maccabees is organized by such a cool narrative. As John Rajchman writes of space and order, when working with architecture, new types of geometry are required in order to understand media literacy. Relying on the essence of space (like its geometric configuration or its literal representation), in fact, limits any ability for movement. It limits how buildings build upon their various spatial meanings.

> "Other geometries" thus require other ways of knowing that don't fit the Euclidean model They are given by intuition rather than deduction, by informal diagrams or maps that incorporate an element of free indetermination rather than ones that work with fixed overall structures into which one inserts everything. Indeed without such intuitive knowledge or informal diagrams, they might well go unseen or unactualized. (100)

My intuition (that is, my imagination) tells me that the Maccabees teaches a new kind of ordering of digital space that is directly related to the narrative I have been telling here about my work and my reflections. This narrative is "cool" because of the participatory gestures it is allowing me to make with secret societies, public schools, and radio and television programming. Participation, in this case, brings together supposed specialized forces within a given structure (like a building and its many histories or attributes). The visual (TV), the written (historical account), and the sense of something (secret organizations) generate an affective feature of space. Separation, McLuhan claims, is the product of print, not media, literacy. Media is tactile and kinetic; sensation rather than logic functions as a linking mechanism, as a tool for clustering. "This separation of the visual from direct tactile and kinetic pressure, and its translation into new dwelling spaces, occurs only when men have learned to practice specialization of the their senses, and fragmentation of their work skills (*Understanding Media* 119). The Maccabees presents a sense-driven structuring of space via many of the elements I present in this chapter. "Any given interaction seems to *overflow* with elements which are already in the situation coming from some other *time*, some other *place*, and generated by some other *agency*" (Latour, *Reassembling the Social* 166; emphasis in original). I sense these elements as together being part of a larger body (the interface of the network). The building's ordering, as I understand it, is media-, not print-structured; in other words, it is affective, not logically structured.

The Affective Interface

The affective dimension I finally introduce suggests a different way, within networked writing, of viewing urban space as well as how the urban's physical structures, like its buildings, function as a computer interface for rhetorical production. "There seems to be a growing feeling within media, literary, and art theory that affect is central to understanding of our information- and image-based late capitalist culture, in which so-called master narratives are perceived to have foundered," Brian Massumi writes (27). Massumi contrasts affect to the reliance on structure as a tool for understanding the conveyance of meaning. "Our entire vocabulary has derived from theories of signification that are still wedded to structure even across irreconcilable differences" (27). Affect, Massumi argues, needs its own vocabulary separate from that of signification. Affect, we learn, is a virtual experience. Rather than being a signified moment or thing, it is a potential, a nonfixed intensity that moves as soon as it occurs. "Something that happens too quickly to have happened, actually, is *virtual*" (Massumi 30; emphasis in original).

Following Massumi's logic, I draw attention to the way media generate affective senses of place because I want to move away from how technology and place have been tied too closely to logical structuring. I also want to distance myself from the specific master narratives that are employed to understand either technology or place. In these gestures I resist, place is not allowed to move; buildings cannot build; interfaces do not change. I am, as McLuhan writes of TV, therefore interested in the imaginative structuring of meaning. In the network, the logical structuring insists on understanding networks as either only computer based or as only a process of connectivity. A network, in this definition, either must be a physical thing or must adhere to specific principles of connectivity. The interface, typically, is limited to some variation of interconnecting strands (which are often weblike) so that one can engage with these understandings. A browser, therefore, serves as an interface for the web. A Facebook profile page serves as the interface for social networking among college students, friends, business associates, faculty, and alumni. An iTunes playlist serves as interface for someone organizing and storing computerized music. In the urban environment, the city network interface is limited to development or destruction stories. Like other features of nonnetworked urban writing, this last interface is limited to master and grand narratives. While this urban interface may be a new media artifact (like a wraparound building), it is not virtual.

Instead of these kinds of interfaces, I am moving closer to a type of interface that teaches how to respond to urban and spatial issues without resorting to an expectation of an argumentative or persuasive result, an interface that is virtual in a way Mitchell did not envision. Such expectations reflect the dependence on fixed points of view McLuhan connected to the invention of the printing press's block printing and that urban planners seem to have settled on with blocks of construction. Instead, as a way to tie together this chapter's focus and add another piece to Digital Detroit, I extend the virtual by moving closer to what Deleuze and Guattari call "a bloc of present sensations" (167). "We are not in the world," Deleuze and Guattari write, "we become with the world; we become with the world by contemplating it. Everything is vision, becoming" (169). An interface that allows place *to become* by affectively building blocks is the interface of digital space's secrecy; it is the cool interface I frame in the previous section; it is the virtual building interface. This interface is the virtual Maccabees I have been constructing in this chapter. The Maccabees, as I put it together here, allows spatial meanings *to become* and not just be. The Maccabees is an affective interface, where sensations, responses, interactions, and encounters drive meaning. This interface *becomes* through the contemplation of its folksonomic meanings brought together: education, secret society, radio, Soupy Sales, Johnny Ginger, and the Lone Ranger. It forms a component of the overall network I am imagining as Detroit. In *How Buildings Learn*, Stewart Brand defines a building's networked layers as an expansion of architect Frank Duffy's "four S's" (the traits of a given building's layers) from its initial four parts to a revised six: Site, Structure, Skin, Services, Space Plan, and Stuff (13). To this list, we might add a seventh s point, as it is informed by the affective interface, sensation. Duffy's layers all affect one another. "Site dominates the Structure, which dominates the skin, which dominates the Services, which dominate the Space plan, which dominates the Stuff" (Brand 14). Sensation, whether dominant or not, moves all of these layers as well. Sensation is what has moved me through Site (Maccabees Building), Structure (literate ordering), Skin (interface design), Services (insurance, TV and radio programming), Space (the building's networked movements), and Stuff (everything that has happened in this one space). Sensation includes my motivations to place specific agents in this building so that each layer is formed and networked to the next; eventually all the agents *do something* and make an interface. My motivations are sensations, intuitions, feelings, emotional choices. Sensations, we can also argue, are generated by curiosity. I *sensed* that the Maccabees might offer an alternative network interface, so I followed the building's connections. Helga Nowotny identifies curiosity as a principle feature of networked relationships.

> Curiosity nourishes itself on questions that point beyond or cast doubt on the usual and given to explore what lies beyond the obvious. It thereby resists premature commitment. It clings as long as possible to the playful and uncommitted impulse, whereas innovation already has allegiance to the introduction of the new and its integration in the given, even if this means the abandonment and disappearance of what already exists. (84)

In networked writings, curiosity is often overlooked in favor of a commitment to the permanent future the writer imagines, a future framed as an improvement. Mitchell, who motivated this chapter, is still too devoted to the progressive qualities of new media as they affect network thinking, concluding his vision of digitally enhanced architecture by urging architects to "be forced to explore the proper respective roles of physically constructed hardware and symbolically encoded software, and of actual space and virtual places" (*City of Bits* 172). That exploration, we are led to believe, will lead to *a better* society, *a better* sense of urban development, *a better* way to design buildings. The desire for something better signifies the very problem Detroit, and buildings like the Maccabees, never solve. "Our space has strange effects. For one thing, it unleashes desire" (Henri Lefebvre, *Production of Space* 97). Desire, though, takes many forms. While promises of something better may suggest a sense of becoming (the verge of a greater achieving being formed), they often do not provide much more than an urban illusion. The urban illusion, as I have already noted, is too dependent on humanistic and moral goals, goals that will fail for their fixed, and not networked, perspectives. In that sense, desire is a failed rhetoric for spatial engagement.[3] Rajchman calls the move away from such promissory rhetorics the move towards the virtual.

> Architects have thought in terms of utopia and ideological program. They have thought in terms of transgression and formal play. The virtual introduces another style of thought. It has nothing to do with an ideology, a belief in an encompassing order, real or utopian. It thinks in terms of arrangements of body and soul, irreducible to any such symbolic order, any such law of possibilities. (119)

This specific definition of the virtual as affective is what I have been trying to uncover; it suggests an alternative to promissory desire. I have been trying to demonstrate the ways conceptual issues evoke other kinds of digital responses not dependent on hardware nor on software, yet fashioned out of the logic the network. Those responses arrange bodies—bodies of ideas, bodies of places, bodies of interactions—in place of representing them as ideological or moral visions. "Every touching experience of architecture is multi-sensory," Juhani Pallasmaa writes, "qualities of space, matter and scale are measured equally by the eye, ear, nose, skin, tongue, skeleton, and muscle. Architecture strengthens the existential experience, one's sense of being in the world" (41). Sensation. Multisensing. These are keywords often associated with the affective dimension of "being." Whether the "being" in a building like the Maccabees is a glorious or dreadful experience is not important; the multisensory quality it projects comes from the ways I engage with the various folksonomic meanings I encounter there. Sensation, in general, is the important spatial attribute of this interface.

Rajchman makes a similar observation regarding architect Peter Eisenman's work. Rajchman comments that Eisenman's skewed geometries "introduce a sort of 'affective space' of unanticipated encounter and connection" (90). Eisenman, Rajchman argues, "conceives the urban setting as an accumulation of superimposed layers in which the partially invisible 'memory' of cities is deposited" (80). Like a multisensory experience of space, these layers generate "a kind of fiction" (80). A story. A narrative. A fiction. Layers of stories and narratives. Blocs of sensations. These are, in effect, interfacial spatial stories driven by the imaginative. But rather than view an architect's already-mapped affective space or already-established narrative—as Rajchman does with Eisenman—I have tried to uncover my own space based on my own physical locale generated from my own interactions. I am writing a layering of narratives out of these spatial interactions. That uncovering reveals a grammar that is imaginative, associative, and affective. In other words, I have found my computer interface. "Content and interface merge into one entity, and no longer can be taken apart" (Manovich 67). The pragmatics of that interface have not been entirely enacted yet here, at least not in the sense of what I might now produce with this interface. By this book's conclusion, the interfaces' role will hopefully be clearer; it is allowing me to produce this chapter as well as the other four.

Nevertheless, the Maccabees, as an affective space for generating meaning, leaves open further possibilities than I previously had at my disposal. This affective interface can open up new usages of buildings or city space than what the single narrative of financial investment or economic downfall has failed to provide. Institutions, like buildings or educational missions, Nowotny notes, initiate secrets like an affective interface. "Institutions are the mediators that either meet the promiscuity of curiosity halfway—or hinder it" (97). An institution either sets a unified order or an affective order. As Rajchman writes, "Once one allows for a world that is disunified, incongruous, composed of multiple divergent paths, one can think in terms of abstract virtualities that, in contrast to such abstract possibilities, are quite real, even though they are not actualized" (65). My interface, therefore, is a virtual map of abstract possibilities. The possibilities are the network I see the Maccabees generating. These possibilities embody what Matthew Fuller calls a "media ecology," that which "describes, mobilizing and mapping, *using* the perspectivalism of particular approaches, materials, and ideas as they intersect" (168). What I have *used* returns me to the initial point I raised regarding the Maccabees, order, and secrets. "The secret," Gregory Ulmer writes, "is not an object to be exposed either by revelation or interrogation, but a relay, a circuit, powering an invention" (*Teletheory* 217). This circuit, motivated by the affective sense of digital literacy, invents a response to the Maccabees at the level of possibilities as well as an overall curiosity regarding how various items connect. One can imagine these possibilities played out heuristically, as I have done here, or in actual technological spaces like weblogs, del.icio.us sites, Flickr accounts, and other emerging writing spaces where writers reimagine space and technology. One could imagine the city, as I am also doing, as a site for these possibilities. One could do so, it is now obvious, as well through buildings. Digital Detroit is in these places, and as I will note in the next chapter, the weblog/discussion space is a part of the Digital Detroit network because of the affective interface I have been creating here. Weblogs, among other online spaces, provide preliminary examples of spatial possibilities because of how they connect technological sites with spatial issues. Unlike Mitchell's vision of a digital future, their usage, as I will show in the next chapter, is not a *bettering* of space. As these sites combine via a number of social networking efforts, they flow and move into one another in ways that may extend what I am calling the affective interface. They contribute to a perspective that frames the urban as a network.

By performing these possibilities, these sensations write spatial encounters as an invention practice. The challenge for the rhetoric of urban planning is to begin to imagine such virtual spaces, to imagine divergence as a new type of structuring, one that shifts attention away from being based solely on logic (like a desktop metaphor) and allows more attention to the possibilities of affective production, to the possibilities of spaces. These possibilities show how the spaces where we work, like Detroit, like the Maccabees, like Wayne State University, move out of fixed positions and are engaged with as becomings. Because the sense of becoming is itself a movement, I turn to this concept in the next chapter. The Motor City has long struggled with its paradoxical identity of movement (automotive industry) and lack of movement (economic stagnation). This point was clear to me when I began this chapter with a building that had moved from various active to stagnant states. In the next chapter, I enter into what has long been the city's most empty space, the abandoned Michigan Central Train Station, because it showcases both characteristics of movement in terms of layering and responses. What is empty and appears not to move, I sense, is itself a site of network flow, a site where various items layered within one another are also responding to one another in a variety of nonseamless ways. The emptiness of the train station is, in fact, not empty but rather an important contributor to Digital Detroit.

4

THE MICHIGAN CENTRAL TRAIN STATION

If you sifted all Detroit in a wire basket the beaten
solid core of dregs couldn't be better gathered.
>   —Jack Kerouac, *On the Road*

*I*n *Urban Encounters*, Helen Liggett writes, "If photography is seen
as the art of making (not taking) pictures, the possibility emerges
for using it as a productive part of city life. From this perspective, photographic images bring memory and experience together, attracting meanings in the process of stopping time and presenting a space" (120). Liggett's
exploration of the urban space's relationship to imagery captures the city
as the everyday, as encounters, as spaces *made* by those who engage with
them, who encounter them, and who respond to them. Liggett situates
photography as a way to "arrest" or stop space so that one might fabricate
relationships (personal or otherwise) with the given space that otherwise would never come into being. In the previous chapter, I outlined
such a feature of the network by developing an affective interface whose
functionality stems from encounter and response (the spaces within the
Maccabees I encountered and work from). Technology, like the camera
Liggett emphasizes, assists in the process of making space because of the
various ways its interfaces allow for experience to mesh with institutional
bodies such as a building. The camera, for Liggett, stops space so that we
(as photographer or viewer) may encounter the space's various components and consequently enter into a rhetorical relationship with the space.

In Liggett's work, photography serves as a tool and interface for encountering space as framed by the city and the everyday. In the moment
of encounter, space is captured as reproduced image but also represented
as something else, something that a photograph may not convey: an emotion, a feeling, an aspiration, a disappointment, a relay for a newly formed

relationship. Encounter, Liggett claims, includes representational and nonrepresentational features of space. The encounter may reenforce or shift understandings of space. Her thesis echoes the project set up by Ash Amin and Nigel Thrift in *Cities: Reimagining the Urban* that "encounter, and the reaction to it, is a formative element in the urban world" (30). Amin and Thrift, like Liggett, work to overcome specific types of spatial representations and the power structures associated with them. "Rather than focusing on the conventional interest in urban studies on the domination and oppression by certain kinds of actors and institutions," Amin and Thrift write, "our concern is with power as a mobile, circulating force which through the constant re-citation of practices, produces self-similar outcomes, moment by moment" (105). The conventional urban image of power, as the previous chapters demonstrate, prevents understandings of spaces, like Detroit, as being anything but victims in larger institutional power struggles. The affective interface, as the Maccabees shows me, does not eliminate power or its image, but instead functions by secrecy, a more ambiguous and affective means for establishing power relationships. Secrecy involves the multisensory layering of moments *without the quest to uncover this layering as the symptom of a greater struggle* (as an investigation of power would require). The notion of secrecy within the network always leaves some elements of a given relationship unsettled and uncertain so that the curious may establish new connections within the interface. A building interface keeps building. Amin and Thrift argue for a type of building interface (without naming it as such) by locating recitations, or rhetorical productions, as contributors to power relations in the city. Photography is one way to recite, or repeat, an image of a space. It is affective, I note following Liggett's work, for what it hides (its power to represent) or keeps secret. "The camera becomes an active tool, not of representation, but of presentation" (Liggett 120). The photograph, like the object it represents, evokes the presentation of sensations. It remakes a given space as the juxtaposition of place, personal experience, affect, and other related moments. "Objects are a vital part of passions" (Amin and Thrift 87). Photographs, themselves objects, are as well.

One of my earliest encounters with Detroit and my ensuing passion—and one shared by many other visitors to the Motor City—was with the Michigan Central Train Station (MCS), a mammoth depot located off of Michigan Avenue and adjacent to the city's Corktown neighborhood. Designed by the same firm that designed New York's Grand Central Station, the MCS opened December 26, 1913. There is nothing secret about this building that stands out among the quaint homes surrounding it in

Detroit's oldest neighborhood. All of the city's residents know the building well. Indeed, one of the first photographs I took of Detroit was of the MCS; I eagerly snapped shots of the fenced in building, the graffiti, and the obvious vandalism. I encountered the MCS, as Liggett argues urban residents and visitors do, with my camera. The encountering, though, may have been an act of reinforcing (rather than remaking) an image, for the picture I took was the same I had seen from afar in various publications. The picture I took was familiar to me before I even took it. The picture I took was of an abandoned train station.

Traveling through Detroit, it is difficult not to notice the MCS. It projects outward from Corktown onto a large, open space. In the era of urban tourism, those who encounter the MCS for the first time, like myself, feel obligated to photograph it because it is so empty and because it is so blatant in its emptiness. Its beastly status, its signs of decay, its obviously lost grandeur attract the camera's eye. "To photograph the material of everyday life is to become an heir to the storyteller," Liggett writes (158). As a part of the spatial story of Detroit I have been recounting so far, the MCS is a material object photographed again and again as a focal point of a communal story. That communal story, in the most obvious way, narrates a city's demise. For those who photograph the MCS, like me, the many who came to Detroit before me, and those who come after me, the story is told as if it will one day be forgotten. We remember Detroit's fall, we almost say, by photographing the MCS. The MCS is recited, and with that recitation, we hear a very familiar story: decay and devastation. The photographic recitations are powerful for how they evoke disgust, pity, or other types of negative feelings. The photographs produce sensations, which are communal, not personal, responses. Merely taking the image, in other words, does not necessarily allow one to make a space. One can just as easily recite a common narrative.

A search for "Michigan Central Train Station" on the image-sharing site Flickr, for instance, produces over one thousand hits. A search on YouTube for "Michigan Train Station" yields over sixty hits. Most of these references recite the story of devastation communally associated with the city. Evidence, like that found on YouTube and Flickr, suggests that a considerable number of people are locating the station in moving and still imagery, and they are reciting that imagery into gestures made to draw attention to Detroit's plight, the forces responsible for such plight, and possibly the ways such plight can be salvaged. Evidence suggests that the station is a centerpiece of Detroit visual encounters. Evidence suggests, I contend, that this repetitive imaging of the MCS produces very similar, and despondent, stories. If there is so much recitation occurring, then, if there is so much posting and sharing of images and text, how is the station empty? How is it not, as circulation suggests, a moving object? The acceptance of the station as empty, it seems, is what makes its meaning communal. Recognizing the movement of the image throughout these circulations, however, might allow for the making, rather than taking, of a picture.

In *No Caption Needed*, Robert Hariman and John Lucaites write that iconic images circulated throughout American culture generate public rhetorics that build and stabilize a sense of citizenry. "The most complicated relationship between the photographic image and public opinion occurs because images communicate social knowledge" (Hariman and Lucaites 10). The public rhetoric surrounding the MCS and that situates a specific social knowledge relevant to Detroit has been a simple one: the station is abandoned, and so is the city. This knowledge produces a certain kind of citizenry, as I will show shortly, that always seems to be leaving the city. It also, as I will show, produces another kind of citizenry engaged in continued response and circulation of its repeated iconic imagery. The iconic image, Lucaites and Hariman also write, "offers a means to tap into the power of circulation and the rich intertext of iconic allusiveness for rhetorical effect" (12). That rhetorical effect, however, depends greatly not only on how a given agent employs the iconic image as allusion (like YouTube and Flickr photography of the station), but on how the employment of the image functions as a type of response. Response is the circulating agent that drives the image's production as well as the various encounters one may have with the image. "The manifold media and messages of the public sphere cohere not by virtue of their content alone, which is always shifting, but because of shared properties of design, addressivity, and circulation" (Hariman and Lucaites 27). These shared properties, which I also want to emphasize via the term "circulation," are, as Lucaites and Hariman argue, emotionally charged.

> One observes social interaction depicted within the frame, those people are put into a social relationship with the viewer, that relationship is embedded in interaction between media course and audience, each of these interactions occur in conjunction with other images and agents in the media environment, and all this is apprehended through the social awareness of the viewer and the interactions of the breakfast table, coffee shop, classroom, or other settings in which media is discussed. (Hariman and Lucaites 35)

Thus, the station's supposed emptiness is a charged experience regardless of whatever material condition it is in or whatever material items it may contain. For that reason, I have taken the same photograph of the MCS as others have. For that reason, I have felt the desire to participate in this shared experience of interaction the first time I visited the MCS. I was already a part of the circulation of response before I had the opportunity to join that circulation as well. The time has come, as I continue to develop the network called Digital Detroit, to join this circulation with other circulations, to create social relationships with and within the image of the MCS.

Images of Response

If there exists only one photograph of the Michigan Central Station within the mass production process of print publications, web sharing, and imagery, it might as well be the same one repeated in almost every representation of the station. The generic photo I identify, and have even taken myself, is no different from any of the others one may encounter in a book, a magazine, on a website, in a private collection, or elsewhere. These various representations are linked and networked for how they repeat the same response to the same building: empty. The repetitive photo I am imagining is the one that graces a 2003 *Metro Times* story on plans to renovate the MCS (Mullen). That photo is also the one that accompanies Kristin Palm's essay on Detroit and its collapse "Ruins of a Golden Age," in *Metropolis* magazine. It is the same photo featured in Thomas Morton's *Vice* magazine critique of Detroit coverage in the news. It is the same photo that graces *Time* magazine's "Detroit's Beautiful, Horrible, Decline" photo essay from March 2009 (Marchand and Meffre). That photo of the MCS is the identical image that Kid Rock stands in front of in his video "Roll On." That photo is the same image Johnny Knoxville drives by in VBS.TV's documentary on Detroit, *Detroit Lives*. That photo is the same image juxtaposed in a promotional trailer for ABC's drama *Detroit 187*. This photo circulates throughout Detroit and those who visit or live in the city. Regardless of photographer, the empty depot looks the same in each picture one encounters in books, in movies, online, and in person. It is an empty building. It is abandoned. If an encounter does exist, one might assume that encounter is the meeting up with what Augé calls the supermodern condition of the non-space. These photographs suggest the building connects to nothing, it is without relationships, despite its repetitive, hyperextended imagery. These photographs suggest the MCS is merely a repeated, vacant space.

The Michigan Central Train Station, 2005. Photograph by the author.

I say "despite" because this imagined (yet very real) photograph of a non-space is, indeed, connected to other similar photographs and encounters. Such a photograph might as well be the one featured in a January 26, 2004, blog post by the anonymous blogger at Detroit Blog.[1] In that entry, the writer snaps a few pictures of the station's vandalized interior on a cold Michigan morning. Damaged walls. Graffiti. Collapsed ceilings. These are the circulated photographs and thus, encounters, of the train station. To know the MCS, in this case, is to immediately recognize the spacious and still palatial looking structure regardless of the damage found in 2007, 2004, or 1984. The Detroit Blog's photographs echo the textual descriptions featured on a July 2007 discussion of the MCS on the Detroit Yes! message board entitled "What Should be Done with the MCS?"[2] Fire a missile into it, one poster commands. Make it into a green space, another suggests. Turn it into an office building is the most common request. As perpetual as the image of the empty station is, so is the question regarding its future. Both the image and the proposals act as empty references, for neither contains within itself a solution, yet all who encounter the station work to project their own sense of power (what to do with it) and sensation (here's how I feel) onto the building. All of these "images" work to keep the station as empty conceptually as it has been kept physically. Yet, in a moment of contradiction, these moments are making the station a nonempty space through the act of photography. Critics, observers, tourists, and loyal city residents lack solutions for filling in the station's emptiness. They lack answers to their own dissatisfying encounters. They lack ways to respond. So they *do* respond by repeating the image of emptiness through photography (and accompanying narratives and proposals).

Responses to urban conditions are often phrased as solutions; there exists a problem, thus, a solution is forthcoming. Lloyd Bitzer famously posed the response as the reason "rhetorical discourse comes into existence" (5). Every exigence, Bitzer claimed, leads to a response. Responses, in turn, generate change. "An exigence is rhetorical when it is capable of positive modification and when positive modification requires discourse or can be assisted by discourse" (7). Responses are framed by rhetorical situations, the various contexts all rhetorical exchange depends upon. The "situation must somehow prescribe the response which fits" (Bitzer 10). Under Bitzer's terms, the many visual responses I or anyone else encounters in the MCS can function as responses to an exigence only when "positive modification" is the intent and when the situation (like taking pictures of a former train station) fits the response (such as disgust, wonderment, confusion, and so on). These responses, Bitzer's work claims about rhetorical situations in general, should alter the reality of the MCS in some way. Yet, despite the plethora of responses to the MCS, visual or otherwise, the reality of the train station's abandonment has not changed. There does not exist a solution or modification for the MCS, though many, as I will show shortly, have tried to modify the building.

Indeed, within the MCS's origins, there is little belief that positive change is possible when faced with a problematic exigence. For instance, during its operational existence, the station lacked a solution for dealing with the challenges urban transportation would eventually pose for train travel, particularly as urban residents moved farther and farther away from city centers. That lack of foresight existed from day one of the station's existence. The MCS never had a parking lot. Built in 1913 without a parking lot, the station was unable to accommodate the early Model T's purchased (and, of course, manufactured) in Detroit. Instead of a parking lot, the station's designers, the New York firm of Warren and Wetmore, built the large Roosevelt park area, which still exists. The park was meant as an environmental display that train passengers would first encounter when setting foot in the city. Eventually, the MCS's designers felt, the main downtown area of Detroit, located to the east, would make its way to the station and Roosevelt Park, and city residents could enjoy the large green space prior to traveling. The city, in other words, would encounter the station on its own terms. Based on these terms, the station, without its parking lot, would then become a central hub for movement and transportation in Detroit. Like much of what the rhetoric of urban planning argues, expansion (generated elsewhere) would fill in the city's spaces. Yet, the opposite occurred. Expansion never arrived. Movement to the station slowed and then faded. The neighborhood around the station never extended to the city's core. In this sense, the station actualized Henri Lefebvre's claim that "the urban space is concrete contradiction" (*Urban Revolution* 39). Somehow, without facilities, the station was asked to create what it wasn't given agency to do. It wanted the city to come to it; the city never arrived. The exigence was never met with its fit.

The city never moved westward as the station's designers imagined. With the growth of private transportation, the ability to arrive at the MCS, thus, was limited. In addition to the transportation of goods and services to the city of Detroit, the transportation of people to a potentially viable economic area suffered. Consumers could not and would not find reason to shop in the area surrounding the MCS. In other words, this central point of movement never experienced the kind of movement (people, retail, services) that most urban areas need for survival and that the MCS's early supporters felt would eventually materialize. That second type of movement activates what Amin and Thrift call "relay points for dispersed networks spaces, not sites of economic containment" (72). Each area of commerce, service, or pedestrian movement affects and prompts the others to grow and develop. A parking lot, obviously, would assist that process. Without the proper prudence to see the folly of not building a parking lot, the MCS's designers imagined the station as a center of commerce, a site of economic containment. Somehow, for some reason, the designers believed, passengers would support the station through their own commercial activity spurred by their encounters with the station's interior; outside commerce would not be needed. Insularity was chosen as the mode for engagement. The planners imagined the city as "an instrument and a means," and not as writers like Amin and Thrift as well as Lefebvre understand space, as "a moment, as an element, as a condition" (*Writings on Cities* 127). Note Michelle Kruz's description of the MCS's interior during its heyday.

> The building's many luxuries included separate men's and women's bathrooms with attendants, smaller individual bathrooms which a traveler could rent and use to clean up for the evening, a restaurant, a

tea room, a lunch room, a smoke room, a mail room, a barber shop, drug stores, and shoe shiners. The three waiting rooms had granite floors and marbled walls. The main waiting room where the ticket office was located had a three-story-high vaulted ceiling. A mezzanine connected the waiting room with the thirteen-story office tower behind. (111)

This splendor, without external accessibility, without relays to other kinds of Detroit activities, without connection to the rest of Detroit commerce, faded quickly over the next fifty years as its entire functionality was reduced to insular relationships (only those who visited the station's interior). The restaurant closed. The shops shut down. The waiting room's pews were sold off for pittances. People stopped having haircuts. Shoe shines were no longer needed.

Today, the station's emptiness, its abandonment and decay, testifies to that failed belief in the building's commercial history. There is more to this spatial story, however, than patrons unable to connect interior purchasing with exterior spending. There is also the element of response. Part of the MCS's history, as popular culture reveals, involves the perpetual practice of leaving Detroit and of making that negative response public. Just as trains left the city daily, just as the station's patrons left its services for services elsewhere, so, eventually, did people leave behind the station's splendor. Despite the interior luxuries of drugstores, beautification, and fine dining the MCS offered with travel, passengers gave up on the station as much as they have given up since on Detroit. Local commerce, in turn, gave up on the MCS. Amtrak, whose lines the station served, moved its operations to a smaller station blocks away from Wayne State University in the New Center. The city, as a whole, moved itself away from the station. These acts of leaving, this cycle of abandonment, cause many Detroiters to feel for this mammoth of a building's demise. A new encounter, therefore, is created as those who leave Detroit understand their own responses as being connected to emotional despair—both their own and others (including the city itself). "There are embodied actions and reactions which, after all, are usually carried out to affect others. Thus action should not be seen as 'individual,' but as a repertoire of practices" (Amin and Thrift 85).

This "repertoire of practices" can be heard in Victoria Spivey's 1936 recording "Detroit Moan" (written long before the MCS's collapse). Spivey excuses her desire to leave the city as an emotional one connected to the various actions she has experienced or participated in. The train, she sings, is good only for taking her away from the unfriendly people she has met, her lack of money, and having little to eat. Detroit leaves nothing for her; so she leaves Detroit. Detroit, Spivey sings, is a "cold place" that recognizes she doesn't "got a dime" to her name. Spivey walks Hastings Street feeling she is not treated right, endures "these cold cold nights" and after meals of beans and days of being hurt, opts "to leave Detroit, if I have to flag number ninety-four." Her final words after this long narrative is that if she can make it home, she "ain't never comin' to Detroit no more."

One can imagine Spivey catching the number 94 out of the Michigan Central Station, looking around the fairly empty area within the station's parameter, and feeling lonely and blue, feeling a reaction to the city's own despair. In 1963, country singer Bobby Bare repeated Spivey's lament in his song "Detroit City." Bare sung of the thousands of southerners' efforts to find wealth in northern, industrial Detroit, and the loneliness that often resulted from this quest. Like Spivey's tale, Bare's narrator "rode a freight train north to Detroit City" only to spend years "wasting my time." When everything seems to have failed and there is no reason to continue on, he'll put his pride "on the southbound freight" and return to "the ones I left waiting so far behind." These encounters with emptiness are connected to the failed commercial efforts I initially highlight of the station (among other transportation endeavors). This encounter with emptiness continues today when people like me stand before the station, take a photograph, and leave. Our reactions are formed by a thematic abandonment that has already circulated in various images, both photographic and emotional.

Always surrounded by unfinished projects and plans, the MCS's construction in an isolated area off of Michigan Avenue was meant to spur investment and development alongside the adjacent Corktown neighborhood. One project included a shopping district sponsored by Henry Ford. But as with the parking lot, nothing was ever built. Another project became the Roosevelt Warehouse, a book depository located adjacent to the station. It stored records, books, supplies, and other materials for the Detroit public school system. The Roosevelt Warehouse connected to the MCS via an underground tunnel (in a previous incarnation it housed the city's main post office, and the tunnel was used to transfer mail from trains to the building). As I noted in the previous chapter, the DPS's narrative of demise is based on an empty connection (economic support and pedagogy). During its usage, the Roosevelt Warehouse served as the DPS's hub for distributing books and supplies to the city's classrooms. Today, the Roosevelt Warehouse is abandoned like its neighbor the MCS. Piles of unused books litter its interior.[3] School supplies have become hazardous waste (due to the breakdown of various chemical compounds).

Metal shelves have collapsed into disarray. Library cards, book binding machines, beakers, and student records have been left in a giant pile of trash, none of it ever delivered to its intended users. Like the musical examples I highlight, abandonment is made public; in this case, it is shown as ruins.

In this abandonment, education and transportation combine to form an unfinished project: failed transportation. Thus, one might point to the train station and, while also recognizing its history as a major conduit of goods, services, soldiers, and passengers, also note its symbolic role in the city's recited grand narrative. "The city has a *symbolic* dimension; monuments, but also voids, squares, avenues, symbolizing the cosmos, the world, society, or simply the State" (Henri Lefebvre, *Writings on Cities* 116). The train station, like its education-based neighbor, suggests, or symbolizes, potential or what might be. It also suggests a space where possibilities failed to be realized because of unrealized relationships (economic relations between a train station's interior and the surrounding area; a failed relationship between transportation and education). This failure symbolizes the failure of relationships within a city network. When Spivey or Bare sing of leaving Detroit, they suggest an unrealized personal goal; the belief that the station and the city would meet it in Corktown suggests an unrealized commercial goal; its past as a warehouse demonstrates an unrealized educational goal as DPS supplies and books are left to rot.

Empty spaces and unrealized relationships discover exigence and, in turn, attract suggestions: how to fix, how to do better, how to make up for lost time or work. For the MCS, these suggestions have, in recent years, also included public proposals of transformation. A public rhetoric responds to the exigence by proposing improvement or development as a way to salvage the lost relationship. A public rhetoric, like its imagery, circulates a communal meaning. "The image appears in the public media, acquires iconic status, and influences collective action and memory because it can mediate the social, political, and cultural contradictions in which a particular people find themselves to a degree that allows them to address common problems" (Lucaites and Hariman 47). Notably, local newspapers address the common problem of "abandonment" by reporting on ideas to transform the MCS into a major hub in American travel or a new police station. One of the most heralded of such suggested efforts was Mayor Kwame Kilpatrick's 2004 promise of up to $130 million to buy the station and transform it into the city police headquarters (Ben Lefebvre). As I have shown in other chapters, claims like Kilpatrick's are hardly new in the Motor City. In Kilpatrick's plan, we hear the repeated topoi of urban renewal as a response to the exigence of decay. "If we are to truly transform our Police Department, we must give them a first-class, state-of-the-art headquarters," Kilpatrick stated ("Mayor Announces Plans"). "This deal [to purchase the station from CenTra Inc.] can make that happen—and it will breathe new economic life into southwest Detroit." By the following year, the mayor's office changed its position and cancelled the plan (King). Indeed, the plan, like other documented plans to turn the station into a casino or shopping mall or new customs house, was dead, as one inspired idea was left behind for another idea elsewhere. Kilpatrick's plan hardly differs from the one to build a hub of urban travel without a parking lot. What is begun, in other words, is never completed to fruition because of a lack of overall planning, but also because response does not always modify space or form a relationship with a given space, though it may affect space in other ways. Just as Spivey's disappointed narrator finds, these proposals seldom settle before they are quickly forgotten or abandoned. Governmental proposals to transform this space into a new fixed site of urban renewal meet repeatedly with failure. Despite an emotional need to fill in the site's vacancy, the emptiness remains.

Still, photography plays a role in keeping the spaces filled in to some extent. "Photographs," Liggett writes, "can function as sites of participatory reading that provoke urban encounters" (118). My own reading of the station images reflects Liggett's claim. These images I draw attention to in this chapter's opening pages allow me to participate in the station's history in a way that going to the station does not allow for. The circulated images allow me to comment, to add opinions, to share my own image of the station, to make observations. These images allow me to form connections with other commentary on the MCS, to realize a relationship. For example, the station's empty spaces are featured prominently in a series of photographs included in Kelii Kavanaugh's short overview of the MCS, *Detroit's Michigan Central Station*. The once ornate, as well as heavily traveled, waiting room now appears in Kavanaugh's documentation as open as an empty cathedral (102–3). What weather, time, and normal decay have not accomplished, vandals have finished. If a waiting room, as Augé argues, is a non-space, the former MCS waiting room has become more than a non-space for the average spectator. Its emptiness suggests not only an absence of meaning relationships, but an absence in general. That absence is profound when one reads through the series of artistic, architectural, and other plans formulated and commissioned over the years to rehab the MCS, plans—similar to contemporary proposals—that conclude Kavanaugh's short book. Exquisite as well as smart, any one of these plans could have refocused the emptiness of the MCS into a fully functional and dynamic space. Office spaces, retail, pedestrian areas, and newly imagined landscaping all are featured in each drawing. The drawings try to forge connections with external commerce in ways the original station could not accomplish. Even when far away from the station—as I am now while I write this chapter—I participate in both the optimism these plans offer and my insider knowledge that they have not yet been engaged with. My own hopes are reflected in the book's final pages. Kavanaugh offers a parting comment on the last plan featured: "One can only hope that someday this plan will come to fruition, and that these renderings will stand as a record of not just another imagined dream, but a reality" (125). That reality is recorded in the circulated image I introduce. The photograph reflects the station's demise and the hope it will have a future. That moment of hope, it appears, that sense of a type of relationship emerging, transforms the waiting room from Augé's non-space into a space. I will return to this point shortly.

In Detroit, the rhetoric of hope is as dominant as the rhetoric of despair. And against, I would assume, Kavanaugh's wish, not a single plan to remake the MCS into something other than a run down and abandoned train station has ever come to realization. Spaces like the MCS continue to attract topoi of the meaningful but seldom-fulfilled promises to make something new, to rehabilitate, to rejuvenate. The absences and emptiness Kavanaugh features in his text on the station maintain the building's presence. Nothing changes. In fact, the only movement stressed in these kinds of scenarios has been the additional topos of replacement. The city needs to replace the MCS with something else, something grander, something alluring. Not just any plan, as I already see via these examples, will suffice. One needs to respond to the rhetoric of replacement with creativity, imagination, and innovation, it would seem, to finally inspire movement in a space that seems bound to forever remain empty. Bitzer dismisses imagination and calls it an inappropriate response to exigence.

> Imagine a person spending his time writing eulogies of men and women who never existed: his speeches meet no rhetorical situations; they are summoned into existence not by real events, but by his own imagination. They may exhibit formal features which we consider rhetorical— such as ethical and emotional appeals, and stylistic patterns; conceivably one of the fictive eulogies is even persuasive to someone; yet all remain unrhetorical. (9)

Bitzer proposes "the fit" in place of the imaginative, arguing that each response to exigence must "fit" the situation it applies to. "The situation must somehow prescribe the response which fits" (10). Prescription obviously negates imagination. Prescription is the desire to build a new police station, shopping mall, or other type of commercial entity. Yet imagination, I noted in the previous chapters, is an important aspect of how networks function interfacially or via fluctuating categories. The imagination is the basis of digital mapping, databases, and interface design, a point I will stress even more so in the final chapter.

Richard Florida's particular response to urban blight connects the imagination to what he labels the "Creative Class," young aspiring individuals who help generate the "Creative Economy." The creative class, too, focuses on the imagination; it connects the urban to imaginative individuals participating in the arts in numerous ways. The creative class has become a buzzword among many urban planners, for it taps into the ways creativity can move urban projects forward in ways "fit" concepts like capital investment and new construction cannot. The creative economy, one might imagine, could be the most appropriate response to the MCS's emptiness because it imagines a hopeful replacement for the city's woes and asks urban residents to form new types of creative relationships with the spaces that they inhabit. Florida gives the creative economy three main characteristics. It comprises "(1) new systems for technological creativity and entrepreneurship, (2) new and more effective models for producing goods and services, and (3) a broad social, cultural and geographic milieu conducive to creativity of all sorts" (48). Detroit, a patron of Florida's inspired "Cool Cities" program, has received a $100,000 grant to follow through on such thinking and make replacement a reality.[4] The grant is meant to replace certain areas of blight with renewable, sustainable housing and businesses. How specific spaces like the MCS will benefit from the "creativity" Florida's ideas evoke, however, is not yet evident. To date, the MCS has not been mentioned in any of Michigan's or Detroit's plans for spending money designated for Cool Cities renewal. It has not been included in this specific response to urban renewal. In 2005, the Greater Corktown Development Corporation was designated a recipient of Cool Cities funding, but the MCS does not appear to be part of the award's plans. This lapse seems to confirm one of Florida's premises regarding the creative class and mass transit. The creative class, Florida writes, "are not thriving for such traditional reasons as access to natural resources or transportation routes" (218). Encounters in the urban, Florida seems to suggest, are not dependent on mass transportation buildings like train stations. Indeed, Florida's image of the creative economy is one where workers do not need to move at all. "People interact most with those located close to them," Florida preaches (125). People, Florida claims, need to be in seamless environments (work and play uniting in one space), not in environments separated by roads, highways, or other conduits of travel. One would think, therefore, that the Corktown neighborhood and the empty train station would be an ideal mixed area for creative development. After all, transportation has vanished from this former transportation hub, and with its displacement, interaction has suffered. The area, public perception notes, is seamless in its own way: everything is in need of repair: homes, businesses, the station. This area, one might assume, could be the place where nonmovement would be appreciated. The station did not move toward the city; the city did not move towards the station. Creativity, thus, has the chance to remain local and without mass movement.

In place of more traditional mainstays like transportation, Florida argues that "quality of place" is one of the most important attributes of place that the creative class requires. Quality of place, where movement is not essential, leads to interaction and relationship building. Quality of place includes knowing "what's there," "who's there," and "what's going on" (232). Without the need to move, one will always be in touch with other areas of experience; one will always be networked, Florida's concept suggests. Florida's quality of place list is intriguing, for it is the basis of Cool Cities and the decision to invest in Corktown. Still, this breakdown, as Cool Cities adopts it, cannot, no matter how alluring it may be nor how much it lifts our emotional commitment to no longer abandon Detroit, account for the station in the rhetoric of renewal or replacement. What's there? An empty space. Who's there? No one (other than vandals, explorers, and film producers). What's going on? Decay. The station, as Cool Cities appears to see it, is asked to remain stationary while the city moves on. The taxonomic breakdown of questions Florida offers does not offer this particular space much. Part of the problem, it appears, is in the seamless, unified image projected by plans like Florida's, a plan that makes continuity the rationale for living within or working within a given space. A single body (creative types) generates a single space. The process, we are told, is seamless. In this case, then, lack of movement does not help, for a seamless body implies one layer of meaning. The imagination the affective interface requires, after all, is multilayered and interactive; it encourages movement (the way I move through the Maccabees building and its various moments and meanings, for instance). The MCS, to date, has been framed neither as multilayered nor as interactive. Cool Cities may induce creativity, but the station cannot do so, this proposal makes clear, unless it fits into a seamless life pattern of work and the personal. If there eventually will be a powerful response to the MCS, it doesn't appear that Cool Cities or Florida's ideas overall will have a different impact than any previous gesture.

Filmic Space

Creative economy is one type of response to the urban plight. The keyword of "response" connects much of the MCS to Detroit; I see this term circulating within a significant portion of this chapter already. Various entities formulate responses and imagine the MCS's potential, speculating how it can be replaced with some other kind of structure or entity. These responses, in a way, photograph the building by generating images that, the metaphoric photographer hopes, will circulate far enough to make a new reality. While the MCS has not secured a place in the creative economy, it has found itself within another contemporary creative space (and response), film. The station serves as an industrial wasteland backdrop to many films, such as *The Island*, *Transformers*, and *Four Brothers*. The topos of replacement the Cool Cities plan circulates moves from the concrete and steel of the physical station to the ephemeral filmic space. These films depict Detroit, and the MCS, as a space that cannot be replaced even if popular discourse requests replacement.

The plot of the Detroit-based film *RoboCop 2*, for instance, parallels the city's longstanding rhetoric of making the station into something other than what it already is. In place of the station, *RoboCop 2*'s narrative offers to replace Detroit in its entirety. In the film's diegesis, the city of Detroit is in default; it owes Omni Consumer Products (OCP) over $37 million. OCP wants to purchase the city's debt, demolish Detroit, and build the new and improved Delta City in its place. "We're taking Detroit private," OCP's CEO states. The public governance of the city has failed. In order to engage with Detroit's empty spaces, as the film's narrative reenforces, one must move through destruction and into renewal. Even when initial ideas have failed, renewal is still the go-to option. "Maybe our plans were overambitious," says Rip Torn's CEO character towards the end of *RoboCop 3*, a film that continues the story of Detroit's takeover. "Let's gentrify this neighborhood. Build strip malls, fast food chains, lots of popular entertainment." Like other narratives of the city, however, the replacement promised in the film's narrative never occurs. Other plots and storylines take over, culminating in another filmic trope, the final shoot-out of good guy and bad guy. Towards *Robocop 2's* conclusion, the two robocops battle one another for supremacy. Detroit remains behind; confusion and destruction reign. The promise of something better fades.

A chase scene over the railroad tracks in the film *Detroit 9000*.

A similar theme plays out in the low-budget 1973 film *Detroit 9000*. A corrupt local government and a racially divided city suggest Detroit on the verge of collapse. The white majority that once ruled the city's institutions has been replaced by a new black leadership unable to deal with its own failures. The film's narrative centers around internal corruption and police impotence, all of which are racially motivated, and, one would hope, can ultimately be replaced by a desegregated city government and police force. As the black Sergeant Williams comments on the film's main protagonist, the white Detective Chalmers, "You got to remember, he's in a minority race. He's white. And in downtown Detroit, he is in a one-to-nine minority. It's a whole new turnaround situation for the honkies. And they got to adjust and it's tough." The film projects a traditional narrative about Detroit and race.[5] One group has moved on; the other has been left behind. The response to urban racial issues is replacement; one ethnic group has been replaced by another. In *Detroit 9000's* conclusion, that familiar storyline of exasperation concludes with(the same trope again) a shoot-out between white and black cops and robbers in the shadow of the MCS. Through back shots of the station's weeds and exposed concrete slabs, the viewer sees just how empty Detroit has become within the process of replacement. Not only do trains not move through this space, but neither, it seems, do justice or racial progress. The film ends with an ambiguous note regarding who did what to whom; who were the real bad guys; who were the urban saviors. How does the city respond to its continuing crisis? The station has not been replaced with a new mode of transportation, but neither has its corrupt, racially divided police.

As these films demonstrate, the MCS as a filmic space can be placed in relationship to its physical space because of its unique photographic presence. The narratives of the films are not dependent on the promise of replacement, Detroit, ruins, or even the station itself, yet they all turn to the presence of each in order to advance a plot. These items project the photographic image's importance onto how we tell a story about a space. A story of police corruption does not need the MCS to tell that story; yet *Detroit 9000* employs the station as backdrop to such a story. "Whatever it grants to vision and whatever its manner," Roland Barthes argues, "a photograph is always invisible; it is not it that we see" (*Camera Lucida* 6). Among the many things we might see in either film is an idea, a concept, an emotion, or some other force that is not as material as the object photographed, be it Detroit or the MCS. "Photography, in order to surprise, photographs the notable; but soon, by a familiar reversal, it decrees notable whatever it photographs" (*Camera Lucida* 34). What is true for the photographic image might also hold true for the filmic image. "The [movie] still offers us the *inside* of the fragment" (Barthes, "The Third Meaning" 67; emphasis in original). As I suggest earlier in this chapter regarding still images and online images, that the station appears in so many films speaks to its filmic qualities, its ability to present moments as fragments circulating within larger narratives. As Robert Ray writes regarding the power of the filmic detail, the station's "filmic-ness" is embodied in an individual scene in an otherwise forgettable movie (9). Its details stand out amidst larger, more complete narratives. The detail's image is decreed notable by the filmic. *The Island*, *RoboCop 2*, *Detroit 9000*, these are hardly examples of quality cinema, nor are they memorable movies. But the detail, the image of the train station circulated in these texts, moves a viewer in very specific ways, be they to fear (dystopic vision) or to metaphor (collapsed culture). While the film is forgettable, the individual scene or object is layered within other moments and ideas. Thus, the film is memorable for the ways it forges viewer associations and relationships.

Barthes describes the punctum (the nonconnotative or denotative meaning) of the photograph (or movie still) in such a manner; the detail relevant or not relevant to the image's overall meaning becomes the focus of an otherwise forgettable picture (Barthes's examples include stills from

Sergei Eisenstein's movies, and photographs of a building, sailors, and Queen Victoria). "A detail overwhelms the entirety of my reading; it is an intense mutation of my interest" (Barthes, *Camera Lucida* 49). I understand the MCS in these forgettable films as such a detail. The building is situated in each film in order to mutate our interests. Via the punctum, "the obtuse dimension of information opens a network of personal associations and memories" (*Electronic Monuments* 84). When watching these films, we don't care about an often-recited story of racial division and corrupt police legislation or the story of two robotic, futuristic policemen as much as we care about the detail of a recognizable building or city because of how each circulates within our own layered network of meanings.

Such details, thus, overwhelm otherwise unmemorable films. I add to Barthes's observations, however, another point. The detail serves to connect bodies of information and experience so that they serve as a response to exigence; in other words, the detail is the basis of rhetorical relationships. Liggett, drawing from Walter Benjamin's work, calls this connection "faithful witness." "The notion of a faithful witness was originally based in a realistic approach to the photographic image, but the idea of witnessing also describes an ethics in which the arrest the camera makes and its connection to the world are used as a site for experience" (Liggett 122). Barthes's punctum connects him to the image and whatever issue or problem it evokes in a way a connotative or denotative reading will not allow for by making the detail a site for experience. A hermeneutic reading is arrested (what the photograph, or we might add, the film means) in favor of a heuristic reading (what the detail might allow one to respond to). The MCS as a filmic detail forges specific connections and experiences based on the detail's relationship to personal experience (how I tie the detail to past circulations of the image I have encountered). These connections allow for responses unimagined in the initial encounter with the image or the initial narrative the image is placed within. Therefore, when I write about the MCS in this chapter as a detail amid various responses (public or filmic), I am writing about another network feature. I am writing about connection once again.

Thus, a scene featuring the station is memorable for its network possibilities. In the age of new media, Lev Manovich argues, film plays a historical role regarding the origins of computer logics as well as functions as a model for contemporary digital work. What, then, is the role of film for networks? Following Manovich's connection between film and technology, I adopt his understanding of the cinematograph (that is, film) as a "writing movement" in order to expand this last point I make about detail and response (Barthes' punctum) (Manovich 24). Part of what Manovich understands as writing movement within cinema is montage, the juxtaposition of unlike images within a single filmic shot. Montage, Manovich writes, appears in digital imaging via the concept of layering. "Rather than *keying* together images from two video sources, we can now composite an unlimited number of image layers. A shot may consist of dozens, hundreds, or thousands of image layers" (152). Movement, within layering, is horizontal and vertical. In such movements, meanings are found within other meanings. For the most part, the recognition of movement in a given space's layers (on film, in a city, in a network) is also a recognition of networks not staying still. Latour insists that networks, and the relationships that they support, be understood as movements.

> We claim that another movement, entirely different from the one usually followed, reveals itself most clearly though the very difficulty of sticking either to a place considered as local or to a place taken as the context for the former one. Our solution is to take seriously the impossibility of staying in one of the two sites for a long period. (*Reassembling the Social* 170)

For the most part, Manovich is not concerned with pursuing the concept of movement. Instead, he devotes attention to the illusion of seamlessness (as Richard Florida does with the creative class) that may emerge from any kind of layered movement. When seamlessness is the objective, a space's movement among images, ideas, concepts, places, and so on is hidden. The relationships among these things, in other words, are not evident because the image is presented as a unified thing. If it is a detail, no matter how complex that detail may be (no matter how many layers it may contain), the image is always presented as singular (like, for example, the story of police corruption or racial division). "The problem," Manovich writes about layering in digital culture, "is no longer how to generate convincing individual images but how to blend them together" (155). Manovich does not find fault with this blending, and, for the most part, neither do I. Instead, what I realize is that the films I note here blend together individual shots and details of Detroit, like the MCS and other urban buildings, with a futuristic or dystopian mise-en-scène so that the end result is seamless. The individual space is layered into another space, and the viewer is supposed to see this layering as a complete blend; that is, Detroit has succumbed to its own narrative of failure. The positioning of an object or concern, like the MCS, within that narrative is not foregrounded; rather, the blending is. One is made aware of this blending by seeing Detroit as not moving, as not responding, as not doing anything but being empty.

This situation resembles that of the always-circulating MCS photograph I began this chapter discussing. While each photograph is, in fact, a response to a previous one, the pictures are never posed as anything other than representative of the overall sense of emptiness. Emptiness, the photographs suggest, is seamless. In that sense, Kavanaugh's images of the station and reproduction of renewal proposals make sense. Detroit or the station is projected as seamless in each project. Neither is shown for its layers, or how its layers respond to one another or how a rejuvenation would have to account for such layers. The presentation of a seamless building makes the project of rejuvenation easier to accept (but, of course, still difficult to accomplish since the layers are not accounted for). The Barthes gesture—a detail moves my understanding of an image so that I can create another type of response to the representation—is unachievable if blending encourages seamlessness.

In terms of movement within the network, it might be more useful, however, to see the film's choice of the MCS as a networked one and not as a seamless one. This particular space, when put in association with the narrative's other elements, helps move the filmic writing, as Manovich might claim for each film I note here. The importance of *RoboCop 2* or *Detroit 9000*, therefore, is not the film's production quality, narrative, or cultural positioning. For Digital Detroit, these films are important for the layering processes they participate in and help generate, and in particular, for the ways details function in these layers (the MCS acting as a primary detail). Even as the station is a circulating image photographed again and again, it does not stay in the same place for too long a period, despite a film's blending of images. The MCS moves narratives of crime, violence, and despair from one film to another. In the end, however, that movement cannot be sufficient, for the movement will eventually stop; when it does stop, the narrative of destruction becomes the dominant topos. The layers of response fall away; the narrative appears seamless. That topos is the one easily recognizable in Kavanaugh's photographs or any of the other images I alluded to previously in this chapter. Instead of focusing on this dominant topos—which, in fact, is the blending of station and city images—I want to focus on the ways such layerings turn into responses, for responses are central to the ways movement works in networks and how this movement forms various types of network relationships. The importance of Barthes's punctum, then, is how it helps shape responses in details. And responses, as I'll argue, do not blend images.

Responsive Layers

The process of digital layering within the network can also be framed as one of response. Layering allows objects within a larger composition, process, movement, or other activity to be in response to one another. Manovich's argument regarding digital layering leaves out the possibility for layers to respond to each other. Instead, Manovich details the instrumental value of software applications like Adobe After Effects or Adobe Photoshop, which allow literal compositing of one image onto another so that the overall space of a given representation is extended. "If film technology, film practice, and film theory privilege the temporal development of a moving image, computer technology privileges spatial dimensions" (Manovich 157). Even more so, I note, spatial dimensions allow elements within a given space to be in interaction with one another, and as I have been exploring Detroit throughout this book, these interactions alter spaces. Otherwise, if all that is at stake in what Manovich calls "spatial montage" (158) is the settling of one image within or onto another, the space would not change but would remain fixed in its overall meaning and representation. In that type of spatial distribution, then, we would be left with unmoving and nonconnecting topoi and not with networks. In the case of a spatial montage, the empty MCS makes sense as an empty building. Filmic meaning, photographic meaning, historical meaning, and so on will never cause the MCS to be anything but an empty space. For this reason, I began this chapter with Liggett, who challenges such assumptions about imagery. Regardless of how the images are layered, the encounter *between* images produces responses that are themselves layers of space. "It is too easy to believe that the photograph resides in the camera," Liggett writes (136). It is too easy, as well, to believe that space resides only in its fixed location, in the city, in the imagination, in a film, or elsewhere. Each layer is responding to the other and thus affecting the so-called spatial montage Manovich describes. "The reading of montage is not only linear," Liggett argues. "It circulates through while making a space. The reader goes back and forth among related image" (129). Circulation through spaces is what interests me, for, in most popular discourse, the station has seldom been conceptualized in such a manner.

When photographed or when filmic layers respond to one another, the space they occupy or portray shifts. Thus, in a network of responses, the representation of what is imaged or imagined is not as essential as what the responses to that representation are and within that representation what they may be. These responses can be located in networked practices. Nigel Thrift, in his theory of nonrepresentation, situates this emerging way of thinking within computer technology, as opposed to photographs or film. Thrift expresses concern over a current state of thought as "a real historical change in which large parts of what were considered as non-representational embodied practice begin to be represented as they are brought into a kind of writing, the writing of software" (86). Similar to Manovich, Thrift's argument places a considerable amount of agency in the software itself. Still, I use Thrift's association of nonrepresentation with computers to further this discussion on response and the MCS. The MCS, after all, is a building that fails to be re-presented as something new despite the calls for such a re-presentation. Even as it is photographed again and again, its layers of responses (as I will show further) are not represented. In addition, the MCS also has a longstanding relationship with computer software.

The train station's connection to software begins in its main office tower. IBM key punchers and verifiers worked for the New York Central Railroad Company's Auditor of Expenditures Department, which operated offices in the station. A photograph in Kavanaugh's book shows several rows of women working at their early adding machines (63). The entire eighth floor, Kavanaugh notes, was devoted to these adding operations. The key punch introduced programming into calculation. On these early adding machines, punch cards fed instructions into the machine the way current programming allows for complex interactions in virtual and computing spaces. I'll extend the role of calculations in networks in the next chapter, but for now I note the linkage between the MCS and computer technology. Not too far away from these IBM workers, the Burroughs adding machine factory produced early computing machines at what is now the intersection of Amsterdam and Burroughs Streets.[6] Blocks away from the former Burroughs factory, Wayne State University's Department of English, my former office space (as noted in chapter 3) can be found. One can imagine adding, key punches, and computing as a variety of responses to early information technology centralized in a part of Detroit. I hear that response in William Burroughs's (heir to the Burroughs adding machine fortune) dystopic technological future, like that explored in *The Ticket That Exploded*. "Now Ali doubled back from above punch cards—There was nothing but a smear of grey substance barring his way to the towers" (155). Or I hear Burroughs's fears of technology in *Nova Express*'s image of punch cards: "Transparent sheets with virus perforations like punch cards passed through the host on the soft machine feeling for a point of intersection" (72). In the MCS, these punch cards as well circulate with the workers who toiled for IBM.

The punch cards they employed in their work formed a layer of information processing within the train station's early, public image.

In the rhetoric of the network, the point of intersection Burroughs describes does not necessarily proliferate the virus. Instead of the metaphoric virus Burroughs writes about, these spaces come together as types of layered reactions, which may or may not be viral in the Burroughs definition. The sites link up, or appear to link up, in a nonrepresentational way. No one force puts them together, nor do they signify the same types of activities entirely, but they can be mapped as a nonrepresentational network (I am describing a layered space, not a physical space one can visit). From the punch card to the adding machine to the office space, computational work occurs. These are networked spaces. In this sense, the MCS at the point of intersection works to situate Burroughs's concerns within the rhetoric of space and networks. My layering in to this chapter of IBM workers at the MCS provides a virtual response to Burroughs and every figure who has called for a replacement of the MCS. "Program empty body—A vast tapeworm of bring down word and image moving through your mind screen always at the same speed on a slow hydraulic-spine axis like the cylinder gimmick in the adding machine" (*Nova Express* 73). Following Burroughs at the New Center intersection I encountered in the previous chapter and this one, I am programming the supposedly empty MCS by bringing together concerns and ides as they might relate to one another. "The local has by no means disappeared in the networked spaces of everyday life," Mark Nunes writes about cyberspace; "rather, it too has become a site of global flows of information" (67). These local flows I identify in the New Center move me from the station (the "local" for this chapter) to other spaces in the city and to the web, the site of contemporary computing. These flows are part of my attempt to work with MCS layers.

In the layering of the MCS, then, I find computing. Just as I have used this chapter to move from the MCS to the photograph to the filmic image, I want to move once again to another technology space, the computer space suggested by Thrift, feared by Burroughs, and expanded upon by Nunes.

> In its most widely accepted form, the virtual agora takes part in a representation of space in which the WWW maps a hypercomplex network of interconnected sites—a matrix of stable, navigable points. In acknowledging the heterogeneous and heteromorphic nature of these sites, one might also acknowledge an alternate arrangement of material, conceptual, and live processes—namely, a network that is emergent and enactive. (Nunes 76)

Thus, I am arranging the punch-card operations alongside Burroughs's adding machines so that I might form a further relationship, one to contemporary computing. Each movement I make reflects a type of imaginative response, for the computational movements in this gesture can be traced to the web. In this last movement, I turn to a specific type of software dominant on the web and hinted at in Nunes's work, the weblog. As networked writing activity, weblogs consist of large spaces of writing interaction where details—comments, posts, images, links—spark responses. Indeed, weblogs are "an alternate arrangement of material" via their focus on responsive mechanisms. Whether through the blogroll (a list of hyperlinked blogs) or through the assumed linkages of larger groups and categories (political, music, food, academic), weblogs support systems of response layered within each other in ways that representation does not always account for. The web, according to weblog search engine Technorati,[7] hosts over 69.1 million weblogs. If any space is generating movement through response, it is the weblog.

The weblog, whether used via free services like Blogger (http://www.blogger.com) or Wordpress (http://www.wordpress.com) or whether enacted by a stand-alone installation such as Wordpress's downloadable version or Movable Type, allows writers to compose daily entries that are time-stamped, to assign categories to those postings, to archive them for later viewing, and to link to other writers' weblogs. "The appeal of each weblog is grounded thoroughly in the personality of its writer," Rebecca Blood notes in one of the first publications on weblogs, *The Weblog Handbook*. "His interests, his opinions, and his personal mix of links and commentary. These links point to anything and everything, from obscure articles about artists, to news analysis concerning current events, to the sites of his friends" (7). At the very least, the weblog is a site where writers interact with information, both personal writing and writing discovered elsewhere. Such writing may be textual, may include visual displays, and may include other multimedia like sound and video. At the very least, then, blogging layers various kinds of activities at once without appealing to seamlessness. And it does so in a digital space. Whether it has to be "personal," as Blood argues, is not definite. Spatial movements and spatial stories are often layered into weblogs responses.

My movement from the MCS to the weblog is also an attempt to work out the ways our personal responses to things, events, moments, and so on function within networks as encounters. Encounter, while a personal activity of engagement, is, as I showed early in this chapter, an engagement with more than one body of information. Weblogs, too, allow for spatial encounters beyond personal engagement. Just as the MCS photograph that continues to circulate from person to person is framed as a "personal" experience as opposed to its already-public presence in an imaginary, personal engagement is typically the focus of attention given to blogs. "Meet Joe Blog," a *Time* magazine article heading readings. In a somewhat condescending tone, *Time* describes blogging as the desire to create individual responses. "In a way, blogs represent everything the Web was always supposed to be: a mass medium controlled by the masses, in which getting heard depends solely on having something to say and the moxie to say it" (Grossman). Having the "moxie" has largely meant solipsistic or hyperbolic sense of one's self. Having the moxie is what makes the MCS, as an independent body, understood as a seamless image of Detroit projected by a single body (and not as a series of layers distributed by various bodies). When the MCS is allowed to be alone, to be stationary as its early planners schemed, it is not seen as part of a larger network.

Blogging, too, typically is understood as an individualized rhetorical act, as a *stationary* experience, and not as part of a network. In this definition, the blog, like the MCS, is described as a fairly empty experience since its focus is largely the self. Even Henry Jenkins, whose work complicates identities among fans, producers, and consumers of culture through the concept of convergence, frames the weblog as largely personal expression by drawing on personal-writing tropes like the diary or privacy. "Blogs are thus more dynamic than older-style home pages," Jenkins writes, "more permanent than posts to a net discussion list. They are more private and personal than traditional journalism, more public than diaries" (*Fans, Bloggers, and Gamers* 179). And writing in the online collection *Into the Blogosphere*, Carolyn Miller and Dawn Shepherd reduce the genre of blogging to the most personal of all public acts: voyeurism. Contextualizing blogging as a kairotic moment, they see weblogs as an extension of late 1990s voyeuristic culture.

> Voyeurism and exhibitionism have been morally neutralized and are on their ways to becoming ordinary modes of being, subject positions that are inscribed in our mediated discourse. The cultural moment in which the blog appeared is a kairos that has shifted the boundary between the public and the private and the relationship between mediated and unmediated experience.

While it is popular to reduce blogging to voyeurism or belletristic expression, as these examples do, my interests in placing blogging within a discussion of the Michigan Central Station involve understanding how response functions in the network and not as an expression of moxie or privacy or even shallow emptiness. We may indeed function as voyeurs when photographing the MCS, but we can also explore the layers that are a part of a given image so that any detail (filmic, physical, or personal) is not understood as being an individualized identity. The station, a centerpiece of various technological responses (photography, film, key punches) seems like an ideal space for such a discussion.

One particular bloglike space, the Detroit Yes! message board, emphasizes my point. Detroit Yes! is not a blog in a conventional sense; it is a message board. Its ability to host posted ideas, images, and threads of discussion, however, allows for a correspondence to be made between it and more traditional blog outlets. The taxonomic difference between the two media forms is marginal given the overall importance of what each does similarly. A 2006 thread on the message board, for instance, begins with the question "Does anyone know what was going on at the MCS today?"[8] Directed at the possibility of another film being shot at the station, responses quickly leave aside the question's focus regarding which film might have been in production, and instead begin layering other kinds of information into the thread. The discussion, overall, layers what production company may be currently filming, the station's history, debates over the station's proper name (Michigan Central Depot or Michigan Central Station), personal asides about driving, speculation over the future state of train transportation in the state, and more proposals to demolish or renovate the station. In other words, this layering of responses demonstrates a movement of ideas, an alternate arrangement of material, and the formation of informational relationships. Very quickly the individualized moment ("is a film being shot?") becomes a layering of ideas. An empty space evokes writers to fill in other ideas about the building, some representational—about the station itself—some not—asides, wanderings, associations. The technology aspect of this discussion cannot be ignored. This movement occurs on a fairly conventional networked medium, the weblog's generic cousin, the message board.

In that sense, the layering I identify on Detroit Yes!—a digital concept I have borrowed from Manovich—is the layering of responses amid one space—the online space. The movement of transportation extends from the empty train station to the digital space that is constantly being filled in. In the rest of this chapter, I want to layer, then, two online spaces: the message board and the weblog. My choice for the weblog stems from its already-established association with Detroit and digital culture. These already-prominent Detroit blogs include: Detroit Blog (http://www.detroitblog.org/), Detroit Funk (http://detroitfunk.com/), Girl from the D (http://girl-in-the-d.blogspot.com/), and Metroblogging Detroit (http://detroit.metblogs.com/). They, and many other blogs, exist to document, critique, comment on, and discuss Detroit. In the last few years, Detroit and the web have overlapped in intriguing ways. Some of these blogs operate within professional contexts (financial news, urban developments); some are esoteric in their approach (photography, forgotten details about the city); some are personal accounts of life in the city (local events the blogger has attended, explorations of abandoned buildings); and some are critical perspectives (the hypocrisy of city actions). "The interaction between the material, the conceptual, and the lived emphasizes that each cluster of processes is inextricably caught up in the produced/producing relation of the others" (Nunes 43). How these spaces generate a network of responses is the focus of the remainder of this chapter.

Blogging, Identity, Space

Longtime Detroit resident Jeff Colby most likely visited the MCS on more than one occasion. As a Detroit resident, Colby may have had much to say about the MCS, in private or in public. Yet Jeff Colby is the kind of blogger, message board contributor, or Internet writer you might not read about. Known in Detroit by the moniker "itsjeff" on the Detroit Yes! message board, Colby died in mid-February 2007.[9] When I first heard of his death, I spent some time searching through archived threads on the popular message board, looking for instances where his name appeared, looking for the kinds of contributions he might have made, looking for what he once might have written about the Motor City, looking for what he might have written about the Michigan Central Train Station. In his Detroit Yes! postings, Colby does not contribute to the thread I noted above, and I have yet to find his overall thoughts on the MCS or how he might have responded to its status in the city. His death, however, became a convergence point for many other kinds of public responses regarding digital writing and Detroit. When I first heard of his passing, I was curious about Jeff Colby's contributions to the online discourse on Detroit, to the "cluster of processes" Nunes describes. Based on the number of posts I found attributed to "itsjeff," based on the kind of memorializing I saw on the same message board after his passing, and based on my own interests in technology, the city, and writing, I felt that I, like many others in the city, should know who Jeff Colby was and why his passing meant so much to so many in southeastern Michigan. And given my own interests in Detroit, I, too, should have already read about this specific online writer. But until his death, I didn't know who he was, and I had never read his writings.

I heard about Colby's passing one morning while listening to NPR on my way to Madison Heights, a northern suburb of Detroit. During the show's eulogy, I listened to other bloggers and local Detroiters discuss the kind of person Colby was, the ways he cared for the urban space he lived in, and his contributions to a larger understanding of how space can be altered, affected, changed, or shaped by technology and writing. Jeff Colby, I thought, could have been a student in a class I teach. Jeff Colby could be the generic blogger written about in any number of studies on blogging and Internet writing. Jeff Colby could have been the prototypical blogger mocked and celebrated in any number of publications on digital writing, like the *Time* article I draw attention to. Jeff Colby could have been the new media writer working to integrate technology into composing practices, tracking down "data spread across multiple media, scanning each and every text for insights into the world" (*Convergence Culture* 95). Jeff Colby could have been these kinds of images we circulate regarding the web and writing, but he never was. Still, Jeff Colby was a member of a digital space responding to a physical space. That final point is one worth further thought.

It might appear crass to think of a person's passing as exigence for a discussion on Detroit, the MCS, and weblogs. I might feel the same way if I were to read another person writing in such a manner. Yet, when I heard this story of the Detroit blogger who invested himself in a digital space, I returned to this project's overall thesis to consider how we, in various areas of study labeled academia (or more specifically, rhetoric, new media, digital studies), often think about space: the spaces we work in, the spaces we live in, the spaces we write to, the spaces we make ourselves heard within, and the spaces we occupy regarding identity (and even this category can be broken down further: personal, disciplinary, institutional, and other types of identities). In the introduction of this book, I begin that thinking with my initial interests in space and rhetoric as well as my initial arrival in Detroit. At the point I first arrived in the city, what I identified as "Detroit" is not what I have come to understand and write about in this book. And elsewhere in this book's early chapters, I locate my identity in the place I once worked, the Maccabees, or the road I've often traveled on, Woodward Avenue. And even in these identifications I break down further identities of each space's overall structure as a part of the network. Still, even as I think about these spaces, and even as I write to them and about them, I ask how such writing functions more explicitly in the networked spaces of the weblog. Knowing the complexity of mapping this space (chapter 1), knowing the folksonomic organization of information in the network (chapter 2), and knowing the affective interface of the network (chapter 3), I now must shift to the ways such characteristics are in response to one another. The exigence of the train station allows me to move to that response by working with the public response to Colby's passing and the ways responses motivate networked writing.

Networked Responses

The story of Jeff Colby, as I heard it on the radio that February morning a few days after his death, highlights a conceptual way new media affects space as responsive networked environment.[10] "I read through thirty-nine pages of Internet commentary," one mourner recounted Colby's writing while speaking at his funeral. "That was just the first day." Thirty-nine pages of Internet commentary suggest a considerable amount of writing for someone who may not have identified himself as a writer. Thirty-nine pages suggest a considerable amount of rhetorical production. Thirty-nine pages extended over multiple computer screens suggest a type of online writing that is expansive, descriptive, and encompassing. As a rhetorical practice, however, blogging is typically not described in such terms; it is often depicted as dangerous and detrimental to professional identity because of a type of "what you say may come back to haunt you" general perception. Often, writers are discouraged from engaging with online media like weblogs, message boards, or related spaces. In the humanities, "Ivan Tribble" alarmed steadfast, academic bloggers when "he" published a now widely circulated diatribe against blogging on the *Chronicle of Higher Education's* online edition that spoke bluntly to these concerns.[11] "What is it with job seekers who also write blogs?" Tribble asks in his polemic's first paragraph. "The pertinent question for bloggers is simply, Why? What is the purpose of broadcasting one's unfiltered thoughts to the whole wired world? It's not hard to imagine legitimate, constructive applications for such a forum. But it's also not hard to find examples of the worst kinds of uses" (Tribble). In this type of discussion, online writing is viewed as dangerous; public discussion may lead to disciplinary retribution ("we disagree with your ideas; therefore, we won't hire you, or we'll fire you"), inappropriate confession (saying the wrong thing regarding one's life), or simply, banalities shared for no reason (posting trivial matters as opposed to lofty ideas). If the MCS signifies danger for a number of dystopian, tech-ridden films, then blogging, too, is treated as a dangerous digital performance. Blogging is empty, critics like Tribble argue. It lacks substance. Its public nature is detrimental to the privacy of communication. The crux of Tribble's argument comes in an anecdote about one specific job candidate's blog, which is read by an exasperated search committee at the school where Tribble teaches. The committee, according to Tribble's narrative, is astonished to read that the candidate has many interests, from public policy to fashion. The candidate has filled in his or her writing space with far-ranging activities and concerns.

> It would never occur to the committee to ask what a candidate thinks about certain people's choice of fashion or body adornment, which countries we should invade, what should be done to drivers who refuse to get out of the passing lane, what constitutes a real man, or how the recovery process from one's childhood traumas is going. But since the applicant elaborated on many topics like those, we were all ears. And we were a little concerned. It's not our place to make the recommendation, but we agreed a little therapy (of the offline variety) might be in order.

This framing of the online space questions why such spaces would be filled in, or layered, with such disparate material. If anything, the blog Tribble is fluxed about is not seamless enough; body adornment, politics, and travel suggestions, if situated in one space, must be blended to the point of clarity and coherence, Tribble argues. Besides this preference for the seamless, what makes the anecdote interesting is its conclusion: those who work through a variety of interests and topics in a writing space, regardless of the topics' relevance to one another, must be crazy (they need therapy, as Tribble argues). Who, the argument goes, other than *a lunatic*, would post thoughts to a public, online space?

In *Postmodernism or, the Cultural Logic of Late Capitalism*, Frederic Jameson outlined the condition of the twentieth century as schizophrenic. In an age where the sign is under question, where we are never sure what refers to what, Jameson argues, schizophrenic writing plays a pivotal role in artistic, communicative, and personal responses. "With the breakdown of the signifying chain, therefore, our schizophrenic is reduced to an experience of pure material signifiers, or, in other words, a series of pure and related presents in time" (Jameson 27). The "schizophrenic" is not a clinical definition; it frames a social condition within a psychoanalytic term. It is exemplified, Jameson notes, in John Cage's music or Andy Warhol's art, but also in architectural design and filmic pastiche. The Bonaventure Hotel is one kind of schizophrenic space, Jameson argues, because of its hyperspatial features, but so might be, we can add, the MCS for its lack of contextual referentiality (a photograph, a filmic detail, a message board thread each carry a meaning of this space to other spaces without specific reference). In the schizophrenic space, Jameson argues, "we seem increasingly incapable of fashioning representations of our own current experience" (21). Schizophrenia results from meanings forming relationships; from the ways meanings respond to one another. "What we generally called the signified—the meaning or conceptual content of an utterance—is now rather to be seen as a meaning-effect, as that objective mirage of signification generated and projected by the relationship of signifiers among themselves" (Jameson 26). The schizophrenic marks a cultural condition that affects a variety of practices where referentiality is questioned. Jameson poses cognitive mapping as a methodology for navigating this condition. "An aesthetic of cognitive mapping," Jameson writes, is "a pedagogical political culture which seeks to endow the individual subject with some new heightened sense of its place in the global system" (54). In later work, Jameson will propose navigating the products of popular culture such as films for such a mapping of the individual's place in a network of meaning. The filmic detail, in this sense, allows for a way to link ideas (the political, the individual, and the filmic narrative). Barthes's focus on the wayward detail or Manovich's interest in layering without representational reference, too, might count as ways to navigate schizophrenic practices. We also might imagine blogging, as Tribble appears to do, as one such navigational practice.

It's not too difficult to see the anonymous blogger Tribble's search committee rejects as practicing some variation of the schizophrenic. That anonymous blogger covers a wide variety of material, form a war in Iraq to the definition of a "real man." But, as Jameson contends, schizophrenic writing is not in need of "therapy" or of a cure; it is not indicative of "morbid content" but rather makes "available more joyous intensities" that displace "older affects of alienation and anxiety" (Jameson 29). In this sense, the hodge-podge of ideas and points Tribble's anonymous blogger frames online exemplifies a broader rhetorical practice that allows for a type of cognitive mapping. "The cognitive map is not exactly mimetic in that older sense," Jameson argues. "The theoretical issues it poses allows us to renew the analysis of representation on a higher and much more complex level" (51). Jameson associates this type of practice with postmodernism, but because the weblog is a part of the web, I feel more comfortable drawing a parallel to a basic component of the web that also allows for such mapping, network writing. The web is one kind of network, a network where various informational identities occupy an ever-changing space. Latour describes the network as a social process, "a very peculiar movement of re-association and reassembling" (*Reassembling* 7). In this rendering of reassociations, social relationships are not contributors to or results of "being crazy"; they are interests established among a variety of information, some of which could possibly appear schizophrenic at first glance because of the odd juxtapositions generated. For example, my juxtaposition of the weblog with the MCS in a book about Detroit and networks may appear "crazy" or, at the very least, out of line with representational reality (the station is not a web space; Detroit is not a weblog). This juxtaposition serves, however, to advance my thinking on response and digital space for how it manufactures a relationship out of a preliminary connection. The juxtaposition serves to generate a social, rhetorical act. I can imagine Tribble's anonymous blogger doing the same through a variety of posted ideas.

The social, as Latour describes it, indicates a situation, combination, association, or some other relationship where information, when put into contact with other information, generates effects. The social, John Law adds, involves "articulating a sense of the world as an unformed but generative flux of forces and relations that work to produce particular realities" (7). The social contains a complex yet moving identity whose mapping is not always easy to do at first. Members of the social are not just connected; they affect each other, and thus, they change identities. The details, as I have noted, of these affects are not seamless. In chapter 3, these affects culminate in an interface. Through that interface, this chapter has been extending the notion of response. Extending Jameson's schizophrenic, the multiple perspectives, roles, beliefs, designs, and so on occupy in a given space comprise not pastiche (as Jameson's critique will reveal, pastiche reflecting another seamless practice), but a network. Following Latour, one could, then, read the anonymous blogger as enacting a network of responses: the posts and comments that seem to Tribble to be either scandalous or banal, in fact, are part of a larger discourse of connections and associations, details layered within other details, each forging various affective positions. Affect, in this case, is neither good nor bad, emotional nor stoic, but rather, following Massumi, virtual. Readers, and in turn, other writers, interact with those connections to generate other responses. In an ironic twist, Tribble's own online, public outcry against public online writing had a comparable effect on the academic blogosphere. Comments were quick and vast, emotional and intense. They became a network of responses. Those responses captured a virtual state of identity (pro and con, angry and in agreement, confused and understanding).

Detroit Responses

In place of the crazy or the dangerous, Jeff Colby's weblog-styled posts demonstrate another aspect of network rhetoric. When I call the online writing done by people like Jeff Colby a network, I think of specific Detroit Yes! threads he participated in. One thread, for example, entitled "The Detroit Banking Thread,"[12] might offer some insight into how I am imagining the responsive nature of weblog writing as a social experience. The thread begins with Colby requesting information on old Detroit banking ads. Colby is working off of a previous thread, one not identified by its name, only by the poster, "Mikem." "Mikem's great scans of Detroit Bank & Trust reminded me of some of our other late banks," Colby posts. "NBD, Manufacturers, Bank of the Commonwealth, Michigan National, Standard Federal." From that memory-inspired introduction, a request ensues. Indeed, many threads, on weblogs or message boards, utilize the request as exigence for extended discussion. Colby frames his request by creating a series of associations other message board members should draw from: "Does anyone recall old ads? I posted 'You outta know, a Detroit banker . . . better!' in the 211 thread. I remember the jingle, 'Manufacturers will help you make it.' And their slogan, 'Manufacturers: That's my bank!' I don't recall any slogan or jingle for NBD." Other participants offer a number of suggestions in response, including personal connections to banks that have come and gone. Eventually, photographs of banks and banking ads are posted by various members; some are archival, some are personal photographs. Colby posts a First Federal Savings of Detroit ad. Others counter with anecdotes. Colby posts a contemporary photo of a bank at Van Dyke and Kercheval that has become a Domino's. Another poster remembers an Empire of America commercial jingle. Another poster quotes *Detroit and Its Banks: The Story of Detroit Bank and Trust* in order to contextualize the thread by drawing attention to the history of the Peninsular Savings Bank. Yet another poster updates Colby's initial photograph by identifying the Domino's as a Detroit Savings Bank as well as providing a series of photographs of other historic Detroit Savings Banks within the city, all in various stages of usage. All in all, this thread situates or maps something called "Detroit" in an online space. The identity of the space we might call Detroit, however, is networked across a series of posts, responses to posts, and updates to posts—each of which connects a piece of Detroit to another piece. These responses are anecdotal, are based on quotations, are visual, and are connected by numerous members of the network. The networked position is a space called Detroit that joins these users as a conversation of various types of responses. The users' identity exists in the responses. It also exists in the various layers that overlap one another. This layering is not seamless, as it is easy to identify the bumps, asides, non sequiturs, and other rhetorical gestures that do not follow linearly, nor reveal the rough connections often formed.

To understand such a networked position, one also has to recognize how a specific new media writing space brings new types of features into relationship with existing features of writing. In this example, the thread provides the space for writers and writings to connect in order to make a new space called Detroit (a space that does not necessarily parallel the actual city that these writers write about). That recognition is not necessarily an obvious one to even those who work within the network. Threads carry writers and their ideas through the process of "connection" or "interactivity" whether they realize such work is being done or not. Whether they foreground the process of creating another space called Detroit or not, another space is coming into being because of the thread's and its posters' interactions. When the Jeff Colbys of on-line spaces compose, they often engage in a process akin to what Steven Johnson has called "the Sleeper Curve." Johnson speaks to the influence certain media, like video games and TV shows, have on composing and thinking. The Sleeper Curve, Johnson writes, is a pedagogical state that occurs when exposure to mass media actually teaches viewers how to write, think, and communicate rather than make viewers passive and dumb, as popular response often declares. "This is the Sleeper Curve: The most debased forms of mass diversion—video games and violent television dramas and juvenile sitcoms—turn out to be nutritional after all" (*Everything Bad Is Good for You* 9). The Sleeper Curve suggests that, in McLuhanist fashion, media content is less important than media structure. Exposure to complex structures, which Johnson poses in terms of narrative and character development, can lead to complex thinking. The Sleeper Curve is an assumption that learning communicative strategies, like networked responses, are generated through both subtle and overt processes. The subtle, however, is stressed in Johnson's theory.

> For decades, we've worked under the assumption that mass culture follows a steadily declining path toward lowest-common-denominator standards, presumably because the "masses" want dumb, simple pleasures and big media companies want to give the masses what they want. But in fact, the exact opposite is happening: the culture is getting more intellectually demanding, not less. (*Everything Bad Is Good for You* 9)

The Sleeper Curve is an argument for how media affect our understandings of and participation in communicative practices in implicit ways. This line of thinking suggests that reading, writing to, and working with weblogs (as well as other digital media like a message board) have effects in subtle ways, even if the reader or writer does not believe such effects are occurring. Johnson's argument is not a deterministic one; instead it acknowledges how, for instance, writers develop sophisticated methods of expression via exposure to specific types of media practices. Johnson's argument also prompts a question regarding weblog usage: What might it mean, then, to understand those who participate in online writing spaces, like weblogs, as not belletristic, crazy, or voyeuristic, but as participants in an increasingly complex space of idea exchange where they must rhetorically map their relationship to this complexity? Even if they are not aware of the complexity of their reading and writing practices, might a multifarious practice be emerging? This practice, the brief banking thread suggests, is based on responses and exchanges. This practice poses other kinds of consequences when it is put into relationship with the MCS.

My question regarding how the weblog exchange might produce a complex understanding of response is not too far removed from questions Henry Jenkins poses in *Convergence Culture*. Jenkins's thesis is that new media practices allow for a convergence, a mixing of spectatorship and participation that blurs how we consume and produce information. "Convergence refers to a process, not an endpoint" (*Convergence Culture* 16). This process, as Jenkins describes it, allows consumers of media to "assume the role of hunters and gatherers, chasing down bits of the story across media channels, comparing notes with each other via online discussion groups, and collaborating to ensure that everyone who invests time and effort will come away with a richer entertainment experience" (*Convergence Culture* 21). One can generalize from Jenkins's focus on entertainment culture and consider convergence's implications for networked rhetoric, particularly for how this rhetoric is influenced via a Sleeper Curve. The banking thread participants collaborate by retrieving and assembling a variety of informational experiences—from the anecdotal to the archival—in intricate ways. The convergence of this collaboration produces relationships at personal and informational levels. For many bloggers or message-board writers, hunting and gathering information across a spectrum of resources so that informational relationships are formed has become part of the writing process they engage with. Following Johnson, the process teaches a type of writing in ways the writers themselves may not be cognizant of; they may or may not see themselves as building a network or producing networked rhetorics. I don't need to claim that the message-board writers know that they are constructing networked spaces (though, they may know this). The hunting and gathering is an integral if not implicit part of the work being done. Liggett's photography gathers images into the digital space by encountering the urban. Manovich's layering gathers images into a seamless space. Jenkins's web writers gather ideas from the media they encounter. If we accept a Sleeper-Curve aspect of networks, one that promotes convergences as opposed to separations of information, then it would be beneficial to focus on spaces where networked writing generates relationships via encounters and gatherings. In this sense, the weblog or the message board, and its various versions of Jeff Colby, are engaging in and creating networked writings. Such a claim deserves further thought.

Convergence Station

In convergence culture, as Jenkins describes it, research (hunting and gathering) provides the basis for responses. "Convergence," Jenkins writes, "represents a cultural shift as consumers are encouraged to seek out new information and make connections among dispersed media content" (Jenkins 3). For Jenkins, convergence occurs "when people take media into their own hands" (17). While such comments reflect the tendency to hyperbolically or romantically stress production over consumption in new media discussions, more important to Jenkins's point is that what occurs in network situations is a process of activity more than it is a dependence on specific tools or applications. "As soon as we begin to talk about participation, the emphasis shifts to cultural protocols and practices" (Jenkins 23). The act of technological convergence occurs as participants in a discussion utilize the network to share, reject, dismiss, supplement, continue ideas, texts, images, and other information. On Detroit Yes! (one such example of this process), writers integrate "multiple texts to create a narrative so large that it cannot be contained with a single medium" (Jenkins 95). Anecdotes, photographs, stories, critiques, all contain the narrative of a forgotten bank. They do so, however, when put into a convergent space.

Another example of this process might come from an additional Jeff Colby thread on Detroit Yes! entitled "WWJ Tiger's Stadium." Tiger Stadium—located across the street from the Michigan Central Station and anchoring Corktown as the "other" empty mammoth edifice identifiable by the endless propositions to remake it into something new—serves as a convergent space. This September 25, 2006, thread begins with a post by board user Bibs.[13] Bibs alerts board readers to an upcoming Kwame Kilpatrick news announcement (hinted at during a local radio show) regarding plans to rejuvenate Tiger Stadium. Since the Detroit Tigers moved to Comerica park off of Woodward Avenue, Tiger Stadium has been unoccupied. Bibs posts:

> There was an interview with Mayor Kilpatrick on WWJ this morning at 7:50 A.M. The interview focused on the success of the Tigers, the economic benefit to the city and it's an image booster for the city. Toward the end of the interview, Mayor Kilpatrick stated that he is having a meeting with the city building and development dept this morning to talk about Tiger's stadium. He alluded that he would like to make an announcement today and that it was a good time to make an announcement due to the success of the Tigers.

Despite the hopeful tone of the post, itsjeff chimes in with his own pessimistic response, the kind typically reserved for buildings like the MCS:

> For those of you coming late to the party, here's the deal: The City dragged its feet for years on deciding Tiger Stadium's fate because the mayor really, really, really wanted big box retail on that site.
> There weren't any takers.
> Earlier this year it was finally announced that the mixed-use proposal, offered years ago, would be adopted.
> But I get the sense that if Wal-Mart finally came around, the City would kick the mixed-use plan out the door. That's why I made the above remark when it was reported that the mayor was very, very happy in discussing Tiger Stadium's fate.

Like the banking thread, this thread, too, opens up various turns and detours in the conversation. Critiques of big box business, Wal-Mart, the previous administration of Dennis Archer, Wal-Mart's wage structure (for whites and for minorities), and opinions regarding Kwame's administration flesh out the thread until the original poster updates the thread with the news that the mayor's announcement has been delayed. Out of this discussion, therefore, there are no conclusions or final statements, only an open-ended thread that converges with the city's still-unresolved politics (similar to the filmic narratives I noted earlier in this chapter). As a space of online writing, such threads, like the banking one, are difficult to decipher for what they achieve. A post on a possible mayoral speech yields to various speculations and eventually to a notice that the speech will not occur. In many ways, this thread functions as an empty space.

Nothing happens. Yet, it, like the MCS as a series of layers, is easily filled in by thread posts and responses. The discussion of Tiger Stadium is networked within itself and to the city it discusses.

I draw attention to this thread because of how various voices and ideas converge, as Jenkins writes, into one space. Jenkins devotes considerable attention to the "collective intelligence" that emerges from convergent culture (spaces and their participants become a broadened thinking that extends from grassroots to corporate bodies). My attention in this chapter is devoted to the responsive networked activity that takes place when agents (texts, ideas, images, people) encounter one another. Just as the photographs one might take of the MCS do not represent the MCS as a reality but rather, as Liggett notes regarding urban photography, as an encounter, so, too, do these voices maintain the sense of encounter I find vital to network response. Through their convergence, the responses, as I initially remarked regarding Liggett's work, make space. We can call this space "real" or "fictional" without any real effect on how the space functions. Its diegesis is responsive.

In *Aramis, or the Love of Technology*, Latour makes a similar claim about the space of science and engineering, that the tracing of a failed research project could be presented only as a mix of fictional and actual accounts, as, in other words, a responsive diegesis. In other words, only a network response would suffice Latour's ability to tell the story of Aramis. *Aramis*'s convoluted narrative of professional discourse, personal narrative, the failure of a technology project, science studies, and fiction resembles, to some degree, a Jameson schizophrenia, a banking or Tiger Stadium thread on Detroit Yes!, or any similar online exchange. At the formal level, the various threads and strands of conversation that make up *Aramis* are nonlinear, responsive (that is, they consist of responses), and personal (the imaginary characters who speak in the name of the narrative's investigation). While the responses are dense and exploratory (Latour is searching for a reason why the Aramis project failed), the end result of this process is not definitive (no one answer for that failure is ever presented). What Latour poses for a research project we see in discussions of Detroit. Resolution is not the aim of the compositional process. Responses are the goal. As opposed to claims or definitive statements, responses make up the identity of the composition.

Latour prefaces his project by noting that in order to tell the story he wants to tell, in order to utilize a variety of styles and responses, he had to invent a new genre called *scientifiction* (ix). It is not too far-fetched, then, to imagine how writers who are not voyeurs or crazy (in Tribble's words) might, too, need to adapt or invent a hybrid medium that allows for networked acts to operate. Like a blog or message board's networked writings, the content of Latour's text, the question of why the Aramis project did not succeed, is a networked investigation. Unlike the preliminary assumptions about blogging I note earlier, which work to settle on a definitive notion of what this writing entails, networked writing is more complex, more layered, and harder to pinpoint as one type of thing (crazy, postmodern, voyeuristic, personal, and so on; while any one of these may be an active component within the network, none stands for the network). In one bloglike exchange in Latour's text, the Norbert character expresses exasperation over the research investigation's networked nature. He sounds as if he would prefer a singular identity (a scientific version of crazy or personal) instead. "But the farther we go, the more crowded [this investigation] is. Every part of the system is as complicated as the systems as a whole. Every plate we unfold is itself made up of plates to be unfolded!" (*Aramis* 243). Networked writings like a weblog-styled thread are, indeed, composed of folds. To get at the conversation in any given thread or to even summarize its value or contribution to writing is analogous to Latour's narrative struggling to understand why Aramis failed. The task is one of exploring connections. The task is creating some type of map. In any given sphere of intricately wound connections, in a given complex situation, it is difficult to arrive at definitive positions regarding what that situation is, what comprises its whole, what caused it to be the way it is. It is difficult, in other words, to separate the responses because they are all bound to one another. Towards *Aramis*'s conclusion, it is evident that there does not exist one single reason for the transportation project's demise. Instead, there are numerous known and still-unknown reasons, each connected to the next, each connected to a larger project called "research." Research, the aim of "professional" examinations of writing and rhetoric (online or otherwise), is undermined as a fixed knowledge or identity. A networked engagement does not promise a stable identity of one "researched" response.

Aramis, in the end, is not as much an investigation into a project's failure as it is a discussion of the networked characteristics of writing and research. Because of that, it helps us understand the limitations of trying to know a space, practice, or user's identity (like knowing who a blogger is, who Jeff Colby was, what Detroit might be, what is the future of the MCS, or what Aramis is). These spaces, layered with response, are not stable images to be captured. They are encounters. Latour calls the networked research process the "collective drift" and explains it as the real project he would like to eventually write: "I'd actually like to do a book where you wouldn't know which is strongest, the sociological theory or the documents or the interviews or the literature or the fiction, where all these genres or regimes would be at the same level, each one interpreting the others without anybody being able to say which is judging what" (*Aramis* 298). One might say, in some ways, Latour's future book is what occurs over a networked thread. Without discursive conclusions, without dominant positions, responses are folded into other responses, and this process generates various relationships of meaning. Each medium incorporated (print, images, video, sound) is composed at the same level; each participant may compose in a variety of genres as well. One cannot get at the meaning of Aramis even when a number of media (interview, fiction, science) are employed because there are too many meanings, each maintaining a different set of relationships. The same can be said of some blogging practices. Like Jeff Colby's postings on the Detroit Yes! board, the responses are the writing itself, and to get at one or two posts' relevance means one also has to unfold the numerous other posts such a post is in relationship with. Unlayering one post often means unlayering many, many others. Understanding the relevance of one medium's form (text) may require understandings its relationship to another medium's form (the image).

What I am writing about in this chapter on the MCS, therefore, is a rhetorical feature of the network that is also a methodology motivated by the network's framing of the response as research. In *After Method*, John Law takes up this kind of methodology, arguing that it "is performative. It helps to produce realities" (143). No doubt that has been true of a certain kind of blogging reality. Blogging, too, might be understand as a method—as opposed to being only a writing space. Blogging, therefore, is a way of generating identity, not at the personal level, as most responses declare, but at the disciplinary, rhetorical, spatial, and other levels we associate as having traits, characteristics, and features of meaning. Blogging, of course, stands as one kind of networked presence that Digital Detroit engages; its importance to the network stems from the very specific types of online exchanges that are generated around and by the MCS. In the network (as blog, message board, or other activity), response "crafts arrangements and gatherings of things—and accounts of these arrangements of those things—that could have been otherwise" (Law 143). Law, like Latour, frames the response as an emphasis on process (152), but in particular, he emphasizes process that consists of the crafting, bundling, or gathering of relations in three parts: "whatever is present, whatever is absent but also manifest, whatever is absent but not manifest" (144). "The issue, then," Law writes, "is imagining—or describing—possible ways of crafting method, obvious or otherwise" (144). The issue is recognizing how rhetorical relationships move across spaces of meaning and writing spaces (when they are present like a current post or when they are absent like a post's response to other posts circulating elsewhere). The issue also involves imagining emerging methods generated by digital technology, methods like writing as a series of responses across a number of spaces. By doing so, we borrow from Law a methodology, similar to Latour's, that always recognizes the difficulty of capturing all relationships in a given moment of rhetorical exchange. For that reason, this type of methodology, which I understand as related to a great deal of blogging and related online writing, stretches the identity of writing while also extending the identity of any given body of information that is being written about.

Thus, I want to remember Jeff Colby for the contributions he made to the conversations informing Digital Detroit about urbanity, space, and related matters. I also want to remember that, through writing like that performed by Jeff Colby and other bloggers, online rhetorical gestures like response challenge perceptions of identity. The identity of a space (Detroit or the MCS), of a person (itsjeff) or a compositional practice (online writing) are all altered by networked responses. To date, the language used to describe that writing has fixated on previously established identities that are either overromanticized, or as is often the case, pejorative. Neither of these gestures is much of a response; they are as ineffective as a discussion or single image of the MCS as an empty building.

As recent as March 26, 2008, the discussion regarding what to do with the MCS continued at Detroit Yes! This thread, "Michigan Central Station,"[14] is a response to the various MCS threads that have occupied Detroit Yes! participants' discussions over the years. Its poster, Burnsie, takes up a never-ending conversation somewhere in its middle and argues that the MCS was built in the right location for its time. Any talk of the station's revitalization, Burnsie argues, cannot be blamed on the station's builders (or, we might assume, on its lack of specific infrastructure as I discuss in this chapter's early pages). "To sum up," Burnsie writes, "the builders of the MC Depot put it there because that was the best spot to serve its trains. Thoughts of 'will this building be in the right spot for revitalization decades from now' did not occur to them."

The thread, after various calls for renewal and critiques of thread members, business owners, and MCS owners, ends in a link to a series of April 2008 MCS photographs published online by the *Detroit News*.[15]

These photographs, like the ubiquitous one I began this chapter with, are of the station's destruction. The photographs are framed by a the newspaper's narrative of the building's usage in movie making. In this sense, despite popular calls for reconstruction, the building's only prolonged usage (film) depends on it remaining vacant, "haunting," and decayed. It must always, to rephrase Law, be absent in order to be part of any kind of layered response. Will this building be in the right spot years from now? That all depends on how future responses are layered. One could counter Burnsie by arguing that the MCS has been in the right spot all along for it has maintained a specific and important presence in the network's ability to layer. Even as it has been stationary, it has moved.[16]

In the introduction to *After Method*, Law questions the identity of science studies and its "assumption that the world is properly to be understood as *a set of fairly specific, determinate, and more or less identifiable processes*" (Law 5; emphasis in original). The same might be said of the MCS. As much as we might argue that the MCS is identifiable, that assumption is put under question through the exploration of the station's identity within other responses. Included, of course, is my own response, in this chapter, which links to other chapters and Digital Detroit features. All of these responses are bordered by me and the specific folkson(me) categorizations I continue to form out of an imaginary series of connections, often without final resolution. My final response to the MCS and the rest of the spaces I collect within this book, then, is to move from the MCS to the city's imagined border, 8 Mile, itself remembered as a response to racial unrest, economic change, and the abandonment of Detroit. Popularized by a film as well, 8 Mile offers a final space for me to build Digital Detroit. My choice to include 8 Mile, as the next chapter will show, is based on the question of choice and decision making in the network. Decisions, as I have shown regarding folksonomies, maps, interfaces, and responses, always play a role in networked rhetorics, and they often do so without fulfilling the request for resolution or conclusion.

5

8 MILE

The ole Detroit perfume / It hangs on the highways.
—Paul Simon, "Papa Hobo"

*I*n *Kick Out the Jams*, a part of Continuum Press's 33 1/3 series on rock albums and contemporary culture, Don McLeese provides a brief commentary and history of one of Detroit's best known bands, the MC5, and their influential album *Kick Out the Jams*. Early in the book, McLeese outlines the MC5's influence as tied to a pivotal moment in Detroit in the late 1960s, a moment when the city had to choose its place within an environment of shifting technological emphasis. "The nuclear-strength power and unbridled urgency of the MC5's musical assault reflected their collective dread at the fate to which assembly-line Detroit had consigned their blue-collar destinies. To escape such imprisonment, a band would have to blast its way out" (47).

Out of all the decisions to be made in 1960s Detroit, "blasting" one's way out might not have been the most prudent choice to make. A city already tense with racial unrest (and about to explode into a riot) needed anything but a blasting out.[1] "A guitar army is what we are," one-time MC5 manager John Sinclair begins in his memoir of the time period (5). Armies. Blasting out. If anything, calm would have been the preferred response to a situation strife with ethnic and economic tension. By 1968, even the most timid of musical voices, Gordon Lightfoot, had already begun what would become a string of public laments for 1967 and its blast. In "Black Day in July," Lightfoot sings of how the riots' blast led to madness and confusion. "The streets of Motor City now are quite and serene," Lightfoot reports. But gutted buildings left over after the riots, he adds, "strike terror" and lead to an overall questioning regarding how such violence begins. By the time the MC5 arrived, the city might have sensed a blast about to occur and madness about to settle in. With the MC5, the city might have anticipated the decision to opt for the violence that Lightfoot later laments.

In contrast to Lightfoot's concerns and unanswered questions, it is likely that the presence of racial tension and frustrated workers in the streets surrounding the Wayne State campus (where the band formed) encouraged the MC5's force. The famous introductory words to the band's biggest hit, "Kick Out the Jams," is, in fact, an act of blasting. The song begins (as often the band's concerts do) with the bands own blast: "Kick out the jams, motherfucker!" In the age of new media, the MC5 declared, the only way to move from the assembly line to the nuclear is with force (the screamed "motherfucker" makes such a point clear). A blast must take place.

The band's first single, "Borderline," is, McLeese writes, indicative of similar understandings of blasts and power. Songs like "Borderline," McLeese argues, pushed "past the limits of convention, playing louder, harder, faster, wilder than rock had ever been played before" (52). Amid such hyperbolic gesturing ("wilder than rock had ever been played"), McLeese pairs the song's debut in 1967 with the riots that happened months later (and that leave Lightfoot somber), commenting that "with the battle lines drawn between 'brothers' and 'pigs,' and 'freeks' against 'straights,' tensions exploded all over again" (62). Tension. Rock. Borders. Battle. These, too, are keywords in any discussion of Detroit, whether we speak about a riot in the center of the city or the city itself. These keywords form the basis of writings like McLeese's association of the MC5 with the city. These adjectives are chosen in order to move audiences in specific ways, but also because writers like McLeese feel that they are good enough terms for describing Detroit or related activities. Terms like *tension*, *rock*, *borders*, and *battle* do not need further explanation or justification; their presentation is satisfying as is, and effective as is because of the specific connotations they raise and readers identify. As any topos-driven discussion dictates, one must decide upon terms good enough to sway or move an audience. These adjectives, I feel, are also as good enough of a description of 8 Mile as any other object they might represent.

Detroit's best-known borderline is 8 Mile. Also known as M-102, "8 Mile" refers to the eight miles the road is from downtown Detroit (other roads, too, bear similar numbers depending on their distance: 7 Mile, 10 Mile, and so on.). Communities such as Eastpointe, Royal Oak, Ferndale, Hazel Park, Warren, and Southfield share the road's boundaries. 8 Mile is a pivotal point within the Mile Road System, southeastern Michigan's navigation scheme for east-west roads. As I began with navigation in chapter 1,

I conclude with navigation as well. 8 Mile serves as a navigational device; its position as a middle point of the Metro area allows residents and visitors to ask which side of the city/suburbs divide they are located. 8 Mile is also a moment of calculation, for it is often used to determine distances and travel times from the center of the city to a given east-west locale. To travel from the New Center to Ferndale requires consideration of traffic leading up to 8 Mile. To travel from Ferndale to Southfield requires a navigation of 8 Mile's east-west lanes. Such maneuvers are common. They allow residents to establish familiar patterns of movement within the Metro environment.

The 8 Wood Motel on 8 Mile, which divides Detroit from Ferndale. Copyright Thomas Hawk, <http://www.flickr.com/photos /thomashawk/4843132333/> (Creative Commons license).

Early surveyors decided on establishing the mile-based distance as a numerical point between two areas within a space. The "best" way to figure that calculation, they decided, was a numerical equation (rather than a common or proper name). The general category of calculation, in turn, makes its way into various spaces of 8 Mile–driven discussion. Like other areas of the network called Digital Detroit, popular culture transfers a space's significance to a general audience, and in the case of 8 Mile, it emphasizes calculation and decision making. In the song "Places to Go," rapper 50 Cent identifies 8 Mile as the intersection of a decision: to live a "normal life" or live the life of a gangbanger. In the end, he opts to live the dangerous life, staying on the road, fleeing from place to place in order to avoid the police. 8 Mile is one place, he sings, that he might be found visiting while on the run. If you want to "holler" at him, 50 Cent argues, don't look to Sunset Boulevard or some expected locale. Instead, you might find him "in Detroit, riding around 8 Mile Road," hanging out at "one of Em's joints and shit."

For 50 Cent, 8 Mile is an imaginary hiding place, an escape from an intense urban life. For those who sustain a rhetoric of the city's improvement (as opposed to a 50 Cent–styled escape), 8 Mile serves economic, imaginary purposes. 8 Mile intersects at Woodward as an imaginary border between the African American city and the supposedly white suburbs as well as the ways the city can negotiate the two sides' economic stasis. At that intersection, various imaginary projects wait to materialize. The long-proposed Shoppes at Gateway would offer 330,000 square feet of retail and commercial development.[2] J. C. Penney, Marshalls, restaurants, and the generic promise of "big box stores" have circulated in newspapers, news reports, and business updates as part of this imaginary.[3] The 8 Mile Boulevard Association boasts projects in the works, including the Shoppes proposal. Its "Rethinking 8 Mile: A Framework for Unifying Elements" imagines 8 Mile as a "series of hubs of community social activity" that unite businesses along the 8 Mile and Woodward corridor (2). Among its several goals, one is to "open communities to new possibilities by changing the 'mind' about the potential of the corridor" (2). Given the road's tumultuous image within public discourse, convincing the population to think differently about 8 Mile, or even to make new decisions regarding when and if to visit the road, might prove difficult. 8 Mile, as the MC5's "Borderline" suggests of borders in general, or as 50 Cent describes in his plea to be on the run, is explosive.

As explosive as 8 Mile may be (it is home to strip joints, after-hours clubs, and XXX-video stores; various retail and entertainment locations; and the bar where rap singer Proof was murdered), and as explosive as the MC5 may have been in their rebellious call to kick out the jams, 8 Mile is not the borderline imagined in the MC5 song I begin with in this chapter. 8 Mile, though, often attracts similar hyperbolic meanings centered around the types of businesses it hosts as well as the boundaries it supposedly protects. Despite the variety of business along the road, storefront names like "Hot Tamales Rocks Topless," "Booby Trap," and "Trumps Gentleman Club" generate the image of 8 Mile as one of depravity and moral collapse. On Tru TV's reality series *Hardcore Pawn*, 8 Mile is the site of Detroit's largest pawn shop, American Jewelry and Loan, where owner Les Gold decides the value of merchandise, chooses who among Detroit's poor to loan money to, and evaluates a mostly African American clientele. Those who shop at American Jewelry and Loan represent the city's rundown neighborhoods; customers are so destitute they must part with knock-off handbags and twenty-year-old television sets in order to survive. In his 1974 inaugural mayoral speech, Coleman Young tapped into that image in order to situate his administration as distinct from such behavior. Young advised "criminals" to "hit 8 Mile Road" and added to that hyperbole by casting the city's white residents as "wrong doers" who should relocate so that black residents could restore order. In his autobiography, Young describes the whites' decision to flee as a fearful response.

> What matters—I'm referring now to the perceptions of the white people who despise my city, which I shouldn't have to clarify but feel that I must—is that upon the election of Detroit's first black mayor, the city effectively became a black enclave. Given the tradition of separatism in the vicinity (ours being the most segregated metropolitan area in the country, according to recent demographic studies), this meant that Detroit, in the minds of many, split off as a sovereign nation virtually overnight.[4] (202)

The decision had been made, Young suggested, and Detroit south of 8 Mile was now going to be all black. Despite its being black, Young also argued, it would not represent the problematic image 8 Mile publically projects.

Amid this historical narrative of a contentious border where racial division plays a dominant role, the MC5's "Borderline" says nothing about 8 Mile or race. Instead, it reflects on love gone bad, a narrator who still needs a woman, a woman who pushes him past his "borderline." While the MC5 may have had to decide, as McLeese claims, whether or not to be assembly-line or nuclear at the pivotal late 1960s moment they belonged within, the narrator of "Borderline" is only responsible for figuring out why: "I just don't know why I have to love you so." By themselves, the song's lyrics feel anything but explosive; their sentimental lament over whether or not a woman will accept a man is more indicative of the love-song genre than an explosive force (like 50 Cent's narrator who explicitly is pimping and threatening violence). "Borderline" is a song about a decision regarding a woman. When read, the lyrics have no "blast." Whatever McLeese reads into "Borderline" or the MC5 in general, it is hard not to be confused over the decision to frame a simple love song within the power chords and explosive guitars of the MC5's high-energy rock.

MC5 audiences, however, assembled the lyrics differently than one might read them. The loud rush of electronic music juxtaposed with political urban turmoil exemplifies in "Borderline" what many critics have called the "revolutionary" quality of the MC5. That revolutionary quality is "Borderline's" choice between staying with a woman or leaving her. That revolutionary quality is the audience's decision to make "Borderline" into a revolutionary tune. That revolutionary quality can be heard in the introduction of the MC5 outside the 1968 Democratic Convention. The event's master-of-ceremonies, "Brother" J. C. Crawford, asked the gathered crowd to decide what their role would be in the coming revolution: "Brothers and sisters, the time has come for you to decide whether you are gonna be the problem, or whether you are gonna be the solution. That's right, brothers. You must choose, brothers, you must choose" (qtd. in Strausbaugh 89). In *Miami and the Siege of Chicago*, Norman Mailer situated the MC5 at the forefront of the mythical 1960s youth-oriented "revolution" that a song such as "Borderline" is associated with. One can read Mailer's description of the MC5 playing to the gathering of protestors at the 1968 convention as a literal opening act for the event or as a metaphoric opening act for a promising and about-to-explode movement. "Borderline" would, we might assume as Mailer seems to do, serve to speed up the revolution, much as rioting African Americans south of 8 Mile might have imagined themselves speeding up a late 1960s revolution. Mailer's hyperbolic description of the MC5's concert resembles McLeese's choice of "electric" tropes in order to narrate his tale of the 1960s.

> The singer's head shaking at the climb like the blur of a buzzing fly, his sound an electric caterwauling of power come out of the wall (or the line in the grass, or the wet plates in the batteries) and the singer not bending it, but whirling it, burning it, flashing it down some arc of consciousness, the sound screaming up to a climax of vibrations like one rocket blasting out of itself, the force of the noise a vertigo in the cauldrons of inner space. (Mailer 142)

Such hyperbole situates songs like "Borderline" and bands like the MC5 as the heralds of a hyped new revolution because they are *electric*. "Music is revolution," John Sinclair declared in 1968 (113). Music allows, he added, control over "the machinery and the technology—especially the communications media" (115). Technology (as music or otherwise), these descriptions make clear, frames an imagined revolution and is the focal point of any decision to join that movement or not. We hear similar framing when Iggy Pop, fronting the Detroit-based band The Stooges a few years after "Borderline" appears, asks us to look out because he's using technology. Writing in *Rolling Stone* in 1969, Lester Bangs identified and critiqued this revolutionary hype in his brief review of the MC5s first album, dismissing its electronic component as nothing more than a cliché. "In the hype [is] the thick overlay of teenage-revolution and total-energy-thing which conceals these scrapyard vistas of cliché and ugly noise" (*Mainlines* 34).

Neither "Borderline" nor the band, of course, was revolutionary. Nor, I tend to think, were they cliché. The MC5, as various writers' choice of words reflects, may have played, however, another role in another kind of revolution, the networked-electronic one. The MC5, like Dylan at Newport, exemplified the coming age of electronic music. Unlike Dylan's insistence that he or the music was still folk (as I note in chapter 2), the MC5 adopted (or were given) the taxonomic tag of revolution because of a hyped-up association between the band and other temporal events that, when all were situated together by audiences and observers, generated a feeling of something *about to blast off*. Whereas the 1967 revolution was based on the speed of violence (the short time it took to burn vast amounts of the city), the MC5-inspired revolution, writers like McLeese seem to believe, was based on the speed of musical delivery. That speed allows meaning to be extended from the literal (love song) to the political (revolution) depending on how audiences restructure the meaning in given contexts. Indeed, Mailer ends his summary of the MC5 and the crowd gathered to see them with the question of revolution and context. In a sped-up and exciting moment, Mailer notes, a *choice* appears to have been made for the revolution. "The reporter took an unhappy look around. Were these odd unkempt children the sort of troops with whom one *wished* to enter battle?" (Mailer 144; emphasis mine).

The battle, whichever side one chose to join, would not be physical, as Mailer implies, but rhetorical. In this metaphoric border war, meanings and how they are distributed or worked with are at stake. Whether the speed of a band's music or the cars that travel down a major road activate meaning, rhetorical movement affects how audiences, agents, and other forces decide to use information at their disposal. In a 1957 essay entitled "Speed of Cultural Change," Marshall McLuhan calls the electronic revolution Mailer and the MC5 tap into a decade later the "Do it yourself movement." Part of the do-it-yourself movement, McLuhan argues, involves the ways information is organized by already-established "editors," but also by the so-called "non-editors," those participants in digital culture who receive information so quickly, and so much at once, that they have no choice but to become "editors" as well (that is, they cannot wait for information to be organized for them, so they do the organizing). These "non-editors," as McLuhan calls them, represent the shift of control from distributed information to those who participate in its distribution and not just its reception. Audiences who heard a call for political power, rather than love confirmation, in the sped-up guitar parts and fast-paced electronic rock and roll of the MC5, too, were editors. They put their own meanings together. And while all reception may involve some degree of editing, one can argue that the nature of electronic music speeds up that reception to reflect McLuhan's notion of do-it-yourself culture. In the do-it-yourself culture of new media, choices are put at the forefront of any informational moment. What do I do? Where does this go? How do I get from here to there? How do I utilize this representation or lack of representation? What did I hear? Or as Mailer ponders, are these the forces I will accompany in a given battle? These were the points I raised in chapter 1 regarding mapping and navigation; how does a given database motivate calculations and decisions? They are points I return to in this final chapter regarding networked decision making in general.

Standing in Chicago in 1968, listening to Detroit's MC5, lacking any symbolic representation to protest against (like the Pentagon, Mailer's subject in *The Armies of the Night*), Mailer remarks:

> In Chicago, there was no symbol for him. Not the Amphitheater in the stockyards, for he had a press pass to enter, and he had entered indeed—it did not seem as much of a protest to march to a building he had entered already. Besides, the city would not allow a march: one was *offered* then *the choice* to be tear-gassed or abstain. (Mailer 145; emphasis mine)

Inside the event, informational networks (the space of a protest, the press pass, the response to the protest) are placed with the participant (Mailer) and not the event (the Democratic National Convention). Mailer's ironic choice (tear gas or apathy) is based on how the borders among these areas collapse as he edits them, as he finds their points of connection, as he chooses where to situate items within the overall network called "protest." Mailer must construct this moment; he must do it himself. Mailer's moment, evoked by the MC5, is the media moment. McLuhan described such moments accordingly. "Participation via television, in Freedom Marches, in war, revolution, pollution, and other events is changing everything" (McLuhan and Fiore 22). In the spirit of what McLuhan will eventually call cool media, the do-it-yourself movement foregrounds a highly participatory media culture. We participate in the media we employ because of choices we make regarding content, form, delivery, and so on. "When news begins to come in so fast that it can't be spelled out, can't be organized editorially, then the editor has to package it in capsulated form by new methods as best he can, and he tosses the final package to the audience and says 'Do it yourself, I have collected the data, it is up to you to put it together'" (McLuhan, "Speed" 17). Detroit events were, as well, put together. "A big part of the problem," McLeese writes of the MC5 in Detroit, "was that the music wasn't allowed to stand on its own" (85). Do-it-yourselfers in the late 1960s in Detroit networked the MC5 (love songs and all) so that the music and lyrics would become various revolutionary gestures, so that neither would stand on its own as a love song. The music was not on its own; electronic culture socialized it for a specific, urban audience that needed to make a rhetorical choice: the music and the cultural period should be linked. Detroit was as much a do-it-yourself revolutionary environment prompted by electronic music as it was a motor city. "The MC5 weren't just a band; they were a movement, the musical vanguard of the militant White Panther Party. In order to embrace this music, you apparently had to commit to the destruction of Western civilization as we knew it" (McLeese 85). Music linked to a time period linked to a political organization equates movement whether the links are intended to move or not. In the twenty-first century, amid the rise of various online applications and global conditions and movements that constitute much of network thinking, the concept is hardly novel. Various organizations and those who follow such organizations utilize the web, social networking, or new media in general to deliver a message. But in the late 1950s, such a notion would have challenged dominant systems of information delivery, from the library to the television, from the radio to the newspaper, in ways that would have been unfamiliar and out of synch with accepted practices. Even the rock concert or rock song would have been challenged. The borders among all these areas are linked as they are sped up. In that linking, the differences among the areas linked do not vanish, but their distinctions are blurred as each is layered with the next.

Amid such linking, a do-it-yourself ethos is circulated. While a 1960s audience seems to have understood how to link up moments with the

MC5, McLuhan's pre–Web 2.0 vision was directed at educators, not pop-culture fans. A pre–Web 2.0 audience hearing that they assemble the media as they receive it no doubt would have found such a proposition absurd, unsubstantiated, and confusing. The topos of information distribution would have suggested that ideas are created by a larger, better-organized body than the individual (fan or otherwise). Such a topos dictates that each idea put into a given circulation is maintained by its own boundary and categorical placement. A love song is a love song. A revolutionary song is a revolutionary song. There are rhetorical boundaries separating the two. Decisions about information reception, therefore, are easy to make.

A do-it-yourself logic operates differently. By the end of "Speed of Cultural Change," McLuhan pushes his do-it-yourself idea a bit further, emphasizing the role of popular culture in this process. As Stuart Hall would do six years later,[5] McLuhan stresses that do-it-yourself new media is tied to the pedagogy of popular culture. Like the Birmingham school of thought Hall headed, McLuhan emphasizes the need to make popular culture and do-it-yourself culture "meaningful" to students. With this point, pedagogy, which previous chapters introduced, returns again to the network. "The entertainment industry is a huge cultural jungle which we have done very little to sort out or make meaningful to our charges, our students," McLuhan and Fiore state. He would continue to connect popular culture to pedagogy throughout the remainder of his writings. In *Medium Is the Massage*, McLuhan and Fiore explicitly chastise contemporary education, which, they critique, is "much like a factory set-up with its inventories and assembly lines" (18). The factory—or assembly line—ideology of education I draw attention to in chapter 2 runs counter to the networked practices I have been describing. The factory method preassembles meanings; the network method allows for practices like folksonomies as well as the various responses that keep meanings in flux and open to be altered. McLuhan and Fiore eventually describe such practices as "electric circuitry, an extension of the central nervous system" (40). I imagine the MC5 entering into that circuitry as they, too, left behind the assembly line for the electronic. "There was nothing subtle or sophisticated about such Motor City music," McLeese writes, "and it seemed out of joint with the times—too hot to be cool, too AM in an FM world, too in-your-face for an era of laid-back peace and love" (17). The out-of-joint feeling that do-it-yourself information projects produce is the "startling and effective" result of information juxtaposition that McLuhan and Fiore emphasize (78). In the electronic circuit, borders are mixed up.

The circuit. The network. These are terms associated with speed and information. "Electric circuitry has overthrown the regime of 'time' and 'space' and pours upon us instantly and continuously the concerns of all other men" (McLuhan and Fiore 16). For some, McLuhan and Fiore's sentiment is translated as a warning that information conflation results in power shifts. Virilio works from that position when he writes that "the reduction of distances has become a strategic reality bearing incalculable economic and political consequences, since it corresponds to the nega-tion of space" (*Speed and Politics* 133). While I understand the political ramifications of information conflation (via suggestion, concealment, generalization, or other means), I am unwilling to yield to the "incal-culable" dimension Virilio stresses because I already notice a sense of calculation at play when distances are reduced. I see that calculation in the early decision to navigate Detroit's east-west divide as a calculation of simple counting (8 Mile, 7 Mile, and so on). I see that calculation in love song/revolution interpretation. I see that calculation in do-it-yourself moments. And as I also have been describing throughout this book, all information affects the concerns of all other information when space is reduced, but in that reduction, decisions regarding information connection or disconnection are made. A love song affects a political gesture. A concert affects journalistic sensibility. A band affects a city. The effects are calculated as much as they are experienced. "The move-ment of information," McLuhan writes, "is instantaneous and there is no mechanism that can do this. It is this astonishing new dimension of the instantaneous that has transformed our human interrelationships into a pattern of conspicuous coexistence" ("Speed of Cultural Change" 18). The instantaneous formation of relationships McLuhan highlights indicates the network drawing together education and popular culture, rhetoric and Detroit, other concerns with other concerns. It is the space where boundaries break down. It is the space where connections may occur so quickly that the most unlikely of objects joins and disconnects in unex-pected ways. The city. The written page. The student. The writer. Rhetoric. Networks. "Borderlines." Boundaries that may have previously kept such categories distinct now merge with one another in complementary and antagonistic ways. In this merger, agency does not vanish. Decisions are made; in the crossing of borders categories break down or expand (that is, they become folksonomic). "Our time is a time for crossing barriers," McLuhan and Fiore famously begin *Medium Is the Massage*, "for erasing old categories—for probing around" (10). In the previous chapters, Digital

Detroit sets up this exploration of crossing perceptual and anticipated boundaries regarding the make-up of Michigan's largest city and its relationship to digital culture. This chapter concludes Digital Detroit by crossing one final barrier, the well-known division of city and suburb that is often metonymic of Detroit's history: 8 Mile Road.

8 Mile

8 Mile is probably the best-known road in Detroit because of the Eminem film of the same name. The film has made 8 Mile a detail that circulates within popular culture similar to how the image of the Michigan Central Train Station circulates in photography. To reference *8 Mile* the move is to reference the road (and vice-versa) as a type of response (one detail leads to another detail's response). Like Victoria Spivey's "Detroit Moan," a song I highlight in the previous chapter regarding the Michigan Central Train Station, "8 Mile," the song from the film and album of the same name, is about leaving. Eminem sings that once he's "over these tracks," he will never look back. He'll hit 8 Mile Road and all will realize that now he is gone. In other words, Eminem will decide to leave by navigating his departure around 8 Mile.

The fame of 8 Mile also comes from the racial mythology that African Americans live on the south side of 8 Mile, and whites on the north side. This mythology, partly encouraged by Coleman Young's legacy, holds that because of the riots, whites *left* one side for the other. Paul Clemens highlights this myth when he writes in his memoir of growing up white on the south side of 8 Mile. "Like 7 Mile and 6 Mile, 8 Mile was so named after its distance from the city center, and referencing these streets as they stood in relation to one's own home was a shorthand way of making clear just how deep into the heart of darkness one still lived" (53). Regardless of the truth of such claims or the ways neighborhoods have remained mixed on both sides of 8 Mile for quite some time, 8 Mile's status is very much one of the borderline. Whether one leaves one side of the border for the other remains a topic of political, social, and economic conversations. Ethnically, economically, culturally—these terms tag bodies that shift border positions. Had McLuhan visited Detroit in 1957, the year before "Speed of Cultural Change" was published, he might not have ventured south of 8 Mile into the supposed "darkness" Clemens racially metaphorizes, nor might he have noticed the supposed flight of whites to the north side of the road. At the very least, those moments of "noticing" are what topos-based tags require of audience reception.

They formed the pedagogical dilemma in chapter 2 that the folksonomic responded to by introducing the "me" of categorization, of the necessity to include a personal dimension to the decision to place ideas within certain spaces for organization.

Altered "Welcome to Detroit" sign. Copyright Cave Canem, <http://www.flickr.com/photos/bewareofdog/2371009332/> (Creative Commons license).

Rather than employ such tags, McLuhan, however, might have continued his interest in speed, popular culture, and media by visiting another type of filmic space than that represented by the Eminem movie, the Bel-Air drive-in at 8 Mile. The "instant" speed of information McLuhan juxtaposed as pedagogy and entertainment would have been on display at the drive-in, where movies such as *Cactus Creek* or *The Delicate Delinquent* would have played. At the height of its usage, three thousand cars could have been accommodated by the drive-in at one time. Viewers could choose between the film being shown and any number of other activities located on the drive-in's grounds (though most of these activities were geared towards children): the kids' train, the merry-go-round, the kiddie-land playground. All at once, entertainment, as the drive-in demonstrated, is divided among a number of spaces, from the passive viewer (the movie) to the active participant (the playground). Decisions about what to do and when in a given space, therefore, become important. If there ever was an opportunity for a "do-it-yourself" electronic revolution, the drive-in, epitomized in the Bel-Air, should have been its focal point. "Put your own entertainment package together," the Bel-Air suggested. "Choose from a number of simultaneous events." Yet, in the age of speed and information, the drive-in died out. Fixed in a specific space on a space location (like 8 Mile), the drive-in's role in a participatory information culture was limited. The space of the drive-in, despite all the activity going on, was too bordered. By the late twentieth century, the website became the new drive-in; it offered a much broader space for numerous activities to occupy at once. Its borders are more fluid and more flexible; its mixture of entertainment, news, and information is triggered by a decision: where to click as opposed as to what to do on a movie theater's playground. One no longer needs to park an automobile in front of the screen to receive information. One needs only to "park" oneself in front of the screen. Like the sped-up effect of electric guitars for a typical audience, information is too fast for the drive-in cinema; it can only be handled by a networked interface.

The introduction to the film *8 Mile*, a montage of scenes of Detroit (the Ambassador Bridge, downtown, storefronts, the 8 Mile street sign) suggests that the only way digitally to introduce the city to an audience is through sped up moments, fragments of urban life, details of the urban, network-styled interfaces of movement. Watching this intro, the viewer decides which fragment, in juxtaposition with which other fragment, represents the city. In this way, the city, too, is an interface for information processing. The acceleration of information is, however, just fast enough for the movie screen or web screen, where simultaneous decisions regarding content, navigation, media, and other factors are being made. Despite the importance of the *8 Mile* film screen and its drive-in predecessor regarding decisions, the web screen is the contemporary space of decision making. It is the partial interface of the network (the affective dimension as outlined in chapter 3). For this reason, decision making plays an important role in this chapter.

Following McLuhan, one might argue, then, that the age of new media affects the age of decision making. In what McLuhan identifies as a preelectronic state, decisions mostly are made by others; in the electronic age, one plays a more active role in informational decision making so that one works among the supposed "others." "We have," McLuhan and Fiore note, "become irrevocably involved with, and responsible for, each other" (24). Involvement. Lack of involvement. This binary is, of course, a commonplace in much of new-media scholarship, from the "choose-your-own-narrative" descriptions of hypertext in the early 1990s to the contemporary fascination with Web 2.0 applications. Despite any hyperbole that may accompany these discussions, one might speculate that moments of involvement—from a song to a drive-in to a film to a website—draw on various modes of decision making regarding the boundaries or borderlines that differentiate between activity and nonactivity. I acknowledge such modes in the chapter 2 discussion regarding folksonomies. Network rhetorics allow for a variety of naming gestures, the bulk of which juxtapose personal information with communal information. Which tag to juxtapose is the focal point of the folksonomic. The rhetor makes specific decisions regarding the abundance of tags at her disposal. While the tag informs the folksonomic, the layer informs response in the previous chapter. In this final chapter, I want to unpack the question of decision making further, focusing on the role of "barriers," as McLuhan calls them, and how they become crossed as decisions are made within networks. The crossing, 8 Mile shows me, is not a simplistic "walking" over or getting around one choice or another, as many describe this road's relationship to Detroit. The crossing, as the MC5 exigence shows me, is a "blast." And as a blast, network decision making suggests explosion outward and inward.

If McLuhan had been at the drive-in in 1957 Detroit, he might have found himself pondering the media crossing (film viewed from a car) at the urban crossing (8 Mile Road). The drive-in, McLuhan might have thought, is in the drive. In McLuhanist fashion, the "drive-in" is an appropriate pun for a digital and "cool" culture.[6] One "drives" into the narrative, as McLuhan might say. "The business of the writer or the filmmaker is to transfer the reader or viewer from one world, his own, to another, the world created by typography and film" (*Understanding Media* 249). In the media-driven environment, one decides: Is this my world or someone else's? Where does the diegesis begin or end? Where are its boundaries? But at a road like 8 Mile, at some point, one also drives away. The diegesis associated with 8 Mile is that the white residents of Detroit fled to its northern side; they metaphorically drove away. They crossed one boundary for another, this diegesis argues. The narrative offers racial makeup on both sides of the road as "proof" or "evidence" of such a claim (each word I place in quotation marks stands for a communal category or tag). According to Thomas Sugrue, the 8 Mile boundary's place in the city's imagination is so strong that by the 1940s, white residents constructed a "foot-thick, six-foot-high wall, running for a half-mile on the property line separating the black and white neighborhoods" on different sides of the road (64). The spatial boundary associated with the city, or the narrative often told, is that whites remained on the northern side; African Americans remained on the southern side. Calls to leave the city, like Coleman Young's, contribute to this version. Sugrue's historical narrative retells this story yet again. When whites moved north, blacks took their places in areas on the north end of the city, areas like those that bordered 8 Mile. "Movement to older, formerly white areas gave black strivers a boost in status, while allowing them to build up equity or savings to fund the purchase of a better home in the future" (Sugrue 190). This is the story of upward mobility; it is an economic spatial story, a true one, but not the only story or diegesis in the age of the network.

In the network, boundaries, like those Sugrue describes collapsing as one ethnic group gains economic ground on another, often don't reflect such fluid movements. Partly, decisions about one's place in a given space can keep one on both sides of the boundary in any given moment. The decision between one side of 8 Mile or the other, for instance, may not be relevant within a given network. For one reason, speed allows both sides to be accessed at once. The speed of decision making affects the way one navigates informational boundaries by presenting both sides as, in fact, one interlinking side (a song, for instance, can be about love and revolution at the same time). Therefore, network decisions do not always result in moving from a good area to a bad one, or vice-versa. Alan Liu portrays networked decision making as an inevitably automated one in which agency yields to the network's ability to "sense the overall systematicity of work" (*Laws of Cool* 109). Liu writes that

> The essence of computerization, we might say, is not speed, flexibility and comprehensiveness in themselves but what these qualities contribute to: the dynamic assemblage of separated pieces of information in an interlinked contextual field that can be grasped whole at the point of action, the rapid and flexible amassing of information in a synoptic frame within which the *systematicity* of technological rationality comes in to view even as one is engaged in practical action. (*Laws of Cool* 108)

In other words, the entire system dictates decision making at the expense of the various assembled parts of that system. The goal, Liu argues, is to engage with systematicity via rationality, making the system or network operate in a rationale manner (one in which a "preferred" state will eventually be settled on). Digital Detroit, however, has not relied on rationality as a principle of network decision making, evident in the opening of this final chapter as well as in the preceding chapters. And rationality, as

8 Mile demonstrates, might not be at the center of residents' decisions to move from one side of the road to the other (fear sparked by irrational concerns like the election of an African American mayor). Liu theorizes digital culture as the desire to be rationale, to make the workplace or any place for that matter systematic. Digital culture, Liu writes, simultaneously suffers from networking's decentralization of systems. Decisions are held hostage, Liu argues, because the "quintessential practice of networking, therefore, now became 'browsing' and 'chatting'" among the massive amounts of information brought into one space (*Laws of Cool* 146). Rather than decide how to navigate information in a given system, Liu flippantly notes, network participants chat and browse in what is called an "epiphany of dissociation" (147).

The role of dissociation in networked decision making, however, may not exist in the ways Liu argues. McLuhan, in particular, does not stress the "rational" as a basic feature of do-it-yourself electronic culture; startling and effective results may not be the result of rational juxtaposition. Indeed, Liu's dissociation is not the dominant act within a network rhetoric; instead, association is the key method. The associations one makes are the departure points for decisions regarding what gets put together and what doesn't (do-it-yourself).

As McLuhan draws from popular culture for explanation and evidence of an emerging information system, so, too, can I provide an example regarding this point. By the end of the movie *8 Mile*, a decision made by the main character Rabbit leaves the narrative open-ended. Rabbit has just won a rap contest in a club. While he does not perform in McLuhan's cool drive-in, film and space interact earlier in *8 Mile* when a pivotal scene takes place in the former Michigan Theater, which is now a parking garage.[7] The suggestion that the car and entertainment are colliding in the age of new media is obvious by this framing, but even more so, the decision making of that scene—to fight or not to fight as two opposing street groups come into contact—is an important moment that carries over into the film's finale where audiences experience the denouement of Rabbit's driven ambition. Both scenes anchor a decision. At the film's conclusion, when Rabbit wins the decisive rap battle the narrative has led up to, and the literal fight in a parking garage becomes a lyrical fight in a club, he is left with the option to further his musical potential or return to the stamping factory where he ekes out a living. Like the fight scene, decision making is the important feature of this moment. The result of that decision is not resolved. The viewers must "do-it-themselves" and figure out which option the brooding Rabbit, who sneaks back into the city's darkness when the battle is over, chooses. Has Rabbit reconciled himself with a blue-collar existence? Will he now be a star? Is he happy? Is he sad? Is any decision made? Audiences form the associations in order to complete the narrative and thus contribute to the overall network of meaning the film's diegesis promotes. Dissociating from the film's ending, as Liu claims occurs in digital environments (like a film), would result in a lack of pay-off for an audience that asks for a satisfying conclusion. Audiences, however, don't dissociate from the film's narrative; they fill the narrative in.

Rabbit making a decision in *8 Mile.*

Rabbit's nondecision calls to mind the interests of Herbert Simon in decision making within information organization, or what he calls "the pay-off" of a decision. Simon's *Models of Man* explores the complexity of decision making regarding "rational and non-rational aspects of human behavior" (1). Key to Simon's work is the concept of the pay-off that accompanies every decision. Within every decision, an individual "must be able to attach definite pay-offs (or at least a definite range of pay-offs) to each possible outcome" (245). Simon introduces one example of the pay-off by the "case of the individual, [who] may be trying to implement a number of values that do not have a common denominator—e.g., he compares two jobs in terms of salary, climate, pleasantness of work, prestige, etc." (251). While it may seem likely that a pay-off (comparison of values) will settle the decision-making process for the individual, Simon argues that the complexity of pay-off judgments reveal that "the actual process is quite different from the ones the rules describe" (246). In contemporary terms, we might interpret Simon's work on decision making and information organization to suggest that no one moment can deconstruct the range of possibilities available regardless of how rationally these possibilities are juxtaposed. Any number of values do not have a common denominator because any number of values are themselves part of larger systems. Nigel Thrift calls this state qualculation, "an activity arising out of the construction of new generative microworlds which allow many millions of calculations to continually be made in the background of any encounter" (90). One characteristic of qualculation, Thrift argues, is "a sense of continual access to information arising out of connectivity being embedded in all manner of objects" (99). The city, the drive-in, the club where the rap battle occurs, all circulate information that Rabbit must choose from. These are the elements of a larger system, what Liu calls "systematicity," that are difficult to separate from one another. They are also part of associations, not disassociations. Even more so, 8 Mile, the road from which the movie takes its name, interjects more objects of information and associations into the network than the film's diegesis does: the various topless bars patronized by rappers,[8] the abandoned storefronts along 8 Mile, the road's cultural meanings, the road's racial meanings captured by the film's throwaway line for Rabbit: "Get on back to 8 Mile". Each object passes on information (within and outside of the diegesis) to Rabbit that affects his decision making. Each object contains a variety of qualculation moments. The system, in fact, is too big for one decision to be made within it. It is however, narrow enough for Rabbit to navigate within. The system (the space of Detroit) is, as Bruno Latour writes, a center of calculation. Centers of calculation are "sites where literal and not simply metaphorical calculations are made possible by the mathematical or at least arithmetic format of the documents being brought back and forth" (*Reassembling the Social* 181). Rabbit must make such calculations as he decides on his fate. Latour notes that centers of calculations occur where there is a "difference of topography," meaning they are not in overreaching or totalizing spaces, but in limited spaces like a cubicle, a war room, or, we might add, a club's rap battle or a filmic narrative (*Reassembling the Social* 183).

In the case of *8 Mile*, the pay-off for Rabbit may be, at first, evident in the film's diegesis (Rabbit will be a rap star), but at the film's conclusion, the pay-off is not as clear as common denominators within a limited space—work in music or work in the factory—are placed side by side. While these may be similar in certain circumstances, we can also ask how they may not hold a common denominator for Rabbit. Work and music. Detroit and popular culture. The city and rap. One influences the other. Working with one may lead to success in the other. Or it may not. Decision making is not a simple process. The qualculation in this given moment is a complex array of other moments. Even in those moments, work and music, Detroit and popular culture, the city and rap, as well as other moments and states, demand calculations regarding a final pay-off. "The behaving organism does *not* in general know these costs, nor does it have a set of weights for comparing the components of a multiple pay-off" (Simon 254). These categories comprise the systems of thought one draws upon within a network in order to organize and arrange material for some sort of result (predicted or not). Simon calls this type of organization "bounded rationality." Bounded rationality, Simon argues, is a social concern. It is based on humans' limitations and their "ability to agree on goals, to communicate, and to cooperate so that organization for them becomes a problem " (199). Bounded rationality highlights "the limits of humans as mechanisms for computation and choice" (200). Given McLuhan's concerns with speed and culture, then, it is no wonder that, as a resident of twenty-first-century Detroit, Rabbit's decision making faces limits when overloaded with information. "It is only because organized groups of human beings are limited in ability to agree on goals, to communicate, and to cooperate that organizing becomes for them a 'problem'" (Simon 199). Because of its focus on limitation, bounded rationality is not, therefore, rationality.

All Rabbit can do as he organizes the best way to negotiate the borders of music and labor is make a bounded "rational" choice. Simon calls this process "satisficing." "The key to the simplification of the choice process in both cases is the replacement of the goal of maximizing with the goal of satisficing, of finding a course of action that is 'good enough'" (205). In that sense, I can understand the choices McLeese, Mailer, and audiences of the late 1960s made regarding the MC5. It felt *good* enough to identify this group as revolutionary, despite the amount of hype and hyperbole involved in reaching this decision. Given the choice of one kind of climate for another, audiences turn to what is good enough. If they were to embrace the rational, on the other hand, they might reject the hyperbolic in favor of a calm, level-headed response. Audiences of the 1960s chose the hyperbolic because it resulted in a good-enough state. In other words, audiences chose between a group of disheveled kids playing guitars and the moment Mailer describes as choosing "the candidate least popular and least qualified by strength, dignity, or imagination to lead"

(145). Given that choice, even when framed in exaggerated manners, the MC5 seemed good enough. Even after a cathartic victory that concludes a tense and emotional experience of having his personal life mocked in a rap battle in front of a hostile audience, walking away into the night seems good enough for Rabbit.

As this chapter argues, 8 Mile is the networked principle of organization whose goal of action is "good enough." Good-enough moments appear when various elements networked within a decision are not common and when they do not necessarily point to rational outcomes. Their juxtaposition or association for a pay-off results not in a value of one or the other but instead in the "good-enough" moment. The moment when Rabbit cannot decide which choice will maximize his financial success and settles instead on the good-enough option of the status quo (no final decision): This is the network moment of good enough. Good enough may feel like an odd trait of network thinking or even a contradiction given the hype often attributed to new media and networks. Good-enough's importance, however, results from the complexity of network borderlines, fuzzy areas of connectivity that are not clearly demarcated (such as the meaning of a rock song or which side of a road is populated by a specific ethnic group). Because of the limitations that exist when navigating these types of social spaces, networks rely on good-enough moments of decision making in order to avoid what Latour calls "the myth of progress" (*Pandora's Hope* 199). The role of good-enough, therefore, is to not frame organization in the network as a "better" or "more advanced" state.

I extend the good-enough gesture satisficing introduces into organization theory in order to conclude without a call for something better, more productive, or final. In my final discussion of 8 Mile and Digital Detroit, I want to avoid the myth of progress popular in many writings on networks, new media, and technology. Digital Detroit, after all, is not a project designed to replicate the topos of rejuvenation. William Mitchell, whose work has informed various parts of my project, for instance, concludes *City of Bits* by claiming that networks will provide a more opportune future.

> Networks at these different levels will all have to link up somehow; the body net will be connected to the building net, the building net to the community net, and the community net to the global net. From gesture sensors worn on our bodies to the worldwide infrastructure of communications satellites and long-distance fiber, the elements of the bitsphere will finally come together to form one densely interwoven system within which the knee bone is connected to the I-balm. (172–73)

In this prediction of the computerized future, Mitchell does not turn to the good-enough dimension of networks. His framing of new media is that network culture will inevitably become a "good." In a sense, Mitchell has framed new media the same way Alan Liu does, only with a different outcome. Neither position (glorious or impoverished future) speaks to what the network shows me. If anything, these value-based decisions regarding network thinking mirror the topoi-bound thinking I have tried to disengage from. My final exploration of one of Detroit's spaces, therefore, is not a return to the very calls of rebuilding and rehabilitation I have been moving away from throughout this book. The crossing of boundaries networks support promises none of these moments that tend to follow a rational decision, like improving a street, remodeling a neighborhood, or investing capital. Instead, network borders are crossed with satisficing motives. To provide the first example of this process, I continue with the themes of speed, popular culture, and music I have begun with in this chapter by returning to Detroit's most famous 1960s band, the MC5, for another short discussion.

Creem

Even as I conclude this book with attention to 8 Mile and decision making, I cross a stylistic border by pausing to reflect on a personal anecdote. In various parts of this book, I pose speculative gestures as central to network decision making. These speculations allow me room to move through a network of meanings so that I may find and create connections among spaces of meaning that feel right or good enough. Such is partly the nature of network decision making; it allows for personalized rhetorical arrangements, many of which challenge or do not correspond to what has become familiar in print culture. As I organize information, I discover connections, some of which emerge from initial speculations rather than from concrete evidence or causality. As Ulmer writes, "Electronic learning is more like discovery than proof" (*Heuretics* 56). These connections feel, for me, good enough, because my intuition is that they may lead to another spatial meaning, that they may allow me to discover what I didn't know, that they may allow me a de Certeau–motivated rhetorical production "whether by making choices among the signifiers of the spatial 'language' or by displacing them through the use [I] make of them" ("Walking" 98–99).

One of those speculations belongs in my childhood. In 1980, as a ten-year-old boy in a Miami suburb far from Detroit, Michigan, I read *Creem* magazine. *Creem* was a major rock magazine published in Detroit. It published writings by, among others, Lester Bangs and Dave Marsh. In honor of the magazine's biweekly contributions to my growing knowledge of rock and roll, I would rip pages from each issue and post them all over my walls. In that sense, I created a filing system outside of the confines of the bounded publication. On the walls of my room, I generated my own information system, my own system of spatial arrangement. Keith Richards was placed above one window, Gene Simmons below another, Ted Nugent next to another. My information was tagged by celebrity figures. Even more so, I was organizing information with rock-and-roll magazines; that is, I used popular culture to understand the world around me. In "A Quick Trip through My Adolescence," *Creem* writer Lester Bangs remembers his own childhood similarly. In a discussion with a college professor, Bangs asks his teacher how, given the demands of teaching, he could keep up with his own work, the news, and the latest magazines. After noting how he divides time for the first two items, the professor responds by asking Bangs a question. "And magazines and all that sort of thing . . . do you *read* magazines?" Bangs responds in the affirmative.

> I thought longingly of my weekly comic book, *Life*, of my always irresistible *Time* and *Newsweek* which I hated and read with some mad compulsion almost weekly, of my twice-a-month *Beat* and my monthly *Hit Parade*, both rock 'n' roll rags and both absolutely essential, I thought of the weekly hippie papers which were my life's blood and the time, the *East Village Other*, the L.A. *Free Press*, and the San Francisco *Oracle*. (*Mainlines* 20)

Bangs struggles with the decision to not study literature, as his professor did, while preferring to concentrate on popular writings and imagery. Bangs's conclusion is that such popular readings helped him "fuck up before we could stand up, and nothing was more relevant than the apparently irrelevant" (*Mainlines* 22). Nothing, then, was more satisficing than the everyday. Bangs's system of information organization relied on a network of magazine publications that focused on the everyday: entertainment, news, local events, and music. Sorting the legitimacy or authenticity of *Hit Parade* from the *Free Press* did not matter to Bangs as he constructed his own information system. The connection between the two types of publications was not based on a value judgment of one over the other, but rather on the overall system created from all of these publications functioning together.

For me, a kid in suburban Miami, nothing was more satisficing than the everyday events, moments, and interests of popular music. Little did I know at the time that Boy Howdy, the *Creem* logo and focal point of my interests, was a Detroit icon. To me, he was just a silly beer shaped logo. *Creem*, based in Detroit in the 1970s and 1980s, epitomized border-music journalism, a journalism that tried to integrate the everyday into industry coverage. The paparazzi of *Hit Parade* and the serious local reporting of the *Free Press* could be claimed as influences on *Creem*'s style. Part humor, part reporting, part criticism, part fan magazine, *Creem* bore little resemblance to other, and more serious commercial music publications like *Circus* or *Rolling Stone*. *Creem* laughed at its readers as it also laughed at itself, the industry it was a part of, and the city it was housed in. Lester Bangs, writing in *Creem* in 1970, summed up the experience as one where the writers "set their audiences up just this way, externalizing and magnifying their secret core of sickness which is reflected in the geeks they mock and the lurid fantasies they consume, just as our deepest fears and prejudices script the jokes we tell each other" (*Psychotic Reactions* 53). The decision to publish *Creem* in, of all places, Detroit, Michigan, stemmed from no rational move. New York or Los Angeles, two major cities for musical production and publishing, would have been more logical choices, for they offered the atmosphere, talent, and finance that Detroit could not. A city partly burned and largely abandoned by both automotive production and the music business (Motown would leave Detroit in 1972), Detroit seemed far removed from the mainstream music scene. It seemed, at best, *good enough* as a space to write about rock and roll. The decision to work out of Detroit, we might imagine, was a bounded one.

"Nothing was more relevant than the apparently irrelevant." The author at fifteen in a "satisficing" rock-and-roll moment. The decision to include the photo is also the decision to accept self-mockery as *Creem* would teach me to do.

"The only real hope is Detroit," Bangs wrote as if in response to such an argument, "where the kids take a low of downs and dig down bands but at LEAST there's no folkie scene and lots of people still care about get down gutbucket rock 'n' roll passionately because it takes the intolerableness of Detroit life and channels it into a form of strength and survival with humor and much of the energy claimed" (*Psychotic Reactions* 69). Bangs's humor and critique, like his initial interest in magazines, is one that organizes the body of information we tag "rock 'n' roll" as something that is "good enough." Rejecting superstars, glitz, and youthful romanticism, Bangs wanted readers to stop treating rock with "any seriousness or respect at all and just recognize the fact that it's nothing but a Wham-O toy to bash around as you please in the nursery, it's nothing but a goddam Bonusburger so just gobble the stupid thing and burp and go for the next one tomorrow" (*Psychotic Reactions* 74). To reach this level of good enough, Bangs altered the topoi of rock and of Detroit.

If any Detroit band carried the topos of seriousness, it was the MC5. As I argue in the beginning of this chapter, McLeese attributes to the MC5 such seriousness, writing that they were the "one band" who "would transform itself into myth, embodying the chaos of a cultural uprising for generations to come" (10). As if writing against this hyperbolic gesturing, Dave Marsh echoes Bangs's disgust with the topos of the serious act and the serious critic. Marsh dismisses the "revolutionary" rhetoric writers like McLeese associate with the band.

> To anyone who is familiar with the first album, the Five's political premise would seem to be musical, in the first place, not rhetorical. They weren't talking revolution, they were making it (as far as they were concerned), and the only 'political' song they cared to put on *Kick out the Jams* was John Lee Hooker's 'Motor City Is Burning.' And if that makes a Marxist revolutionary, then both Hooker and Gordon Lightfoot can be hung on your bedroom wall next to Mao and Huey. Marsh 38)

The topos of revolution, as Marsh frames it, resembles that of the networked future Mitchell proclaims. Both promise something better, something that is progressive, something that will liberate, and neither tends to deliver on the promise. Instead of a fulfilled promise, good-enough states emerge out of network situations. We could argue, for instance, that along the same lines as Marsh's suspicion of the MC5, Rabbit, at the end of *8 Mile*, seems disenchanted with the promise that rap will bring a better future and, therefore, he returns to the good-enough state of factory work, or, at the very least, city life. The promise of "something better" does not translate as actual improvement or progress.

It is not odd that do-it-yourself 1960s audiences yearned for something better and looked to revolution as the answer. Nor is it odd that contemporary Detroit critics and residents yearn for something better to finally happen in their city. Nor is it odd for the 8 Mile Boulevard Association to imagine the road's intersection at Woodward as a space on the verge of a revolutionary improvement, to new shopping. Nor is it odd to contextualize Detroit with revolutionary gestures like the MC5, the 1967 riots, or a networked future. Revolution, the urban, and technology often become hyperlinked in various discussions. Henri Lefebvre, after all, situated decision making and the urban in terms of revolutionary struggle and the stage that will follow the industrial when the revolution is accomplished.

> The revolutionary transformation of society has industrial production as ground and lever. This is why it had to be shown that the urban centre of decision-making can no longer consider itself in the present society (of neo-capitalism or of monopoly capitalism associated to the State), outside other means of production, their property and their management. Only the taking in charge by the working class of planning and its political agenda can profoundly modify social life and open another era: that of socialism in neo-capitalist societies. (*Writings on Cities* 179)

Lefebvre, we might argue, is merely repeating a commonplace regarding space and worker revolution. In 1963, Malcolm X shifted the worker topos associated with urban decision making that Lefebvre highlights to the topos of race and revolution; he did so in Detroit. "Message to the Grassroots," Malcolm X's speech on this issue, was delivered at Cobo Hall in the same year the MC5 formed. "Message to the Grassroots" is a speech concerned with decision making, directed to a mostly working-class audience of Detroit African Americans. The speech asks its audience to question why they should engage with revolution and makes race the focus of all revolutionary decisions. "I would like to make a few comments concerning the difference between the black revolution and the Negro revolution. There's a difference. Are they both the same? And if they're not, what is the difference? What is the difference between a black revolution and a Negro revolution? First, what is a revolution?" In chapter 2, I noted another event at Cobo Hall, Bob Dylan's singing of "Masters of War," a song that focuses on a revolution against the military industrial complex. One way to address these moments of revolution and how they relate to a networked rhetoric is to identify their connection to a Detroit tradition of *choosing* subversion or resistance as response mechanisms when confronted with various difficult problems or conflicts. Such is the gesture Dan Georgakas and Marvin Surkin choose in their collection of stories about Detroit workers. The movement known as "Detroit Revolutionaries," they argue, "attempted to integrate within itself all the dissident threads of the rebellious sixties in order to create a network of insurgent power comparable to the network of established power" (5). Indeed, every story Georgakas and Surkin present in their study is a revolutionary one, a rebellion against some kind of established order in the hope that a new political decision will be made, one that will improve the city's race and labor relations. This revolutionary framing of the city can be extended to the founding of the White Panther Party just outside of Wayne State University in the Cass Corridor by John Sinclair (the MC5's first manager) or to Norman Mailer's watching the MC5 play at the Chicago Democratic Convention in 1968, deciding that he "would probably not vote—not unless it was for Eldridge Cleaver" (Mailer 223).

Malcolm X's Detroit-delivered topos of revolution belongs in that tradition as well. "A revolution is bloody. Revolution is hostile. Revolution knows no compromise. Revolution overturns and destroys everything that gets in its way" (Malcolm X). As a film, *8 Mile*—being about a poor white singer subverting the black tradition of hip hop by destroying other rappers in a battle without compromise (anything can be said against your opponent)—belongs in that tradition. These traditions, though, are limited when decision making functions as hyperbole. I find all of these rhetorical exchanges too dependent on this gesture of exaggeration. The same hyperbole is heard in Malcolm X's speech when he argues against civil rights by associating civil-rights leaders with slave mentality: "These Negroes aren't asking for no nation. They're trying to crawl back on the plantation." The same hyperbole is there in Rabbit's disdain for success. The same hyperbole is there in the MC5. That same hyperbole is what *Creem* dismissed.

Hyperbole is not vital to networked decision making because it focuses too strongly on the fate of a situation being better or progressive. In the hyperbole of a revolutionary rhetoric—particularly as it is tied to the city—a situation, condition, or problem is exaggerated so that something "better" might be established. When John Watson founded the *Inner City Voice* newspaper on the Wayne State campus in 1967, he, too, embraced hyperbolic rhetoric as the solution to the various practices that—when networked—create a moment such as racism, the riots, or something similar. Watson, like the MC5, embraced the exaggerated gesture of "the blast." Only Watson's hyperbole, like that of others around him, did not recognize its position within a larger network of meaning. "Michigan Slavery," the paper's first headline read below a masthead that proclaimed "Voice of a Revolution" (Georgakas and Surkin 16). Reading these headlines, one could have been hearing Malcolm X or listening to Norman Mailer; any of these moments places a decision within the same type of framework, one in which a moment—whatever its related meanings might reveal—is tagged as revolution. Hyperbole, through its emphasis on improvement (or worsening), ignores the collective agents involved in decision making. Obviously, we want to improve racial relations in any given space. Among these various revolutionary gestures I draw attention to (the worker, networked future, music, Malcolm X), however, the hyperbolic gesturing does not recognize the collective, the gathering of items like those that Bangs gathered as a youth or that I have been gathering throughout the preceding chapters. Each member of that collection may not recognize the others (Watson, for instance, may recognize his masthead as connected only to Malcolm X and not other temporal or spatial moments), but they are all in the same collective assemblage. Declaring "revolution" on its own, a declaration like that of Watson's reflects a nonnetworked decision. Latour defines the collective in terms other than revolutionary; he uses the language of conversation (the focus point of the previous chapter's final section on weblogs and message boards). Conversation is not a negative feature the way Liu frames chatting and related networked conversations. "The only way to recognize the 'citizenry' within the collective that may be relevant for public life," Latour argues, "is to define the collective as an assembly of beings *capable of speaking*" (*Politics of Nature* 62). Capability is agency. Potentiality is agency. Satisficing, the feeling of good enough, is one kind of potentiality regarding networked decision making because it has not yet settled on the outcome of the decision (better or worse, revolution or capitulation); rather it allows the elements collected to speak with one another. In chapter 2, I also utilized the concept of capability to imagine Dylan at Cobo Hall. In that brief digital diegesis, I engaged with what never occurred (a folksonomic Dylan performance) by forming a fictive conversation with the various items my research has presented to me. I also allowed those items to speak with each other.

A revolution, despite the hyperbole relied upon over the years, never did occur in Detroit, at 8 Mile, at Cobo, or anywhere else in southeastern

Michigan. *Conversations* about revolution did, of course, occur. Yet capability or potentiality was not enacted because the topoi of Detroit were not and still have not been allowed *to be capable* of speaking (as I try to make them do in this book), nor have they been allowed to be capable of speaking with each other. Whatever has been rhetorically circulated regarding revolution, Detroit has remained in the capitalist system it always belonged within, and the city has participated in various democratic processes like any other city in the nation, sometimes prospering (if only briefly) and sometimes failing (like other cities).[9] A capability has been neither enacted nor moved the urban space's position.

Hyperbole is the rhetorical gesture of what has not happened yet. The gesture exaggerates a story or situation, much as my own diegesis of Dylan did as well, in the hopes of finding the right "fit" to a problematic rhetorical situation. Hyperbole, however, does not need to promise a better situation, as revolutionary rhetorics do, nor does it need to be considered entirely irrelevant to networked rhetorics. Its presence in this part of Digital Detroit *tells* me to use it regardless of its problematic position in Detroit discourse. Victor Vitanza writes that hyperbolic rhetoric can produce what he calls "curative fiction," "comic jabs against the dominant tragic, sickly philosophical view of things" (56). The curative fiction, like the digital diegesis, does not define a philosophical topos such as revolution because its intent is to bring "about the liberation from the hierarchically arranged prevailing 'truth'" (Vitanza 56). The so-called "truth," that class, race, or even musical revolution will decide the progress of the urban, is a failed gesture. If anyone, therefore, was projecting revolution or mythic status in 1960s Detroit, *Creem* insisted, it wasn't the MC5. Revolution, *Creem* wrote, was too serious a topos, and finding a fit to the exigence of that topos, the magazine argued, was not the best response to the problems of the 1960s. Curative fiction, as we might imagine *Creem* performing it, was a satisficing response for the magazine. As Michael Kramer writes, "The key to *Creem*, and its larger significance to the story of rock music and the counterculture, was that the publication 'struggled for fun' with a mixture of affection and wit that the magazine linked discursively to its Detroit locale" (45–46). The *Creem* struggle was based on fun, not fighting. It was the struggle for an exaggeration without promise. It was the struggle for good enough, not revolution. It was the struggle for, what Barthes might call pleasure, or what I identified in chapter 3 as a bloc of sensations. Pleasure, in decision making, is not a trivial moment of enjoyment, but rather can be found within associations, capability, humor, and other spaces of meaning that interact.

Diegetic Spaces: The Good-Enough Diegesis

Part of that pleasure is found in location choice, or in finding the appropriate space. While its locale was Detroit, *Creem* was not published on 8 Mile. Instead, it was published in a small loft on Cass Avenue, the avenue that runs through Wayne State University, the space where the MC5 formed, the space where the *Inner City Voice* was published. As I noted in chapter 1, I often mapped my route to Wayne State from Ferndale (where I lived) by crossing 8 Mile. Once I would arrive at Wayne State, I worked in an office just on the outskirts of Cass Avenue (I taught in a building on Cass). This networked connection of associations is fuzzy at best. Its fuzziness does, however, offer me an insight regarding networks and decision making because satisficing is never a clear outcome of networked thought. One difficulty I have experienced while writing about 8 Mile and the various associations I discover is that the hundred or so copies of *Creem* I owned as a kid, and that I drew so much pleasure from, have long been thrown out. While mentioning that my former employment and *Creem* once occupied the same street does not feel like a good-enough connection between 8 Mile and *Creem* (or even a good-enough for a topos-driven argument), I insist on believing that this connection can be found in one or more of those trashed magazines forever lost to me. In my own mapping scheme, I imagine *Creem* as a space on the route to Detroit and Wayne State. Even though I no longer have the magazines to prove to me so, this space is a part of my database whether or not its position is obvious or clear in relationship to other items in my overall database. Writing this final chapter and including *Creem*, therefore, leaves me with an organizational decision: how to include what is missing?

In the network, this dilemma poses the problem of where items connect or belong in a given space, particularly when the goal of connection is not necessarily a progressive state. Loss, it appears, can play a central role. David Kolb notes that, in networks, organizational choices can be tied to a loss of place. "One effect is a growth of social settings and actions divorced from any geographical place" (13). Kai Erikson writes that this divorce of action and place results from how borders and boundaries shift within networks. "The boundaries are calculated according to the network's functioning" (311). Erikson elaborates: "Therefore, it is thinking of a relation without an interior, or communication without a centre, that seems to constitute a key to the ontological field that network has occupied in the era of vanishing unambiguous borderlines" (313). When *Creem* left Detroit, it settled in Birmingham, far beyond the 8 Mile border. If the magazine made a decision that was "good enough," it was probably the one to move from the heart of Detroit, Cass near Wayne State, to Birmingham, an expensive and suburban area at least four miles to the north of 8 Mile. The decision, it would seem, left a type of empty interior to the magazine's claim to be from Detroit. I understand *Creem*'s decision to be like the one Rabbit makes at *8 Mile*'s conclusion. Asking which side of 8 Mile to live on is like asking whether one wants to be a star or to go back to the factory (as Rabbit asks). It is to choose between connecting with actual agents (as I ask about *Creem*) or with the idea of an agent (as with my memory of a lost *Creem*). Even *Creem* itself could not decide on whether to write from Detroit (Cass) or the suburbs beyond 8 Mile (Birmingham). Still, *Creem* framed its own narrative as being the magazine in Detroit. It decided to create its own diegesis. It formed a curative fiction.

Ulmer writes that "A diegesis involves time as well as space and my plan is to represent not just a place but an event" (*Heuretics* 100). Ulmer frames the diegesis as networked based. "The 'field' or network I must construct, within which an invention, or the premises of inventive thinking, might appear has all the qualities of a diegesis in a film" (*Heuretics* 98). The connection between the filmic and the drive-in I began this chapter with (and worked with in the previous chapter) is not lost on me; the digital diegesis appropriates imaginative rhetorics from film (logics of layering and association) for purposes of invention (what I quote Robert Ray in the previous chapter as attributing to the filmic detail). Invention, this thinking allows, is an imaginative creation of an event. The event I imagined in chapter 2 was a folksonomic Dylan performance. The event I imagine here is the lost *Creem* magazine dedicated to 8 Mile. "Given equal competence (no longer in the acquisition of knowledge, but in its production)," Lyotard writes, "what extra performativity depends on in the final analysis is 'imagination,' which allows one either to make a new move or change the rules of the game" (52). Performativity, Lyotard writes, deemphasizes professional positions in database culture, particularly of those who teach knowledge, like professors and teachers. "A professor is no more competent than memory-bank networks in transmitting established knowledge, no more competent than interdisciplinary teams in imagining new moves or new games" (53). Agency, then, distributes among a number of agents; a networked narrative (or digital diegesis) is produced by a number of forces (not only the professor or "author" categories I might claim for myself). Invention is a networked process. The reason to produce a Digital Detroit, as I have been arguing, is not to recite or repeat the narrative of Detroit, but to employ the network in order to perform Detroit as a network, to imagine the city as a network, to change the rules of the game regarding how we write about an urban space like Detroit. It is to make a new move. While decision making could be the force that drives revolutionary gestures (like the MC5's performances or Malcolm X's speech), I find instead that satisficing has been my method in this project as each item I decide to work with helps me change a variety of rules regarding writing about place, space, and cities in general. In other words, I do not imagine Digital Detroit as a revolutionary gesture ("network rhetoric will save us all"), but as a satisficing gesture ("it is good enough"). Satisficing involves agents producing capability rather than actuality. Satisficing involves exploring networked capabilities to discover what they might produce, rather than what they have produced already. In the moment of capability, there is room for further options to be weighed, included, or excluded (and this is how I read Rabbit walking away; he performs the capable; the audience imagines what will be). There is room for imagination in the database structure of networks.

In the moment I cannot find an issue of *Creem* featuring 8 Mile, I have to imagine it. "The nonhuman quality of networks is precisely what makes them so difficult to grasp," Alexander Galloway and Eugene Thacker argue (5). The nonhuman involves the material but also the imaginary. Galloway and Thacker suggest that network decision making is also done by non-humans whose engagement joins with that done by humans. "Network power is additive, not exclusive. It propagates through 'and' not 'or.'" (18). In the "and" of additive power, there exists the "this "and "this" and "this" of satisficing (the array of choices). The opposite gesture of the additive would be a move towards better "or" worse, status quo "or" revolution. Within the additive, we imagine further connections. "What if freedom consists in finding oneself not free of a greater number of beings," Latour asks, "but attached to an ever-increasing number of contradictory propositions?" (*Politics of Nature* 227).

With that in mind, networks are not revolutionary gestures. They are (at times) the gathering of contradictory propositions. Throughout Digital Detroit, I have found the contradictory to be the source of most of my inventive strategies. Connections may, indeed, contradict one another while also providing me with further information to explore and build from. To make a contradictory connection, I gather to the lost magazine a found body. In this final section, in what might be described as a final digital diegetic event or as a curative fiction, one connection I add to 8 Mile is the murder of Amjed Abdallah and the eventual discovery of his body at the border that divided the two *Creem* offices. One well-known recording studio in Detroit is the Studio 8 recording studio at

430 W. 8 Mile, where Eminem recorded portions of his first album, *The Slim Shady LP.* On January 4, 2005, the Studio 8's owner, Amjed Abdallah, was killed apparently for his mixing board.[10] Among the many murders Detroit witnesses each year, this one perplexed residents more than most do. Why would a man be killed for a mixing board? In his confession to the murder, Terence Terrell Moore stated that he shot Abdallah over an argument concerning charges for studio time. Moore admitted to stealing the mixing board in order to make the crime *look like* a robbery. The board was merely a side thought; it played no role in the actual event that occurred. A narrative had to be invented or made up.

In this networked moment, the imaginary is the focal point of its rhetorical exigence. Moore made the murder scene appear other than it was when he *decided* to fabricate an exigence. In that decision, Moore imagined his rationale. Moore also invented himself into a revolutionary figure in order to argue for why he killed Abdallah. According to an *Oakland Press* report, in court, Moore called himself "13," as in the 13th disciple of Jesus.[11] While he eventually scribbled "I CONFESS TO THIS KILLING" at the bottom of a police report,[12] even that act of representation does not solve the mystery of "why" he killed the studio owner or even why he felt compelled to make up his involvement in the crime. No rational decision existed. In the overall scope of a networked rhetoric and the decisions I must make as I gather information, the mystery of Abdallah is the mystery of my missing *Creem* magazine. The lack of concrete evidence does not deter, but rather propels me forward.

Following Ulmer and the work I have done in the previous chapters, I might explore a bit more the Abdallah murder as a diegesis of decision making. Detroit and murder are already connected via a public narrative of crime, from the Purple Gang of Prohibition times to 1970s drug gangs like YBI. (Young Boys, Inc.) and the Chambers Brothers to the mythology of "Devil's Night" generated by journalist Zeev Chafetz. This connection is one of perspective: The streets are safe or the streets are violent. Each act of crime pushes communal perspective towards the category of violence. Richard Cherwitz and James Hikins employ the term *perspectivism* as one rhetorical approach for moving outside such binaries. Perspectivism questions "the nature of 'the objects of knowledge' and the means by which these objects are apprehended" (249). Cherwitz and Hikins present perspectivism as a rhetorical act formed by relations. "At best, the rhetor can make us aware of a relationship, possible or actual, that we were not (or are not) conscious of prior to rhetoric. But the rhetor cannot, strictly speaking, 'create' a world of both relations and relata in defiance of relations actually existing" (259). Cherwitz and Hikins argue that relationships already exist in the world, regardless of how we understand them. The task is to locate these relationships and to utilize them for rhetorical production in order to move outside of binaries that often regulate rhetorical expression. For Cherwitz and Hikins, one binary is the mental/physical debate (where the world exists). Such binaries represent "an unfortunate 'category mistake,' that is, an artificial categorization of the objects of experience" (258). To counter binaries, Cherwitz and Hikins call their theory perspectivism, the idea that "all phenomena are what they are because of their relationship to all else" (260). Where the world exists, for example, could be rephrased as "Where does Detroit exist," "Why is Detroit digital," "What is the relationship between Detroit and networks," or even "Why does Detroit suffer from so many murders" and "Why did Moore murder Abdullah?" Each question prompts a categorical shift based on how a new set of relationships is imagined. I don't want to sustain a "category mistake" regarding space and Detroit (as I claim has long been the case) by forming a binary division of one answer in opposition to the next. Nigel Thrift's nonrepresentation theory (briefly noted in the previous chapter) shows that such categories do not depend on representational relationships; nor do they need to continue to claim that the world exists in referents of "things" and not on their relationships. Nonrepresentation theory includes "a sense of mutability; of the moments of inspired improvisation, conflicting but still fertile mimesis, rivalrous desires, creative forms of symbiosis" (Thrift 21). Nonrepresentational theory is the digital diegesis. It is the capability of a moving narrative.

In the digital diegesis, relationships drive narrative by making audiences aware of existing relationships. Relationships also frame the Abdullah murder and the missing *Creem* magazine as a mental/physical debate of perspectivism and imagined relationship. Did either exist? Can we make that decision and respond negatively or in the affirmative? Did the relationships I imagine between both these items and Digital Detroit "already exist in the world," or does their taxonomic presence (a murder, a magazine) depend on an imaginary gesture performed in a large database of information? The only way to decide, it seems, is to allow the potentiality that each of these two moments are capable of affecting the other. In that sense, perspectivism is a central element of the digital diegesis because it allows the writer to tell a rhetorical situation as a story, and even more specifically, as a story of relationships that already exist in the world. Imagination is not, then, fabrication; instead it offers a final arrangement of material within a rhetorical space.

The relationship I tell in these final pages is that of the taxonomic category called "trial." Trials are the categories for decision making; they constitute the final pay-off of a verdict's settlement on proof or argument: guilty or innocent, right or wrong, better or worse. Aristotle indicated as much when he dismissed nonlogical evidence because of its inability to provide final evidence. When affective (emotional) evidence dominates, Aristotle argued, decisions could not accurately be made. "It is clear that the opponents have no function except to show that something is or is not true or has happened or has not happened; whether it is important or trivial or just or unjust, in so far as the lawmaker has not provided a definition, the juryman should somehow decide himself and not learn from the opponents" (*On Rhetoric* 1.6). A trial suggests conclusion as all items within a given relationship are resolved. Even with resolution, as the Abdullah murder demonstrates, a final decision still can elude, a moment of satisficing can suggest the irresolvable, yet settled decision of network rhetoric. At one networked location within Detroit I find the Abdullah murder at 8 Mile and the subsequent trial. On the other end, I find Henry Ford's 1916 libel lawsuit with the *Chicago Tribune*, a case that bears resemblance to Moore's trial and his outburst of "13." As Ford biographer Douglas Brinkley tells the story, Ford was incensed over the newspaper's association of his political beliefs with the taxonomic category of "anarchist" (or we might, add, revolutionary) in an editorial, so Ford sued the newspaper for libel. Ford, who spent a lifetime perfecting the assembly-line categorization of parts in a larger system, rejected himself being categorized within a specific political system. Brinkley repeats a portion of the trial in order to showcase Ford's odd testimony. When put on the stand, Ford opted for a nontaxonomic response, one that made a final verdict difficult to obtain. One particular part of the trial has *Tribune* defense attorney Eliot Stevenson questioning Ford.

> "How can you tell what the future should be in regard to preparedness [for war] if you don't know history"
>> "I live in the present," Ford wavered.
>> "Are you ignorant of the fundamental principles of this government?"
>> "I suppose it's the Constitution."
>> "What does 'fundamental principles of government' mean?" Stevenson persisted.
>> "I don't understand," Ford insisted.
>> "What is the fundamental principle of government?"
>> "Just you," Ford replied. (245)

In this case, the taxonomy does little to help understand the motives of a trial, of a wrong doing, or of an exigence. Ford decides to respond to the trial in a way that makes little sense. Calling Ford an anarchist; Ford's treating a question-and-answer session as something other than the category of Q&A would prompt one to treat it; and—in the Moore case—even the mystery of the motive of a murder despite a presented confession: All fail to generate an understanding of the situation. Deciding which taxonomic reference will properly explain the outcome of an important deliberative issue remains perplexing even though we may desire resolution. Aristotle, on the other hand, stresses that judicial resolution must be based on taxonomic breakdowns: The types of wrongdoers, the characteristics of who is being wronged, and the traits of just and unjust actions (*On Rhetoric* 1.12–14). In the Ford trial, the jury returned with a good-enough verdict to accommodate its taxonomic confusion. the *Chicago Tribune* was found guilty of libel, but "the court reduced the suggested assessment of damages from the $1 million requested to a symbolic six cents" (Brinkley 247).

Beyond their taxonomic confusion, the Abdullah and Ford cases are also stories of resolution at a loss. Burke addresses Aristotle's preference for completion (diegetic conclusion) by equating such an end with "actuality." "Since an action contains some ingredient of purpose, or end, Aristotle uses the term 'entelechy' ('having its end within itself') as synonym for 'actuality'" (Burke, *Grammar of Motives* 262–63). Completion (a final decision) may be understood as motive or actual finalization of a moment or thing, but regardless, "the *generic* factor here resides in the fact that the aim is to give the work the form proper to its kind" (*Grammar of Motives* 263). Among the two trials I highlight (one of which is anchored to 8 Mile physically, and one which is anchored by the automotive industry and its roads), completion plays little role regarding narrative construction. A digital diegesis, like the one I build here, does not perform entelechy since its concerns are not with actuality, the expected response (whether Abdullah, in fact, murdered the studio owner or whether, in fact, Ford was really an anarchist). Purpose is the basis of expectation, of a final, decisive moment. Purpose, the most communal taxonomic reference to entelechy in rhetorical instruction, does not allow for the satisficing gesture I find in these two trial moments as well as the other moments this chapter discusses. The digital diegesis, on the other hand, may feel as if it is without purpose—either in its brief, fragmented narrative or my own motivation to include these different events. Being without purpose, however, does not prevent the diegesis's performance.

A final moment of crime completes the example and attempts to clarify that last point. As the 1984 World Series drew to a conclusion, Detroit residents celebrated the Tigers' victory with a riot. Bubba Helms, a resident of nearby Lincoln Park, drove to Tiger Stadium in Corktown in order to join the celebration. All night, he had been drinking a fifth of liquor and smoking some marijuana at home. In a *Detroit News* photograph, Bubba is captured waving the Tigers pendant in front of a burning police car. He holds a pendant over this head; his belly protrudes from his zip down sweatshirt. The ground around him is covered in fire and empty beer cans. The first questions the photograph raises are: Why would one pose for a crime? Why draw attention to a criminal act? What prompted this decision? Seven years later, after achieving a fairly infamous notoriety for this photograph, Helms attempted suicide by shooting himself in the face, did not manage to kill himself, and finally two weeks later swallowed a bottle of pain pills that ended his life.

Helms's narrative, like the others that precede him in this chapter, offers no sense of purpose or rationale for eventual decision making. A misdirected photograph, notoriety, depression, and death, these are all results of some type of decision, results networked over a space called Detroit or the World Series. The items form a relationship that exists without justification (there is causality, but causality does not lead to a value-based decision). One can assume that Helms went to the celebration because it seemed "good enough." Without trying to be callous or insensitive to his very legitimate suffering, I suggest that a similar decision ended his life without a satisfactory conclusion, only a satisficing one.

Nor does the communal representation and circulation of Helms's crime settle the matter of why he posed in front of the photographer or participated in the riots. While Helms is *remembered* for his posturing through this specific image that the *Detroit News* published, the newspaper, which owns the photograph, no longer makes it publically available; Google searches for the photograph come up empty, and only a 2006 Detroit Yes! thread offers a copy of the image.[13] Unlike the proliferation of Michigan Central Station images noted in the previous chapter, circulation of Helms's is limited to single hard-to-locate image. The discussion of the image is mostly reduced to a circulated category: Someone was once photographed in front of a burning police car. Contributors to the Detroit Yes! thread discuss the image's scarcity by focusing on the ambiguity and obscurity of the event. The final comment of the thread notes, "I had also always heard he had just stumbled upon the scene and jumped in front of the camera. It makes the story that much more tragic."

Like the various items Rabbit must choose from to make a decision in *8 Mile*, those who come to Helms's case years later can only choose from a variety of informational bits (missing photograph, story of the riot, Helms's suicide attempt, the possibility of chance encounter) in order to arrive at a good-enough moment.

Like the other two trial-based moments I present, the case of Bubba Helms appears to have no relationship to my lost (hypothetical) *Creem* magazine; it merely reflects a lack of overall purpose regarding a given spatially bound decision (such as, what is my purpose to include a magazine that I no longer own or may have never existed or why would someone pose to be photographed while committing a crime). "In view of the fact that the term Purpose is so especially susceptible to dissolution," Burke argues, "we should be particularly on the look-out for its covert retention even on occasions where it is overtly eliminated" (*Grammar of Motives* 290). Burke continues by adding, "When the pentadic functions are so essentially ambiguous, there is always the possibility that one term may be doing service for another" (*Grammar of Motives* 291). It may seem as if I am merely juxtaposing random moments, but my purpose is to make aware a perspectivism of 8 Mile that finally unites these various moments into a concrete relationship in which they do service for each other. The relationships do exist in the world even if their purpose is not evident. My purpose, however, is in fact evident. I decide that they exist in the network of decision making. I choose to demonstrate their relationship as not evidentiary, but rather performative of a diegesis that moves through unresolved moments without offering narrative resolution to their connections: winning a rap battle, murdering a man, suing for libel, and rioting. I decide that these moments demonstrate 8 Mile's contribution to networked rhetorics. I am the generator of a networked rhetoric.

The Purpose of the Network

The lost *Creem* magazine I am compelled to mention does not show me 8 Mile, nor does it reveal the secret relationship between 8 Mile and decision making. Instead it confirms my own satisficing decision to conclude this discussion of resolution within Digital Detroit with the MC5. To find some semblance of completion for this project (no matter how strong the lack of resolution is, readers still need completion), I return one final time to this fabled Detroit band. As this chapter has revealed to me, decisions often begin and are supported via hyperbole. John Sinclair positions the founding of the MC5 within such hyperbole. "We started out as cultural revolutionaries, with the belief that our way of life would inevitably replace the Amerikan [*sic*] way of death" (42). Sinclair adds, "The MC5 actually functioned as rock and roll guerillas," (43) and "It was our culture which represented a real threat to the hegemony of the established order" (44). This is the language of exaggerated gesture. It is the language Lester Bangs rejected.

I do not avoid a hyperbolic gesture such as situating a final chapter around a lost *Creem* magazine; I also do not depend on this gesture to propose a myth of progress like revolution or hegemonic overthrow. Instead, I work within a mythical MC5-ish hyperbole borderline. Within the networked decision, there always exists an element of hyperbole, for hyperbole allows bounded rationality to occur; we are limited in our abilities to depend solely on rationality. The challenge is to not give in entirely to hyperbole, as the examples I present demonstrate. Networked rhetorics employ various exaggerated elements so that the intuition relevant to decision making (how to navigate, how to categorize, how to build an interface, how to respond) may take place. With a lost magazine, therefore, I can conclude this discussion of decision making and digital diegetic events. I can conclude Digital Detroit with a bit of hyperbole.

I have chosen one final hyperbolic Detroit figure for that task, Ted Nugent. Nugent, a longtime Michigan resident and a Detroit son, is among the most hyperbolic figures in rock and roll. Nugent, whose image once graced the walls of my Miami bedroom, is often known as the Motor City Madman. McLeese quotes Nugent as an early admirer of the MC5. "I can't describe in words what it meant to witness that band live. Seeing them made us realize we had to play better, harder, than anyone on the scene. We began practicing likes boys possessed. In Detroit, you'd die if you played it like the record—you had to add something . . . We channeled the MC5 best" (qtd. in McLeese 54). Eventually, the MC5 did not live up to Nugent's initial expectations. Likewise, *Creem* itself could not live up to its own decisions. In 1988, *Creem* ceased to function.[14] Whatever the actual reasons for its demise may be, the magazine affords me its lost status by no longer publishing its print magazine. *Creem*, therefore, is now truly lost, no longer existing in its original form. Its cessation grants me a purpose and a return to the hyperbolic. Four months prior to the end of its publication, the magazine interviewed Nugent. When asked about the MC5 and the band's famous drug use, Nugent distanced himself from the "explosive" history of Detroit music that begins this chapter with the fascination McLeese depicts him as having with the band. In the republished, extended online version of the original Nugent interview,[15] Nugent rejects the MC5 for the band's exaggerated drug use.

"I used to go to the Five all the time and try to be friends with them, but they were so stoned it was like talkin' to a fuckin' log" (Morgan). Nugent continues his disdain, framing his experience with the band as a political one. In particular, Nugent's relationship to the MC5 ends in disillusionment with the band and its flamboyant leader, John Sinclair of the White Panther Party.

> Many people, many times. I was fascinated by it because I was a major fan of the Five, and I was a major fan of what I thought was a camaraderie there. Not a commune. Not a bunch of dope smokin' pieces of ass fuck. I said, "I want to know about this people's party." And, you know, he's gagging on a joint, and I realized there wasn't a whole lot to talk about. You know, he smelled like a fuckin' hippie, he looked like a fuckin' hippie, he smoked all kinds of fuckin' dope and I said: "No, John. Fuck you." And I was outcast. (Morgan)

Not every decision must end in fascination, completion, or resolution. Sometimes the result of such decisions is to be outcast. Sometimes, as with the case of the MC5, the result is to witness the revolutionary rhetoric one has popularized fade from public view. Sometimes, a deliberative act does not end with a trial's justified conclusion. Nugent's remarks are relevant for Detroit as a network.

The political topoi of Detroit, Michigan, too often make the gestures of completion their purpose or objective. Such topoi construct a perspectivism dependent on the narrative of binary divisions: ruin or prosperity. The argument for any kind of urban renewal or examination of space ends with the call for "improvement." Towards the end of *The Urban Revolution*, Henri Lefebvre's response to such calls is to frame the next stage of the urban as "practice." Practice, Lefebvre writes, fulfils the final stage of urban development, of which we might assume Detroit belongs within. Practice is an ongoing critical gesture related to decision making. "It systematically extrapolates and concludes, as if it held and manipulated all the elements of the question, as if it had resolved the urban problematic in and through a total theory, one that was immediately applicable" (157). While Lefebvre never defines how this gesture might be preformed or what it might look like, I take the ambiguity of practice as central to what Digital Detroit is about: allowing the meanings of a space to overcome the hyperbolic binaries that limit spatial understanding or narrative to "this" or "that" rhetorical motions; allowing spatial meanings to avoid the total theory or grand narrative gesture (Detroit is in ruins/Detroit is about to be rejuvenated).

If we look at the various urban urbanist proposals, we find that they don't go very far. They are limited to cutting space into grids and squares. Technocrats, unaware of what goes on in their own mind and in their working concepts, profoundly misjudging what is going on (and what is not) in their blind field, end up minutely organizing a repressive space. (*Urban Revolution* 157)

The politics of 1960s rock and roll (drugs or sobriety) or racial divisions (to live south or north of 8 Mile) reflect technocratic binaries as much as architectural and urban planning–driven design might do. Space must, this technocratic position demands, be resolved. A decision must be made. "These ideologies," Lefebvre writes of the desire to plan space (whether capitalist or Marxist desire), "confuse practice with ideology, social with institutional relations" (*Urban Revolution* 164). In the space of planned order, the practice (a rock-and-roll performance or the decision to live somewhere), becomes confused with an ideological stance (drug use equates rock and roll or a space equates a specific racial habitation). A good-enough moment works otherwise; it recognizes the formation of relationships in the network as a practice without purposeful order. Nugent declares as such when he realizes he was "outcast." Without regret or joy, he passes off his result as good enough. He has fulfilled no purpose by being outcast. Within the network of late 1960s and early 1970s Detroit rock and roll, Nugent is outcast from leftist politics and drug use. He is not sorry to have earned this status.

And even now, as I write this from my own position of academic outcast—living in Columbia, Missouri, no longer in Detroit—I understand that a relationship to space (rock and roll or an urban city) does not depend on the final feeling of joy or sorrow. My decision to leave Detroit is a good-enough one as well. When Wayne State declined to accommodate a spousal hire for me, I chose to join a department in Missouri where my spouse and I would both be hired. Outcast from Michigan, I have no regrets. I also have no joy in my departure from the Detroit area. There are consequences for the decision I made (new work opportunities, a house that could not be sold in the devastated Detroit market), but in the network of relationships constructed around me, Detroit, rhetorical studies, and all of the other elements within this book, I experience a satisficing moment. My own decision was not a singular moment within an academic career. It belonged within various calculative moments. Like Rabbit's gesture in *8 Mile*, it is a decision among decisions, among information, among moments, among further decisions.

I conclude this chapter on 8 Mile and this book overall with Ted Nugent because traditionally the rhetorical gesture of scholarship demands the writerly decision to opt for resolution. That resolution may promise further work, may wrap up the story the writer has worked hard to tell, or may point to another situation or problem still in need of being addressed. I could, for example, offer a hopeful or sorrowful note regarding Detroit's future, the role of technology in the Motor City, or rhetoric and networks in general. Nugent, however, performs his own final gesture differently. Nugent ends the print run of *Creem* with a statement lost to the magazine's original readership; it was never printed in the first version of the interview. *Creem* is lost to me; Nugent is lost to *Creem's* original audience. Nugent represents the lack of completion most writing demands. This metaphoric lack also is present in the online version of the interview. In that version, when asked if his ideas will be understood the way he wants them to be, Nugent responds: "The only way it'll happen is if someone does more of a commentary. If you try quotin' me, it'll come off . . . (pauses) It'll come off funny . . . (laughs) They're always funny. But the essence is gone with the fuckin' wind." Only more commentary, more relationships, more associations, more assemblage of the collective of the network will allow for more understanding. "We no longer expect from the future that it will emancipate us from our attachments," Latour argues. "On the contrary, we expect that it will attach us with tighter bonds to more numerous crowds" (*Politics of Nature* 191). The purpose of collecting attachments is not resolution, but further decisions. What we don't need are declarations or promises, but collections of information, databases, we navigate within.

I can quote the planners, designers, architects, pundits, proponents, opponents, and anyone else regarding Detroit, but such quotes eventually are heard, in our age of do-it-yourself reception, as metaphorically funny because they are left to stand on their own. The quotes, by themselves, without relationship to one another, without perspectivism, don't make sense. They are absurd. They are the absurdity of a love song being read as a song of revolution. They are the kind of absurdity *Creem* sought to publish during its Detroit run. They are the kind of absurdity that is demonstrated in a pseudojournalist-novelist's proclaiming grand gestures at the Democratic convention in 1968. And yet, that so-called whimsy has produced problematic results for the urban city like Detroit, the space within the network that is not treated as a network. The absurd promise of a singular decision—what any quote I can collect regarding the urban would provide—has not produced resolution in Detroit; on the contrary, it produces more promise. Like the 8 Mile Boulevard Association's continuing promise to renovate 8 Mile at Woodward, the city becomes overdependent on promises of resolution and ignores the overall network. Digital Detroit is a project that has attempted to position Detroit—and space in general—as the site of a broader comprehension than what we currently allow for when we depend on decision making as the generation of a resolution or the fulfillment of a promise. This broader comprehension, I have learned, is the network and the rhetoric it embodies in various moments, conversations, movements, and space in general.

NOTES

WORKS CITED

INDEX

NOTES

Introduction

1. While I am aware of the differences various discussions of space and place often draw between the two terms, I am also aware that many of these differences quickly become muddled and contradictory. Thus, I will often move between the two terms without distinction. Edward Casey traces some of the distinction to Greek philosophy (Aristotle and Philoponus), where place suggests an enclosed area, and space suggests an extended one (94–95). Still, as Casey also notes, the two terms can be ambiguous.

1. Networks, Place, and Rhetoric

1. See <http://www.nbc.com/Video/videos/snl_1432_narnia.shtml>.

2. <http://detroit.metblogs.com/archives/2007/02/view_realtime_d.phtml>.

3. See: http://www.google .com/search?hl=en&q=google+maps+site%3Ahttp%3 A%2F%2Fatdetroit.net&btnG= > Search.

4. In *Detroit Is My Own Home Town*, Malcolm Bingay claims that the French priest Father Gabriel Richard set up the first printing press in this part of the country.

5. <http://www.smh.com.au/news/web/google-launches-embeddable-map-feature /2007/08/18/1186857828212.html >.

6. See <http://www.wayfaring.com/ and http://www.rrove.com >.

7. <http://bluweb.com/us/chouser/gmapez/start.html>.

8. Choose "Yellow Pages" in Amazon's search box, and you will be taken to this site.

9. See <http://outside.in/>.

10. See the *Detroit Free Press*, July 20, 1967.

11. The radio show was once recorded in the Maccabees Building, the building where the Department of English now resides.

12. <http://www.techtownwsu.org/>.

13. See the embedded YouTube video at TechTown's website: <http://www .techtownwsu.org/htm/techtown_video_a.htm>.

14. See both Bizdom U's "About Us" site(<http://www.bizdom.org/program/>) and TechTown's news report(< http://www.techtownwsu.org/techtown/news/detail .asp?ContentId=D666D97F-CFB3-42BC-965D-24A0BCFD4D10&bk=%2Ftechtown %2Fnews%2Findex%2Easp>).

15. See the website: <http://www.bizdom.com/students/2006/page1.html>.

2. Woodward Avenue

1. The song was originally recorded by John Lee Hooker.

2. For readings on the "people" aspect of social networking, see Thomas Vander

Wal's blog InfoCloud and its post "Explaining and Showing Broad and Narrow Folksonomies" at <http://www.personalinfocloud.com/2005/02/explaining_and_.html>.

3. I use the word "things" deliberatively. Latour's Actor-Network-Theory traces the connections among ideas, people, and things. Folksonomy is too often only associated with people and social networking, not with concepts or things.

4. My usage of "choral" comes mostly from Gregory Ulmer's work in *Heuretics: The Logic of Invention* and *Electronic Monuments*. Chora, Plato's other term, which—while not popular among the Greeks, has been rehabilitated by contemporary scholars—is the fluid, moving receptacle of information; topos signifies the fixed place of meaning.

5. The photograph is from Wayne State University's Virtual Motor City Collection: <http://dlxs.lib.wayne.edu/cgi/i/image/image-idx?sid=a3c1d9769108544b809830b86a4c85eb;med=1;c=vmc;q1=Detroit%20Day;rgn1=vmc_ti;size=20;lasttype=boolean;view=entry;lastview=thumbnail;subview=detail;cc=vmc;entryid=x-12109;viewid=12109;start=1;resnum=1> .

6. I am aware of how difficult it is to present examples of an idea in practice (or what I imagine the idea in practice to look like). I ask, therefore, that one read the example as brief, as a possibility, and not as a complete response to my query regarding folksono(me) and digital writing. Future work (by myself and others) will extend the gesture into fuller, though never-to-be-settled, practices.

3. The Maccabees

1. See: <http://www.lib.wayne.edu/resources/digital_library/index.php>.

2. While not sporting a digital display, the downtown Cadillac Tower office building hosted, for years, a mural of Red Wing great Steve Yzerman. The building interface it projected was sports celebrity, not technology. Such an interface makes sense for a city nicknamed "hockey town." The mural has since been replaced by a Pontiac advertisement.

3. Desire and sensation are not necessarily the same. While desire can be affective, moving with sensations or employing sensation for rhetorical purpose does not necessarily impose desire on the situation. In this specific situation, I am connecting promise to desire; my usage of sensation as a mediator, however, offers no promise. It only builds.

4. The Michigan Central Train Station

1. See the entry entitled "Seven Below" at <http://www.detroitblog.org/?m=200401>.

2. See <http://atdetroit.net/cgi-bin/foroum/discus.cgi?pg=prev&topic=107211&page=106353>.

3. See the very graphic photography posted by James D. Griffoen of the weblog Sweet Juniper at <http://www.sweetjuniper.org/BookDepository/>.

4. See <http://www.southwestdetroit.com/Home%20Items/Cool%20Cities/Cool%20Cities%20Press%20Release.htm>.

5. This point is evident in the original movie poster for the film, which reads: "It's the Murder Capital of the World. And the Biggest Black Rip-Off of the Decade. It's gonna get solved . . . or the town's gonna explode."

6. See <http://www.xnumber.com/xnumber/hancock7.htm>.

7. See <http://technorati.com/about/>.

8. See <http://atdetroit.net/forum/messages/76017/84449.html?1161229149>. In addition to the similarities that exist between blogs and message boards, the writers I will discuss, particularly Itsjeff, were described in mainstream Detroit media as "bloggers," not as message board writers. Thus, I use the generic term "blog" here.

9. See the *Detroit Free Press*, <http://www.freep.com/apps/pbcs.dll/article?AID= /20070219/BLOG07/70219045> and the Detroit Yes! message board, <http://atdetroit .net/forum/messages/5/94176.html?1172123090>.

10. For the full audio story of Colby and his passing, see <http://www.wdetfm. org/article.php?id=1528>.

11. I use scare quotes here because the gender and name of the author are not revealed in the essay; a pseudonymous identity is used instead.

12. See <http://atdetroit.net/forum/messages/62684/73427.html?1149212287>.

13. See <http://atdetroit.net/cgi-bin/foroum/discus.cgi?pg=next&topic=76017& page=78639>.

14. See <http://atdetroit.net/forum/messages/5/130786.html?1207863657>.

15. See <http://multimedia.detnews.com/pix/photogalleries/newsgallery/0408200 8trainstation/>.

16. Another new thread on the station was begun on April 8, 2009. Entitled "Michigan Central Depot Ideas," the thread recirculates the same imagery and discussions found on previous threads. Once again, historical reflection, new ideas, investment possibilities, and many of the previous posters continue the layered discussion of the building. While the conversation and the ideas it sparks are not new, the participants do not feel prevented from circulating these ideas once more. See: <http://www.detroityes.com/mb/showthread.php?t=291>. A day earlier, the Detroit Council voted to demolish the Michigan Central Station. See the *Detroit Free Press*, <http://www.detnews.com/article/20090407/METRO/904070421/Detroit+Council +votes+to+demolish+Michigan+Central+Depot++charge+owner>.

5. 8 Mile

1. See Google's posting of unpublished *Time-Life* photos of the riots: <http: //images.google.com/images?q=detroit+riots&q=source%3Alife>.

2. See <http://www.crainsdetroit.com/article/20070713/SUB/70713072/-1> and <http://www.modeldmedia.com/inthenews/gateway9607.aspx>.

3. See <http://www.detnews.com/apps/pbcs.dll/article?AID=/20071006/BIZ/ 710060367>.

4. In the same autobiography, Young dismisses charges that he was antiwhite or that he helped create any antiwhite sentiment after his inauguration. Public memory and accounts of that time period, however, often disagree.

5. See Hall and Whannel's *The Popular Arts*, and in particular, their discussion of pedagogy and James Dean.

6. McLuhan calls film a hot medium. He also, however, attributes a number of cool experiences to filmic watching. See the "Movies" chapter of *Understanding Media*.

7. See *Time* magazine's pictorial "The Remains of Detroit" for a photograph of the theater turned into a parking garage: <http://www.time.com/time/photogallery /0,29307,1864272_1810106,00.html>.

8. For an example, we might consider Proof, Eminem's acquaintance, and his murder at the CCCC topless club on 8 Mile in 2006.

9. One can consider the 2008 bailout request made by GM, Ford, and Chrysler and see how the hyperbole of revolution lost out to other conditions.

10. See "Detroit Rapper Charged in Death of Ferndale Studio Owner," *The Detroit News*, Tuesday, January 25, 2005.

11. See <http://theoaklandpress.com/stories/031205/loc_20050312021.shtml>.

12. See <http://theoaklandpress.com/stories/110805/loc_2005110802.shtml>.

13. See <http://atdetroit.net/forum/messages/85961/82413.html?1161517838>.

14. It has since been revised in a new format and with a new supporting staff. It is not, however, the same magazine it once was.

15. It was published as "Crime and Punishment: The Ted Nugent Interview" in June 1988. The reprinted online version claims that original language was cut from the first version for having too many obscenities.

WORKS CITED

Amin, Ash, and Nigel Thrift. *Cities: Reimagining the Urban*. Malden, MA: Blackwell, 2002.

Aristotle. *The Metaphysics*. Trans. Hippocrates G. Apostle. Bloomington: Indiana UP, 1966.

——— . *On Rhetoric: A Theory of Civic Discourse*. Trans. George Kennedy. New York: Oxford UP, 1991.

Atwan, Robert. *Convergences: Message, Method, Medium*. N.p.: Bedford, 2005.

Augé, Marc. *Non-Places: Introduction to an Anthropology of Supermodernity*. Trans. John Howe. London: Verso, 2000.

Bahree, Megha. "Map Mania." *Forbes.com* June 5, 2006. <http://www.forbes.com/business/global/2006/0605/062.html>. July 26, 2006.

Bangs, Lester. *Mainlines, Blood Feasts, Bad Taste: A Lester Bangs Reader*. New York: Knopf, 2003.

——— . *Psychotic Reactions and Carburetor Dung*. New York: First Vintage Books, 1987.

Barabási, Albert-László. *Linked: The Science of Networks*. Cambridge, MA: Perseus, 2002.

Bardini, Thierry. "A Utopia Realized: Cyber of All." *Ctheory*. Article 146. <http://www.ctheory.net/articles.aspx?id=433>.

Bare, Bobby. "Detroit City." *Classic Country: 1950–1964*. Time Life Records, 2002.

Barthes, Roland. *Camera Lucida*. New York: Hill and Wang, 1981.

——— . "The Eiffel Tower." *The Eiffel Tower and Other Mythologies*. Trans. Richard Howard. New York: Hill and Wang, 1979.

——— . *Roland Barthes*. Trans. Richard Howard. New York: Hill and Wang, 1977.

——— . "The Third Meaning." *Image-Music-Text*. Trans. Stephen Heath. New York: Hill and Wang, 1977.

Battaglia, Tammy Stables. "Bing Knocks Glenn Beck for Detroit-Hiroshima Comparison." *Detroit Free Press* Mar. 1, 2011. <http://www.freep.com/article/20110301/ENT03/110301012/1003/news01/Glenn-Beck-compares-Detroit-Hiroshima>. Mar. 1, 2011.

"Believe in Detroit." *Detroit Believer's YouTube Channel*. N.d. <http://www.youtube.com/user/DetroitBeliever>. Jan. 2011.

Benkler, Yochai. *The Wealth of Networks: How Social Production Transforms Markets and Freedom*. New Haven: Yale UP, 2006.

Berlin, James. *Rhetoric, Poetics, and Cultures*. West Lafayette, IN: Parlor, 2002.

Bing, Dave. "Mayor Dave Bing's Inauguration Speech." Jan. 8, 2010. <http://www.myfoxdetroit.com/dpp/news/local/mayor-dave-bing%27s-inauguration-speech>. Jan. 8, 2010.

Bingay, Malcolm W. *Detroit Is My Own Home Town*. Indianapolis: Bobbs-Merrill, 1946.

Bitzer, Lloyd. "The Rhetorical Situation." *Philosophy and Rhetoric* 1 (Jan. 1968): 1–14.

Blaire, Carole. "Contemporary U.S. Memorial Sites as Exemplars of Rhetoric's Materiality." *Rhetorical Bodies*. Ed. Jack Selzer and Sharon Crowley. Madison: U of Wisconsin P, 1999. 16–57.

Blake, Blind Arthur . "Detroit Bound Blues." *Complete Recorded Works*. Vol. 2 (1927–1928). Document Records.

Blondie. "Detroit 442." *Plastic Letters*. Capitol.

Blood, Rebecca. *The Weblog Handbook*. New York: De Capo, 2002.

Bolter, Jay David. "Theory and Practice in New Media Studies." *Digital Media Revisited*. Ed. Gunnar LiestØl, Andrew Morrison, Terje Rasmussen. Cambridge: MIT P, 2004.

Booth, Wayne C. *The Rhetoric of Rhetoric: The Quest for Effective Communication*. Malden, MA.: Blackwell, 2004.

Borgmann, Albert. *Holding onto Reality: The Nature of Information at the Turn of the Millennium*. Chicago: U of Chicago P, 2000.

Brand, Stewart. *How Buildings Learn: What Happens after They're Built*. New York: Penguin, 1995.

Brinkley, Douglas. *Wheels for the World: Henry Ford, His Company, and a Century of Progress*. New York: Viking, 2003.

Brooks, David. "The Splendor of Cities." *New York Times* Feb. 7, 2011. <http://www.nytimes.com/2011/02/08/opinion/08brooks.html>. Feb 7, 2011.

Bruns, Axel. *Blogs, Wikipedia, Second Life, and Beyond*. New York: Peter Lang, 2008.

Buchanan, Richard. "Design and the New Rhetoric: Productive Arts in the Philosophy of Culture." *Philosophy and Rhetoric* 34.3 (2001): 183–206.

Bunge, William. *Fitzgerald: Geography of a Revolution*. Cambridge, MA: Schenkman, 1971.

Bunkley, Nick. "Urban Village Taking Shape." *Detroit News* Mar. 14, 2006. <http://www.detnews.com/apps/pbcs.dll/article?AID=/20060314/BIZ/603140344/1001>. July 25, 2006.

Burke, Kenneth. *Attitudes toward History*. Boston: Beacon, 1961.

——. *A Grammar of Motives*. Berkeley: U of California P, 1974.

Burroughs, William. *Nova Express*. 1964. New York: Grove, 1992.

——. *The Ticket That Exploded*. 1962. New York: Grove, 1967.

Casey, Edward S. *The Fate of Place: A Philosophical History*. Berkeley: U of California P, 1998.

——. *Getting Back into Place: Toward a Renewed Understanding of the Placed World*. Bloomington: Indiana UP, 1993.

Cash, Johnny. "One Piece at a Time." *Sixteen Biggest Hits*. Sony Legacy, 2009.

Castells, Manuel. "Materials for an Exploratory Theory of the Networked Society." *British Journal of Sociology* 51.1 (Jan.–Mar. 2000): 5–24.

Chambers, Jennifer. "Michigan Orders DPS to Make Huge Cuts." *Detroit News* Feb. 21, 2011. <http://detnews.com/article/20110221/SCHOOLS/102210355/Michigan-orders-DPS-to-make-huge-cuts>. Feb. 21, 2011.

Cherwitz, Richard A., and James W. Hikins. "Rhetorical Perspectivism." *Quarterly Journal of Speech* 69.3 (Aug. 1983): 249–66.

City on the Hope: Detroit on the Move. Detroit: Handy (Jam) Organization, 1965.

Clark, Gregory. "Writing as Travel, or Rhetoric on the Road. *College Composition and Communication* 49.1 (1998): 4–23.

Clemens, Paul. *Made in Detroit: A South of 8 Mile Memoir.* New York: Anchor, 2005.

Coats, Nigel. *Guide to Esctacity.* Princeton, NJ: Princeton Architectural Press, 2003.

Collins, Randall. *Interaction Ritual Chains.* Princeton, NJ: Princeton UP, 2004.

"Compuware and Detroit Public Schools Make Major Deal to Manage the District's Information Technology Services." Aug. 16, 2000. <http://www.compuware.com/pressroom/newse/2000/1168_ENG_HTML.htm>. Aug. 16, 2000.

Davis, Sammy, Jr. "Hello Detroit." Motown, 1984.

Dawsey, Chastity Pratt. "DPS Budget Worse than a Year Ago." *Detroit Free Press* May 19, 2010. <http://www.freep.com/article/20100519/NEWS01/5190456/DPS-budget-worse-than-a-year-ago>. May 19, 2010.

———. "Up to Fifty Schools Could Close in Detroit." *Detroit Free Press* Apr. 2, 2009. <http://www.freep.com/apps/pbcs.dll/article?AID=2009904020357>. Apr. 2, 2009.

de Certeau, Michel. "Walking in the City." *The Practice of Everyday Life.* Trans. Steven F. Rendall. Berkeley: U of California P, 1984.

DeLanda, Manuel. *A New Philosophy of Society.* New York: Continuum, 2006.

Deleuze, Gilles, and Félix Guattari. *What Is Philosophy?* New York: Columbia UP, 1994.

Derrida, Jacques. "The Future of the Profession." *Deconstructing Derrida: Tasks for the New Humanities.* Ed. Peter Pericles Trifonas and Michael A. Peters. New York: Palgrave Macmillan, 2005. 11–24.

Detroit 9000. Miramax, 1973.

"Detroit's Torn Lifeline." *Newsweek* Sept. 1984, 59.

Dickinson, Greg. "Memories for Sale: Nostalgia and the Construction of Identity in Old Pasadena." *Quarterly Journal of Speech* 83.1 (1997): 1–27.

Dourish, Paul. *Where the Action Is: The Foundations of Embodied Interaction.* Cambridge: MIT P, 2004.

Dylan, Bob. *Chronicles Vol. 1.* New York: Simon and Schuster, 2004.

Eminem. *8 Mile: Music from and Inspired by the Motion Picture.* Interscope, 2002.

Enos, Richard. "Ciceronian Disposito as an Architecture for Creativity." *Rhetoric Review* 4.1 (1985): 108–10.

Erikson, Kai. "The Ontology of Networks." *Communication and Critical/Cultural Studies* 2.4 (Dec. 2005): 305–23.

50 Cent. "Places to Go." *8Mile: Music From and Inspired by the Motion Picture.* Interscope Records, 2002.

"The Fire This Time." *Time* Aug. 4, 1967. <http://www.time.com/time/magazine/article/0,9171,837150,00.html>. June 10, 2006.

Florida, Richard. *The Rise of the Creative Class.* New York: Basic, 2002.

Fuller, Matthew. *Media Ecologies: Material Energies in Art and Technology.* Cambridge: MIT P, 2005.

Fuller, Matthew, and Florian Cramer. "Interface." *Software Studies: A Lexicon.* Cambridge: MIT P, 2008.

Galloway, Alexander, and Eugene Thacker. *The Exploit: A Theory of Networks*. Minneapolis: U of Minnesota P, 2007.

Georgakas, Dan, and Marvin Surkin. *Detroit: I Do Mind Dying. A Study in Urban Revolution*. Cambridge, MA: South End, 1998.

Glazer, Sydney. *Detroit: A Study in Urban Development*. New York: Bookman, 1965.

Goody, Jack. *Domestication of the Savage Mind*. New York: Cambridge UP, 1977.

Gopwani, Jewel. "Navigating Technology: Map Mission." *Detroit Free Press* May 26, 2006. <http://www.freep.com/apps/pbcs.dll/article?AID=/20060526/NEWS09/605260378>. May 26, 2006. Graham, Stephen, and Simon Marvin. *Splintering Urbanism: Networked Infrastructures, Technological Mobilities, and the Urban Condition*. New York: Routledge, 2001.

Greenfield, Adam. *Everyware: The Dawning Age of Ubiquitous Computing*. Berkeley, CA: New Riders, 2006.

Grossman, Lev. "Meet Joe Blog." *Time* June 13, 2004. <http://www.time.com/time/magazine/article/0,9171,650732,00.html>. June 13, 2004.

Grusin, Richard, and Jay David Bolter. *Remediation: Understanding New Media*. Cambridge: MIT P, 2000.

Guest, Greta, and Marisol Bello. "MGM Bets Big on Detroit: $765 Million, a Thousand New Jobs." *Detroit Free Press* Apr. 7, 2006. <http://www.freep.com/apps/pbcs.dll/article?AID=2006604070327>. Apr. 7, 2006.

Hall, Stuart, and Paddy Whannel. *The Popular Arts*. London: Hutchinson Educational, 1964.

Hariman, Robert, and John Louis Lucaites. *No Caption Needed*. Chicago: U of Chicago P, 2007.

Harmon, Katherine. *You Are Here: Personal Geographies and Other Maps of the Imagination*. Princeton, NJ: Princeton Architectural Press, 2004.

Harris, Joseph. *A Teaching Subject: Composition since 1966*. Upper Saddle, NJ: Prentice Hall, 1997.

Hayles, Katherine N. *My Mother Was a Computer: Digital Subjects and Literary Texts*. Chicago: U of Chicago P, 2005.

Herron, Jerry. *Afterculture: Detroit and the Humiliation of History*. Detroit: Wayne State UP, 1993.

Horan, Thomas. *Digital Places: Building Our City of Bits*. Los Angeles: ULI—The Urban Land Institute, 2000.

"How Munched Is That Birdie in the Window." *The Simpsons*. Season 22, episode 7, Nov. 28, 2010.

Jacobs, Jane. *The Death and Life of Great American Cities*. New York: Random, 1961.

Jameson, Fredric. *Postmodernism or, the Cultural Logic of Late Capitalism*. Durham: Duke UP, 1999.

Jenkins, Henry. Convergence Culture: Where Old and New Media Collide. New York: New York UP, 2000.

Johnson, Steven. *Emergence: The Connected Lives of Ants, Brains, Cities, and Software.* New York: Scribner, 2001.

——. Everything Bad Is Good for You: How Today's Popular Culture is Actually Making Us Smarter. New York: Penguin, 2005.

Jones, Thomas. "Up in Smoke: Cigar Making in Detroit." *Detroit News* Dec. 10, 2007. <http://info.detnews.com/history/story/index.cfm?id=24&category=business>. Dec. 10, 2007.

Kavanaugh, Kelii. *Detroit's Michigan Central Station*. Charleston, SC: Arcadia, 2001.

Kilpatrick, Kwame. "Mayor Announces Plans to Transform Train Depot into New Police Headquarters." City of Detroit. Mar. 4, 2004. <http://www.detroitmi.gov/mayor/releases/2004%20Releases/Police%20Headquarters%20at%20Central%20Depot.htm>. Mar. 4, 2004.

———. "State of the City Address." City of Detroit. Mar. 14, 2006. <http://www.ci.detroit.mi.us/mayor/speeches/State%20of%20the%20City%202006.htm>. Mar. 14, 2006.

King, R. J. "Train Depot Won't House Police Hub." *Detroit News* 1, 2005. <http://www.detnews.com/2005/metro/0507/01/B01–233908.htm>. July 1, 2005.

Kiska, Tim. *From Soupy to Nuts! A History of Detroit Television*. Royal Oak, MI: Momentum, 2005.

Kittler, Friedrich. *Gramophone, Film, Typewriter*. Trans. Geoffrey Winthrop-Young. Stanford, CA: Stanford UP, 1999.

Kolb, David. *Sprawling Places*. Athens: U of Georgia P, 2008.

Kramer, Michael. "Can't Forget the Motor City: *Creem* Magazine, Rock Music, Detroit Identity, Mass Consumerism, and the Counterculture." *Michigan Historical Review* 28 (2002): 42–77.

Kruz, Michelle. "Michigan Central Railroad Station, Vernor and Michigan Avenue." *Detroit and Rome: Building on the Past*. Ed. Melanie Grunow Sobocinski. Dearborn: U of Michigan-Dearborn, 2005. 110–13.

Landow, George. "The Paradigm Is More Important than the Purpose." *Digital Media Revisited*. Ed. Gunnar Liestøl, Andrew Morrison, Terje Rasmussen. Cambridge: MIT P, 2004. 35–64.

Lanham, Richard. *Economics of Attention*. Chicago: U of Chicago P, 2006.

Latour, Bruno. *Aramis, or the Love of Technology*. Cambridge: Harvard UP, 1996.

———. *Pandora's Hope: Essays on the Reality of Science Studies*. Cambridge: Harvard UP, 1992.

———. *Politics of Nature: How to Bring Sciences into Democracy*. Cambridge: Harvard UP, 2004.

———. *Reassembling the Social: An Introduction to Actor-Network-Theory*. New York: Oxford UP, 2005.

———. *Science in Action: How to Follow Scientists and Engineers through Society*. Cambridge: Harvard UP, 1987.

Law, John. After Method: Mess in Social Science Research. New York: Routledge, 2004.

Lefebvre, Ben. "National Briefing Midwest: Michigan: From Train Station to Police Station." *New York Times* Mar. 6, 2004, A9, col. 2.

Lefebvre, Henri. *Production of Space*. Malden, MA: Blackwell, 1974.

———. *The Urban Revolution*. Trans. Robert Bononno. Minneapolis: U of Minnesota P, 2003.

———. *Writings on Cities*. Trans. Eleonore Koffman and Elizabeth Lebas. Malden, MA: Blackwell, 1996.

Lessenberry, Jack. "Detroit's Future, and Ours." *Metrotimes* Nov. 9, 2005. <http://www.metrotimes.com/editorial/story.asp?id=8460>. Nov. 9, 2005.

Levine, Philip. "What Work Is." *What Work Is: Poems*. New York: Knopf, 1992.

Lévy, Pierre. *Collective Intelligence: Mankind's Merging World in Cyberspace*. Cambridge, MA: Perseus,1997.

Liggett, Helen. *Urban Encounters*. Minneapolis: U of Minnesota P, 2003.

Lightfoot, Gordon. "Black Day in July." 1970. *Classic Masters*. Capitol, 2008.

Liu, Alan. "The Humanities: A Technical Profession." *Teaching, Technology, Textuality: Approaches to New Media*. Ed. Michael Hanrahan and Deborah L. Madsen. New York: Palgrave, 2006. 11–26.

———. *The Laws of Cool*. Chicago: U of Chicago P, 2004.

Logan, Sam. "Time for New Leaders, New Thinking." *Detroit Free Press* July 31, 2008. <http://www.freep.com/apps/pbcs.dll/article?AID=/20080731/OPINION05/80731071>. July 31, 2008.

Lynch, Kevin. *The Image of the City*. Cambridge: MIT P, 1960.

Lyotard, Jean-François. *The Postmodern Condition: A Report on Knowledge*. Trans. Geoff Bennington and Brian Massumi. Minneapolis: U of Minnesota P, 1997.

Madrazo, Leonardo. " Net City: A Collaborative Environment to Promote the Contemporary City." *Journal of Urban Technology* 12.1: 21–47.

Maffesoli, Michael. *The Time of the Tribes: The Decline of Individualism in Mass Society*. London: Sage, 1996.

Mailer, Norman. *Miami and the Siege of Chicago: An Informal History of the Republican and Democratic Conventions of 1968*. New York: Signet, 1968.

Mailloux, Steven. *Disciplinary Identities: Rhetorical Paths of English, Speech, and Composition*. New York: MLA, 2006.

Malcolm X. "Message to Grassroots." Oct. 10, 1963. Teaching American History. <http://teachingamericanhistory.org/library/index.asp?document=1145>. Oct. 10, 2009.

Manovich, Lev. *The Language of New Media*. Cambridge: MIT P, 2001.

Marchand, Yves, and Romaine Meffre. "Detroit's Beautiful, Horrible Decline." *Time* Mar. 2009. <http://www.time.com/time/photogallery/0,29307,1882089_1850974,00.html>. Mar. 15, 2009.

Marsh, Dave. "MC5 Back on Shakin' Street." *Creem* 3 (Oct. 1971): 37–46.

Massumi, Brian. *Parables of the Virtual: Movement, Affect, Sensation*. Durham, NC: Duke UP, 2002.

Mast, Robert H., ed. *Detroit Lives*. Philadelphia: Temple UP, 1994.

Matheu, Robert. *Creem: American's Only Rock 'n' Roll Magazine*. New York: Harper Collins, 2007.

Mattalart, Armand. *The Invention of Communication*. Trans. Susan Emanuel. Minneapolis: U of Minnesota P, 1996.

McClelland, Edward. "Kwame Kilpatrick Exits, with Barack Obama Holding the Door." *Salon.com* Sept. 4, 2008. <http://www.salon.com/news/feature/2008/09/04/detroit/>. Sept. 4, 2008.

MC5. "Borderline." *Kick Out the Jams*. Elektra, 1969.

McCullough, Malcolm. *Digital Ground: Architecture, Pervasive Computing, and Environmental Knowing*. Cambridge: MIT P, 2005.

McGraw, Bill. "Today's Detroit Has Little to Do with 1967." *Detroit Free Press* July 20, 2007. <http://www.freepress.com/apps/pbcs.dll/article?AID=/20070720/COL27/707200367/1161>. July 20, 2007.

McLeese, Don. *Kick Out the Jams*. New York: Continuum, 1995.

McLuhan, Marshall. *The Gutenberg Galaxy: The Making of Typographic Man*. Toronto: U of Toronto P, 1962.

——. "Speed of Cultural Change." *College Composition and Communication* 9.1 (1958):16–20.

——. *Understanding Media: The Extensions of Man.* Corte Madera, CA: Gingko, 2003.

McLuhan, Marshall, and David Carson. *The Book of Probes.* Corte Madera, CA: Gingko, 2003.

McLuhan, Marshall, and Quentin Fiore. *The Medium Is the Massage: An Inventory of Effects.* Corte Madera, CA: Gingko, 2001.

Miller, Carolyn. "The Aristotelian Topos: Hunting for Novelty." *Rereading Aristotle's Rhetoric.* Ed. Alan G. Gross and Arthur Walzer. Carbondale: Southern Illinois UP, 2000. 130–46.

Miller, Carolyn, and Dawn Shepherd, "Blogging as Social Action: A Genre Analysis of the Weblog." *Into the Blogosphere: Rhetoric, Community, and Culture of Weblogs.* Ed. Laura J. Gurak, Smiljana Antonijevic, Laurie Johnson, Clancy Ratliff, and Jessica Reyman. June 2004. <http://blog.lib.umn.edu/blogosphere/>. July, 15 2004.

Miller, Henry. *The Air-Conditioned Nightmare.* New York: New Directions, 1945.

Mirel, Jeffrey. *The Rise and Fall of an Urban School System.* Ann Arbor: U of Michigan P, 1999.

Mitchell, William J. *City of Bits: Space, Place, and the Infobahn.* Cambridge: MIT P, 1997.

—— *E-topia: Urban Life, Jim—but Not as We Know It.* Cambridge: MIT P, 1999.

——. *Placing Words: Symbols, Space, and the City.* Cambridge: MIT P, 2005.

Morath, Eric. "State Stuck in Stalled Economy." *Detroit News* Aug. 16, 2007. <http://www.detnews.com/apps/pbcs.dll/article?AID=2007708160344>. Aug. 16, 2007.

Morgan, Jeffrey. "Ted Nugent: Crime and Punishment." *Creem* June 1998. <http://www.creemmagazine.com/_site/BeatGoesOn/TedNugent/CrimeAndPunishment001.htm>. Apr. 2005.

Morton, Thomas. "Something, Something, Something Detroit: Lazy Journalists Love Pictures of Abandoned Stuff." *Vice* Aug. 2009. <http://www.viceland.com/int/v16n8/htdocs/something-something-something-detroit-994.php?page=1>. Aug. 15,2009.

Mrozowski, Jennifer. "Detroit Schools Face $45M Deficit." *Detroit News* May 16, 2008. <http://www.detnews.com/apps/pbcs.dll/article?AID=/20080516/SCHOOLS/805160404&imw=Y>. May 16, 2008.

Mullen, Anne. "On Track: Hope Gains Steam for Renovation of Train Station." *Metro Times* Nov. 26, 2003. <http://www.metrotimes.com/editorial/story.asp?id=5221>. June 22, 2003.

Murray, Billy. "The Little Ford Rambled Right Along." N.p.: C. R. Foster, 1915.

Nowotny, Helga. *Insatiable Curiosity: Innovation in a Fragile Future.* Trans. Mitch Cohen. Cambridge: MIT P, 2008.

Nunes, Mark. *Cyberspaces of Everyday Life.* Minneapolis: U of Minnesota P, 2006.

Ong, Walter J. Orality and Literacy: The Technologizing of the Word. New York: Routledge, 1982.

——. *Ramus, Method, and the Decay of Dialogue.* Cambridge: Harvard U P, 1983.

Osgood, Dick. *Wyxie Wonderland: An Unauthorized Fifty-Year Diary of WXYZ Detroit.* Bowling Green, KY: Bowling Green U Popular P 1981.

Pallasmaa, Juhani. *The Eyes of the Skin: Architecture and the Senses*. West Sussex, England: John Wiley and Sons, 2007.

Palm, Kristin. "Ruins of a Golden Age." *Metropolis* Oct. 15, 2006. <http://www .metropolismag.com/html/content_0502/pol/>. Oct .15, 2006.

Park, Kyong. *Urban Ecology: Detroit and Beyond*. Sheung Wan, Hong Kong: Map Book Publishers, 2005.

Perec, Georges. *Species of Spaces and Other Places*. New York: Penguin, 1997.

Pennebaker, D. A. *Don't Look Back*. Warner Bros., 1967.

Poremba, David Lee. *Detroit: City of Industry*. Chicago: Arcadia, 2002.

Proctor, Robert E. *Defining the Humanities: How Rediscovering a Tradition Can Improve Our Schools*. Bloomington: Indiana UP, 1998.

Rajchman, John. *Constructions (Writing Architecture)*. Cambridge: MIT Press, 1998.

Raskin, Jef. *The Human Interface: New Directions for Designing Interactive Systems*. Boston: Addison-Wesley, 2000.

Rasmussen, Terje. "On Distributed Society: The Internet as a Guide to a Sociological Understanding of Communication. *Digital Media Revisited*. Ed. Gunnar LiestØl, Andrew Morrison, Terje Rasmussen. Cambridge: MIT P, 2004Ray, Robert. *The Avant-Garde Finds Andy Hardy*. Cambridge: Harvard UP, 1995.

"Rethinking 8 Mile: A Framework for Unifying Elements." Detroit: Archive Design Studio, 2005.

Reynolds, Nedra. *Geographies of Writing*. Carbondale: Southern Illinois UP, 2004.

Ronnick, Michele Valerie. "From Rome to Detroit: Augustus Woodward and the Campus Martius." *Detroit and Rome: Building on the Past*. Ed. Melanie Grunow Sobocinski. Dearborn: U of Michigan-Dearborn, 2005. 13–16.

Sassen, Saskia. "The Global City: Introducing a Concept and Its History." *Mutations*. Ed. Rem Koolhaas, Stefano Boeri, Sanford Kwinter, Nadia Tazi, and Hans Ulrich Obrist. Barcelona: Actar, 2001. 104-23.

Schneider, Keith. "Across the Great Divide: Woodward Avenue as a Link to Regional Cooperation." *Metrotimes* July 5–11, 2006: 10–12.

Schramm, Jack E., William H. Henning, and Thomas J. Dworman. *Detroit's Street Railways*. Vol. 2: *City Lines 1922–1956*. Chicago: Central Electric Railfans' Assoc., 1980.

Schumacher, Patrik, and Christian Rogner. "After Ford." *Stalking Detroit*. Ed. Georgia Daskalakis, Charles Waldheim, and Jason Young. Barcelona: Actar, 2001.

Shaviro, Steven. *Connected, or What It Means to Live in the Networked Society*. Minneapolis: U of Minnesota P, 2003.

Shirky, Clay."Ontolongy is Overrated: Categories, Links, and Tags." Shirky.com. N.d. <http://www.shirky.com/writings/ontology_overrated.html>. May 1, 2006.

Simon, Herbert. *Models of Man: Social and Rational: Mathematical Essays on Rational Human Behavior in Society Settings*. New York: Wiley, 1957.

Sinclair, John. *Guitar Army*. New York: Douglas Book Corp., 1972.

Slack, Jennifer Daryl. "Logic of Sensation." *Gilles Deleuze: Key Concepts*. Ed. Charles Stivale. Montreal: McGill-Queen's UP, 2005. 131–39.

Smith, Terry. *Making the Modern: Industry, Art, and Design in America*. Chicago: U of Chicago P, 1993.

Spivey, Victoria. "Detroit Moan." The Complete Recorded Works Vol. 4 1936–1937. Document Records, 1995.

Sterling, Bruce. "Order Out of Chaos." *Wired* Apr. 2005. <http://www.wired.com/wired/archive/13.04/view.html?pg=4>. Apr. 15, 2005.

Stevens, Albert Clark. *Cyclopaedia of Fraternities*. New York: E. B. Treat, 1907.

Stewart, Kathleen. *A Space on the Side of the Road: Cultural Poetics in an "Other" America*. Princeton,: Princeton UP, 1996.

Strausbaugh, John. *Rock 'til You Drop: The Decline from Rebellion to Nostalgia*. New York: Verso, 2001.

Sugrue, Thomas. *The Origins of the Urban Crisis: Race and Inequality in Postwar Detroit*. Princeton: Princeton UP, 1998.

Svenonius, Elaine. The Intellectual Foundation of Information Organization. Cambridge: MIT Press, 2000.

Talbot, Bryan. *Alice in Sunderland: An Entertainment*. Milwaukie, OR: Dark Horse, 2007.

Taylor, Marc C. *The Moment of Complexity: Emerging Network Culture*. Chicago: U of Chicago P, 2001.

Thrift, Nigel. *Non-Representational Theory: Space, Politics, Affect*. London: Routledge, 2008.

Tidwell, Jennifer. *Designing Interfaces*. Sebastopol, CA: O'Reilly Media, 2006.

Tribble, Ivan. "Bloggers Need Not Apply." *Chronicle of Higher Education* July 8, 2005. <http://chronicle.com/jobs/2005/07/2005070801c.htm>. July 8, 2005.

Ulmer, Gregory. *Electronic Monuments*. Minneapolis: U of Minnesota P, 2005.

———. *Heuretics: The Logic of Invention*. Baltimore: Johns Hopkins UP, 1994.

———. *Teletheory*. New York: Atropos, 2004.

Vander Wal, Thomas."Folksonomy." Vanderwal. net. Feb. 2, 2007. <http://www.vanderwal.net/folksonomy.html>. Mar. 15, 2007.

Virilio, Paul. "Architecture in the Age of Its Virtual Disappearance." *The Virtual Dimension: Architecture: Representation, and Crash Culture*. Ed. John Beckmann. New York: Princeton Architectural P, 1998.

———. *The Art of the Motor*. Minneapolis: U of Minnesota P, 1995.

———. *Speed and Politics: An Essay on Dromology*. New York: Semiotext(e), 1986.

Virno, Paolo. *A Grammar of the Multitude: For an Analysis of Contemporary Forms of Life*. Los Angeles: Semiotext(e), 2004.

Vitanza, Victor. "Critical Sub/Versions of the History of Philosophical Rhetoric." *Rhetoric Review* 6.1 (1987): 41–66.

Walter, Eugene. *Placeways: A Theory of the Human Environment*. Chapel Hill: U of North Carolina P, 1988.

Weinberger, David. *Everything Is Miscellaneous: The Power of the New Digital Disorder*. New York, Times Books, 2007.

———. "The New Is." *JoHo* Sept. 12, 2005. <http://www.hyperorg.com/misc/thenewis.html>. Sept. 12, 2005.

———. *Small Pieces Loosely Joined*. Cambridge, MA: Perseus, 2003.

"What Is TechTown." *TechTown*. Mar. 15, 2007. <http://www.techtownwsu.org/techtown/>. Mar. 15, 2007.

White, E. B. "Farewell, My Lovely." *New Yorker* May 16, 1936. <http://www.newyorker.com/archive/1936/05/16/1936_05_16_020_TNY_CARDS_000161110>. Sept. 2, 2009.

White, Jack. "Courageous Dream's Concern." *Detroit Free Press* July 6, 2008. <http://www.freep.com/apps/pbcs.dll/article?AID=/20080706/ENT04/807060599/1039/ENT>. July 6, 2008.

Widick, B. J. *Detroit: City of Race and Class Violence.* 1972. Detroit: Wayne State UP, 1989.

Wilkinson, Mike. "Fifty-One Thousand Opt Out of Detroit Schools." *Detroit News* Jan. 15, 2007. <http://www.detnews.com/apps/pbcs.dll/article?AID=/20070115/SCHOOLS/701150362>. Jan. 15, 2007.

Williams, Raymond. Keywords: A Vocabulary of Culture and Society. New York: Oxford UP, 1985.

Wood, Denis. *The Power of Maps.* New York: Guilford, 1992.

Wood, Denis, and Robert Beck. *Home Rules.* Baltimore: Johns Hopkins UP, 1984.

Woolgar, Steve. "Five Rules of Virtuality." *Virtual Society? Technology, Cyberbole, Reality.* Ed. Steve Woolgar. Oxford: Oxford UP, 2002. 209–29.

Yates, Francis. *The Art of Memory.* Chicago: U of Chicago P, 1966.

Young, Coleman. *Hard Stuff: The Autobiography of Coleman Young.* New York: Penguin, 1994.

Young, Jason. "Line Frustration Detroit." *Stalking Detroit.* Ed. Georgia Daskalakis, Charles Waldheim, and Jason Young. Barcelona: Actar, 2001.

INDEX

*J*eff Rice is the Martha B. Reynolds Chair in Writing, Rhetoric, and Digital Media and an associate professor at the University of Kentucky. He is the author of *The Rhetoric of Cool: Composition Studies and New Media* (2007) and a coeditor of *New Media/New Methods: The Academic Turn from Literacy to Electracy* (2008) and *Keywords in Markup: From A to <A>* (2010). He blogs at Yellow Dog (http://www.ydog.net) and at Make Mine Potato (http://makeminepotato.ydog.net).